Disintegrating Empire

FRANCE OVERSEAS:
STUDIES IN EMPIRE AND DECOLONIZATION

Series editors:
James D. Le Sueur and Cindy Ermus
Founding editors:
Philip Boucher and A. J. B. Johnston

Disintegrating Empire

*Algerian Family Migration
and the Limits of the
Welfare State in France*

ELISE FRANKLIN

University of Nebraska Press · Lincoln

© 2024 by the Board of Regents of the University of Nebraska

Acknowledgments for the use of previously
published material appear on page xvii, which
constitutes an extension of the copyright page.

The University of Nebraska Press is part of a land-grant institution
with campuses and programs on the past, present, and future
homelands of the Pawnee, Ponca, Otoe-Missouria, Omaha,
Dakota, Lakota, Kaw, Cheyenne, and Arapaho Peoples, as well as
those of the relocated Ho-Chunk, Sac and Fox, and Iowa Peoples.

Library of Congress Control Number: 2023053681

Designed and set in Adobe Caslon Pro by L. Welch.

To my family

Presented in this manner, private life allowed itself to be seen, visited, rifled through, and yet it never showed its true face with any certainty. . . . It will not unmask itself to our overly curious and often distorted prying.

—Arlette Farge and Michel Foucault, *Disorderly Families*

Before arriving, I imagined the French administration as an elegant, kind lady. Reality is harder. I never thought it could be so exhausting to get papers in order.

—Anonymous, quoted in Catherine Wihtol de Wenden, "Les immigrés et l'administration"

CONTENTS

ILLUSTRATIONS

TABLES

ACKNOWLEDGMENTS

My first debt in this work is to a moment of profound mortification. As a graduate student, I took part in a conference on the Algerian War in Paris. Eager to share my dissertation research with some of the people who had assisted with it, I invited Nelly Forget to attend. Forget, a social worker in Algeria during the war and personal assistant to famous ethnologist Germaine Tillion, had graciously welcomed me into her home to photograph her archives the year before. To see her in the audience brought past and present into tension, and I became uneasy with my decision. How would she react to my analysis of the colonialist nature of social work—work she had engaged in—during the Algerian War? I was right to be worried. In short, she did not agree with my interpretation. In a public rebuttal that I thought would never end, she claimed that I had flattened the dimensions of care work. She argued that I misunderstood and devalued the efforts of social workers who often put their lives on the line in the service of their clients and their profession. In Forget's case, this self-abnegation was especially true, as she had been detained and tortured for her care of the Algerian civilian population during the war.

I was initially indignant at her comments. Nelly had personal connections to Algeria, and my doctoral training taught me that she could not be objective about her own history. It would, of course, be difficult to see oneself historicized, I thought, believing myself gracious. Over time, my position has evolved. I've asked myself some questions: Who am I to say that I know better? What is lost in synthesis? After a decade of research and engagement on these issues, am I even an objective "outsider" anyway? In what follows, I have attempted to render social work in its multiplicity in the years surrounding Algerian independence during the long period of decolonization. This is not to say that I have changed my mind about the imbrication of colonialism and welfare, but rather that I've complicated my story. I tell this history by foregrounding dramatic irony, suggesting what historical actors could not possibly have known or intuited about their actions, revealing a larger picture of which they were (sometimes unwittingly, sometimes woefully) unaware, and which shapes our reading of their actions. I hope this effort holds as true for agents of the welfare state as for the Algerian clients who sought their aid. Nelly's comments remind me of the tension between the stories of individuals from the past and the structures they bumped up against, a tension inherent in all history writing and that is particularly clear at our own historical juncture. I have taken this opportunity to reflect on the way my historical actors, like all of us, are caught up in institutions much larger than ourselves.

This is equally true when conducting archival research. I owe many thanks to the archivists who helped me access this material, much of which was tied up in bureaucratic morass, some of which required dérogations or personal permissions, and select pieces of which were temporarily unavailable as they underwent abatement after coming in contact with asbestos. The archives of the Fifth Republic at Fontainebleau, which collapsed under their own weight during my research year, are a maze of boxes cataloged by year of deposit rather than office or ministry. So much remained opaque to me as I worked there. I am thankful to Vivien Richard in particular, who helped me find what I needed as the boxes were transferred to Pierrefitte. I am also especially grateful to Gérard Petitjean at the institution formerly known as the BDIC, who helped me receive permission from Cimade to view its archives, including their case files. I thank the staff at the Archives du Nord for searching for a VHS player so I could watch the videos stored in the archives of the SSFNA, as well as their help receiving permission to view the case files conserved there. I thank Anne-Marie Pathé at the Institut d'Histoire de Temps Présent, who made Monique Hervo's archives available to me; Tatiana Sagatni at Génériques, who helped me access AMANA's archives; and Laurence Le Bras at the Bibliothèque Nationale, who granted me permission to view Germaine Tillion's uncataloged papers.

In years of decreasing or nonexistent funding for humanities research, I am grateful to the institutions that made this work possible. At Boston

College, I thank the Morrissey College of Arts & Sciences and the Clough Center for Constitutional Democracy. This research was also supported through a partnership with the École Normale Supérieure, by the Social Sciences Research Council, the Society for French Historical Studies, and the American Historical Association. I completed research on the book project thanks to funding from the Jamie & Thelma Guilbeau Charitable Trust at the University of Louisiana at Lafayette. The Commonwealth Center for the Humanities and Society at the University of Louisville helped support publication. Bridget Barry and the team at the University of Nebraska Press offered valuable support and clarity of vision.

I am indebted to wonderful colleagues. At the University of Louisiana at Lafayette, I especially thank Ian Beamish, Sara Ritchey, and Sarah Cook Runcie. At the University of Louisville, I thank two supportive chairs, Blake Beattie and Chris Ehrick, as well as Terri Keeley, Katie Kleinkopf, Susan Ryan, and Jen Westerfeld. I am also thankful for the insightful and pivotal feedback provided by my fellow fellows at the Commonwealth Center for the Humanities and Society at the eleventh hour of this project. Virtual audiences at the French Empire Workshop and the Migration Studies Working Group provided important feedback on earlier iterations of chapters. I thank the editorial boards at *French Politics, Culture & Society* and *Gender & History*, their anonymous peer reviewers, and especially Herrick Chapman and Maud Bracke, whose feedback improved two articles that shaped the development of this larger work. A portion of the latter article is included in chapters 4 and 5. I am also appreciative of Margie Andersen and Melissa Byrnes, who helped me formulate ideas for another essay, a portion of which comes from the final chapter of this book.

I'm grateful to the people who make up my history network, who engaged with my work and made it better, and who helped me find belonging when I felt adrift. I offer profound thanks to those who have read parts of this work, talked me through analytical cul-de-sacs, or commented on talks, papers, and drafts in various iterations: Margie Andersen, Nimisha Barton, John Boonstra, Julian Bourg, Megan Brown, Melissa Byrnes, Brooke Durham, Darcie Fontaine, Sarah Griswold, Burleigh Hendrickson, Jennifer Johnson, Ethan Katz, Amy Limoncelli, Alessandra LaRocca Link, Amelia Lyons, Emily Marker, Shannon Monaghan, Minayo Nasiali, Jess Pearson, Terry Peterson, Ginny Reinburg, Sarah Cook Runcie, Miranda

Sachs, Sandrine Sanos, Todd Shepard, Jill Slaight, Alexandra Steinlight, and Owen White. I thank Anaïs Faurt, who prepared the index. Amelia gave me the very important tip to head to Lille for the regional archives of the Nord SSFNA and has graciously shared advice and expertise.

Julian Bourg taught me to quiet my impulse to complicate every claim and imparted advice that has become central to my historical ethos: understand first and critique second. Laura Frader's careful attention to detail has made me a better writer and strengthened every argument. Thomas Dodman offered critical framing advice at my defense that shaped my entire revision. Thank you to members of my cohort at BC who have remained friends long after, especially Pete Cajka, Erica Hodes, Amy Limoncelli, Shannon Monaghan, and Carolyn Twomey.

My deepest thanks go to mentors and friends who have supported me through the emotional journey of writing. Ginny Reinburg and Sylvia Sellers-García model the kind of scholar and teacher I want to be, and they have remained the most thoughtful of interlocutors. Melissa Byrnes and Burleigh Hendrickson have each illuminated some of the more shadowy aspects of publishing and academia. I thank Lisa Tankanow, my oldest friend, and Ali Link, one of my newest, who both encouraged me to get out of my own head. I cannot put into words all that I've learned from Alexandra Steinlight, a perceptive reader and steadfast friend whose timely interventions balanced careful judgment, unparalleled writerly instinct, and heartfelt support.

Especially during and after COVID, the pains of parenting and performing an all-consuming task like writing made our children's caregivers among the most cherished people in our lives: Dianne, Lisa and Aline, and Molly and Benita, among many others have made this book possible.

I thank my wonderful family, who did not ask me when this book would be finished. Marisa and Raph, my nieces Genevieve and Vivienne, and brand-new nephew Grant, Garth and Anna, Steph and Conor, and my dad, Mark, and Mary Ann. I miss Joan and John Durkin, Millie Moreland, and Carrie Dolmat-Connell. My mother, Patricia, has been my role model every day of my life. I have tried to write this book so it reflects the qualities of hers that I most like to think I inherited: her persistence, clarity of thought, and uncanny ability to put her finger on a structural problem.

I thank my darling daughters, Calla and Adele, for the inspiration and awe they have filled me with over the years of completing my dissertation and then this book. I've said it before, but it is no less true: before them, I was a historian who did not understand time. They've made me grateful for every minute.

Finally, Scott, who has been my family for two decades. Without his support, none of this would be possible. He makes everything in my life more joyful, vibrant, and wonderful.

Part of chapter 2 was previously published in "A Bridge across the Mediterranean: Nafissa Sid Cara and the Politics of Emancipation during the Algerian War," *French Politics, Culture & Society* 36, no. 2 (Summer 2018): 28–52.

Parts of chapters 4 and 5 were previously published in "Defining Family, Delimiting Belonging: Algerian Migration after the End of Empire," *Gender & History* 31 (October 2019): 681–98.

Part of chapter 6 was previously published in "Inessential Labor: Reproduction, Work, and Algerian Family Migration after Independence," in *Fertility, Family, and Social Welfare between France and Empire: The Colonial Politics of Population*, ed. Margaret Cook Andersen and Melissa K. Byrnes (Palgrave Macmillan, 2023).

ABBREVIATIONS

AMANA Assistance morale et aide aux nord-africains (Moral
Assistance for North Africans)

ASSFAM Association service social familial migrants (Migrant
Family Social Service Association)

ASSRA Adjointes sanitaires sociales rurales auxiliaires (Social
and sanitary rural auxiliary assistants)

ATOM Aide aux travailleurs d'outre-mer (Association for Aid to
Overseas Workers)

CADAF Centre de documentation et action familiale (Center for
Documentation and Familial Action)

CAF Caisse d'allocations familiales (Family Allowance Fund)

CANAM Commission d'aide aux nord-africains dans la metropole
(Commission for Aid to North Africans in the
Metropole)

CGT Confédération générale du travail (General
Confederation of Labor)

CIMADE Comité Inter-Mouvements auprès des Evacués (Inter-
Movement Committee for Evacuees)

CLAP Comité de liaison pour l'alphabétisation et la promotion
(Liaison Committee for Literacy and Promotion)

CNMF Comité national pour les musulmans français (National
Committee for French Muslims)

CTAM Conseillers techniques pour les affaires musulmanes
(Technical advisers for Muslim affairs)

DDASS Direction départementale des affaires sanitaires et sociales (Departmental Office for Sanitary and Social Affairs)

DOM Départements d'outre-mer (Overseas departments)

DPM Direction de la population et des migrations (Bureau of Population and Migrations)

EEC European Economic Community

EMSI Équipes médico-sociales itinérantes (Itinerant Medico-Social Teams)

ESNA Études sociales nord-africaines (North African Social Studies)

FAS Fonds d'action sociale (Social Action Fund)

FLN Front de libération nationale (National Liberation Front)

GPRA Gouvernement provisoire de la république algérienne (Provisional Government of the Algerian Republic)

HLM Habitation à loyer modéré (Low-income housing)

IGAME Inspecteur général de l'administration en mission extraordinaire (Inspector general for the administration)

INED Institut national d'études démographiques (National Institute for Demographic Study)

INSEE Institut national de la statistique et des études économiques (National Institution of Statistics and Economic Study)

JO *Journal officiel de la République française* (Official Journal of the French Republic)

MRAP Mouvement contre le racisme, l'anti-sémitisme et pour la paix (Movement against Racism and Antisemitism and for Peace)

MSF Mouvement de Solidarité Féminine (Women's Solidarity Movement)

OAS Organisation armée secrete (Secret Army Organization)

ONI Office National d'Immigration (National Immigration Office)

SAMAS Service des affaires musulmanes et de l'action sociale (Service for Muslim Affairs and Social Action)

SAS   Sections administratives spécialisées (Specialized Administrative Sections)

SAU   Sections administratives urbaines (Urban Administrative Sections)

SGI   Société Générale d'Immigration (General Immigration Society)

SLPM   Service de liaison et de promotion des migrants (Liaison Service for Migrant Support)

SONACOTRA   Société nationale de construction de logements pour les travailleurs (National Society for Construction of Housing for Workers)

SONACOTRAL   Société nationale de construction de logements pour les travailleurs originaires de l'Algérie et leurs familles (National Society for Construction of Housing for Algerian Workers and Their Families)

SSAE   Service social d'aide aux émigrants (Social Service for Aid to Emigrants)

SSFNA   Service social familial nord-africain (North African Family Social Service)

TOM   Territoires d'outre-mer (Overseas territories)

A NOTE ON LANGUAGE

Throughout the book, I use "Algerians" to refer to those legally designated as "French Muslims of Algeria" or "French with North African roots" during the late colonial period. While this is anachronistic in the sense that some metropolitan French referred to French settlers as "Algerians" during the colonial period and that Algeria did not exist as an independent country until 1962, it also reflects some nationalists' contemporary usage. If I follow French usage, I have put it in quotes because "North African" and "Muslim" are purposefully and historically vague signifiers created to legislate segregation and inequality. Following Laurent Dubois, I note that without proper historical analysis, we risk misunderstanding these discriminatory and racialized terms as "categories that can generate explanations rather than as social artifacts that demand them."[1]

Second, I also purposefully use the terms "migrant" and "migration" to express the multidirectionality of migration as well as the uncertain length of relocation during this period. I understand this uncertainty as an outcome of French policy decisions aiming to prevent migration from Algeria.

All translations from the original French are my own unless otherwise noted.

Disintegrating Empire

Introduction

Threads of Decolonization

In the summer of 1969, Madame Sahra K., an Algerian woman living in Roubaix, France, forgot her fabric in a classroom. She was learning to sew in a weekly stitching class offered by the regional office of the North African Family Social Service (SSFNA), a specialized social aid association created in the years after the Second World War. Seven years after Algerian independence, Madame K. was still among the many Algerian women to whom the SSFNA provided services. Upon realizing she had left her fabric behind, Madame K. asked her SSFNA social worker for help locating it. In the subsequent inquiry, the social worker wrote with clear pride at once self-referential and on behalf of Madame K.: "Since we just gave her a sewing machine, she is full of keenness for sewing."[1]

Madame K.'s request, like most social work, is quite ordinary, but we can nonetheless learn a surprising amount from this quotidian event. The broadest insight: French administrators continued to support sewing courses for North African and especially Algerian women despite Algerian independence and a wave of decolonization across North Africa. What accounts for this continuity? Then, I note Madame K., who still attended these weekly courses where she learned to use the sewing machine. What did she gain week after week, month after month, year after year? Finally, there is the social worker, whose correspondence asserts a certain level of trust between provisioner and client. While we never hear from Madame K. directly, in this letter written on her behalf, we sense Madame K.'s attachment to what she learned and her belief that the SSFNA could help her resolve at least this small problem.

The letter I cite comes from the K. family's dossier compiled by a social worker. Theirs is just one of over 2,700 family casework files held at the Archives du Nord in Lille, France, which contain the records of the regional SSFNA offices of Lille, Roubaix, and Tourcoing. The sheer number overwhelms, and her family's story reveals only one perspective of a much larger interventionist project on behalf of Algerians, the largest North African community in the area. In fact, the missing fabric is the least remarkable part of Madame K.'s file, which is full of the family's paperwork documenting the difficulties they faced receiving Monsieur K.'s promised disability benefits, the details of the couple's separation, and their children's temporary placement with another family. These records make up a dossier overstuffed with legal documents and procedural letters, representing years of advocacy on behalf of the K. family.

More to the point, through this missing fabric we can begin to understand the relationships at the center of the French welfare state—a pursuit at the heart of *Disintegrating Empire*. Families such as Madame K.'s usually met their specialized social workers and the social work team at moments of crisis or change, moments that had the potential to become what Arlette Farge and Michel Foucault famously called "family stories."[2] These stories, as I understand and relay them here, are fashioned from incomplete translations, case notes about families' intimate lives rendered in the social worker's hand. They function as an important—if not unmediated—opening for investigation. The stories also help me address the primary historical questions of this study: If Algeria gained independence in 1962, why did French social services for families from Algeria persist and even grow after independence? How do these services help us understand the social-historical process of decolonization?

To answer these questions, I follow three primary "threads" of analysis: the history of the midcentury welfare state, family migration from Algeria, and the social work relationships created by these phenomena. I take this metaphor from the sewing and stitching classes offered to students like Madame K., which were among specialized social aid associations' most popular offerings during the late colonial era and well into the post-independence period.[3] They functioned as a space for sociability among women, and, in French social workers' minds, as a place for potential integration to French society. There, newly arrived women from Algeria could observe their French teachers and begin to emulate more integrated fellow Algerian and North African students. I follow these threads throughout the book to illustrate that French welfare institutions evolved after Algerian independence in a way that preserved empire at their core.

These three threads also slowly (and somewhat incompletely) disintegrated as various offices and ministries sought to erase administrative holdovers of French Algeria. I have chosen these specific threads to understand how this imperial relationship worked loose. In doing so, I find that some threads frayed faster than others. For example, guaranteed free circulation migration agreements between France and independent Algeria ended quickly. Other threads took longer to unravel, unmaking the empire slowly rather than all at once. Historians have insisted upon 1962 as an important point of rupture *and* on the long-lasting effects of the French Fifth Republic's birth during the Algerian War.[4] I am deeply interested in continuity and rupture, as this book shows. I also engage with these issues to make a methodological argument: I take up Frederick Cooper's invitation to think of decolonization as a process, one that I might add was uneven, altered by the threads one pulls.[5]

For this reason, *Disintegrating Empire* examines the entangled history of the French midcentury welfare state and the specialized social aid associations created to assist it, family migration from Algeria, and social workers who mediated between the state and its clients as they carried out their care work. After the Second World War, welfare policy experts stitched social services for Algerians into the structure of the midcentury welfare state. Once the Algerian War began in 1954, two French republics, many successive administrations, and ultimately two independent states—France and Algeria—continuously tailored welfare to support specialized social aid services for Algerian families migrating across the Mediterranean. These last-ditch efforts pulled the threads tauter, making it more difficult to eventually separate them. I pursue this story beyond Algerian independence. Algerians became the largest migrant population on metropolitan French soil in 1972, but they had long been the specific focus of legal regimes seeking to prevent their migration or their access to social benefits while in France. I end with French disinvestment in specialized welfare services on the eve of the election of Socialist François Mitterrand to the French presidency in 1981.

Through this metaphor, I also imply something deeper. These threads made up the fabric that had once tethered Algeria to France. While I follow the threads of midcentury welfare, family migration, and the resulting social work relationships separately, they were also entwined, reinforcing each other. I therefore find it necessary to follow the relationship between these threads as well. After years of colonial racism and efforts that aimed to "civilize" Algerians under empire, the French welfare network for Algerians did not come apart so quickly.[6] Specialized welfare services for Algerians and their colonial-era goals were embedded in the infrastructure of the French midcentury welfare state. The persistence of these services—maligned, understaffed, and underfunded though they were—"unsettled" the republic, as Mayanthi Fernando has suggested.[7] They attest to the continued centrality of Algerians and Algeria to France's welfare state during this long period of decolonization.[8]

With the collapse of empire, some of the welfare state's prodigious benefits also belatedly unraveled. In the late colonial period, French policy experts at many levels—welfare provisioners, mid-level bureaucrats, ministers of health, population, immigration, and even the Interior, charged with the Algerian question—agreed that specialized social services for Algerians supported French empire and unburdened metropolitan welfare offices. Despite, or perhaps because of this connection, the specialized welfare network grew after Algerian independence. This growth led these same architects to try to tailor welfare services exclusively to French citizens.[9] The collapse of these specialized services for Algerians in the 1970s, over a decade after Algerian independence, shows that defunding social services has a much longer history defined by exacting controls on colonial citizens and migrants of newly independent countries while in France. The welfare state's story was not merely one of rise and fall, but of winnowing "deserving" clients. The techniques of restriction they used—the bureaucratic webs woven to deny coverage and stopgap partnerships of private organizations staffed by teams far too small for jobs much too large—connected the end of empire to the transnational politics of neoliberalism in the 1980s and 1990s. Administrative vestiges of empire as well as the logics that propped them up persevered in France after Algerian independence. The family migration prompted by Algerian independence ultimately reveals the limits of the midcentury welfare state.

I begin with Madame K. for a final reason: this is a book about Algerians' and Algeria's particular place in the midcentury welfare state and the French imaginary at the end of empire. My study makes three interventions to this end. First, by connecting the periods following the Second World War and Algerian independence, I chart the slow evolution of institutions fostered through empire as they disintegrated.[10] Second, social histories of this longer period have tended to be place- or policy-based, as is the case for Minayo Nasiali's study of welfare for migrant populations in Marseille after the Second World War or Muriel Cohen's analysis of Algerian families' housing in Paris.[11] I build from these important studies to focus on the intermediary space between high-level policy decisions headquartered in Paris and the "street-level bureaucrats'" of the Nord who translated these policies on the ground.[12] Finally, and to my mind most importantly, I analyze the relationships established between social workers, specialized social aid associations, and their clients to insist upon their centrality to decolonization. Though I often illustrate this claim through individual family stories, my intent is not to suggest that individual social workers or associations were simply "bad apples" that upheld colonialist and racist ideologies. To the contrary, I see these discrete stories as proof that the midcentury state owed its structure to empire. *Disintegrating Empire* is not just about the state or associations or migrants, but rather the dynamic, conflicting, and often messy nature of the relationships that were nurtured through the midcentury welfare state and that circumscribed Algerians' belonging.

Algeria and France: A Case for Specificity

Algeria, Algerians, and the Algerian War hold a unique place in the history of French empire, independence movements, and decolonization. The invasion of Algiers in 1830 began a history of imperial conquest unlike many others on which France embarked.[13] In 1848 France made Algeria a legal territory of France, effectively extending France across the Mediterranean.[14] This unique history of territorial assimilation led to a large-scale effort to settle Algeria with French and other European settlers who eventually became known as *pieds noirs*.[15] To promote this settlement scheme, French law and local government expropriated the land of indigenous populations of Algeria, including descendants of other empires spanning from the Romans to the Ottomans. Many other French territories remained colonies or protectorates without large settler populations or territorial integration. A French monarchy, an empire, and two republics all denied citizenship and political equality to Algerians until 1946, nearly a century after Algerian land had become French.

Historians have attested to the scars and silences that mark this history and, later, the brutal war for independence.[16] I also make the argument for the singularity of the Algerian case by investigating Algerians' interactions with the welfare state. During the final years of empire and after Algerian independence, Algerians were exempted from the bilateral treaties that governed other foreign nationals' and current and former colonial citizens' migration to France. As "paradoxical citizens," Algerians had access to French nationality cards and social rights under empire.[17] They also posed a real and metaphorical challenge to French borders.[18] The Evian Accords signed by France and the Provisional Government of the Algerian Republic (GPRA) guaranteed independent Algerians free circulation across the Mediterranean. This agreement stood in contrast to post-independence guarantees with other former French colonies, matched only by promises of open borders made in the 1957 Treaty of Rome for members of the European Economic Community.[19] This laxity led the French government to single-mindedly pursue a policy of limiting Algerian migration, and especially Algerian families' migration, after independence in the 1960s. This pursuit led to a disproportionate focus on Algerian family migration as a "problem."

Though I show that empire came apart slowly, I do not mean to deny the importance of independence as a political event. For anti-colonial actors, pro-colonial protectionists, and everyday citizens, the end of empire in Algeria represented a sea change in France's and Algeria's standing in the world and their reputations at home and abroad. It also allowed France to position Algerian independence as the logical and predetermined endpoint of empire, as historian Todd Shepard has argued.[20] I sort through narrative threads about the end of this empire to untangle the long period of decolonization.[21] The unique services the midcentury welfare state offered to Algerian families during the late colonial period ultimately made limiting their migration after independence even more crucial. By pulling apart these three separate and important threads, I ask how and for whom the midcentury welfare state worked. I endeavor here not only to show Algerians' specificity in light of other migration agreements and bilateral treaties but also to argue that their specificity led French policymakers to undermine the midcentury welfare state.

Thread One: The Midcentury Welfare State

Building on the work of Philip Nord and Herrick Chapman, I draw out the remarkable continuities of care and provisioning of services that spanned the Third, Fourth, and Fifth Republics as well as Vichy.[22] The midcentury welfare state also sustained interwar familialist and racist policies. When welfare services were first established in France following the late nineteenth-century Bismarckian invention, the French business class helped shape early French welfare according to a male breadwinner/female homemaker model, a model that also restrained wages and promoted the birth rate, as Laura Frader has shown.[23] Paternalism was intrinsic to this design, as was the belief that benefits would prompt workers to have more robust families.

Though the French state progressively took over these responsibilities from private enterprise, evidence of welfare's earlier imprint remained. In 1932 a law mandated family benefits for all employees, linking the right to welfare to the nuclear family. Slowly, over the course of the 1930s, and especially with the establishment of the Fourth Republic in 1946, the French welfare state included benefits as varied as social security, health care, pensions, family and maternity benefits, and unemployment and workers' compensation. Far from unified, these benefits were managed cooperatively by workers and employers and funded by both parties' contributions.[24] The law also included the creation of public-private specialized social aid associations for North Africans, finally citizens of France but requiring, in the French administration's eyes, additional social support.

Following historian Amy Offner, I characterize this set of services as the midcentury welfare state.[25] This focus on the "midcentury" redirects the European historiography's insistence on a simple and unproblematic "post": after the war, after the empire. While the history that *Disintegrating Empire* recounts primarily takes place after the Second World War, I emphasize the recurring conflicts that characterized this midcentury welfare state across administrations. These administrations were all committed to protecting the family to preserve French society. Vichy's emphasis on the family was a through line for the welfare state, as was its populationist and xenophobic thinking (themselves holdovers from the Third Republic).[26] Indeed, social benefits for citizens of France were meant to encourage a demographic boom in the 1950s and 1960s and laid the groundwork for a welfare state based explicitly around the conjugal family as the primordial unit of French society.

By using this term, I also mean to broaden our understanding of what constituted welfare administratively. The reach of the French welfare state is well known—covering birth to death—but the midcentury welfare state included more than pensions, social security, and health care. It was also a decentralized and ad hoc administration, which was not simply directed by French government officials. The midcentury welfare state included para-state and non-state social service associations that had their own agendas and that nonetheless scaffolded the welfare state to provide specific remedial support. From the perspective of Algerian families, the midcentury welfare state was a bricolage of offices, comprising the central administration and sprawling outward to para-public specialized social aid associations that served North African populations.

Racial difference—or religious and ethnic difference *imagined* as racial difference—was also crucial to the midcentury welfare state.[27] Particularly as France became the capital of migration in the interwar period, welfare services delimited deserving from undeserving, whether according to lines of nationality, politics, or colonial status. Pronatalists and familialists inside government were concerned with promoting the French birth rate while managing costs.[28] While Nimisha Barton underscores the welfare state's relative largesse on behalf of migrant women "so long as they be mothers," in my reading her study also reveals the growing conflation of Europeanness, whiteness, and deservedness.[29] As Amelia Lyons has powerfully shown, specialized social aid associations for Algerian families that developed in the postwar period represented an attempt to erase Algerians' supposed racialized, gendered, and religious differences through a "civilizing mission in the metropole."[30]

My study traces the transformation of specialized welfare services in a dynamic triangular relationship with its clients and the state *across* the period of Algerian independence, rather than ending with this pivotal moment. These public-private partnerships were born from need during the 1940s and 1950s as Algerians moved to France to rebuild it after the

Second World War. While in France, Algerian workers—who, according to the gendered recruitment practices of the French state, were mostly men—also theoretically gained access to these provisions while taking part in France's economic and social revival. Social services were not just aimed at workers but also their families.[31] Migrant men, women, and children could also become objects of the welfare state's alleged reformative powers if not always recipients of its reputed benefits. During the Algerian War, Lyons and others have demonstrated that welfare also functioned as a weapon.[32] Efforts to win the "hearts and minds" of the Algerian population and to preserve French Algeria took root in the Algerian home. Metropolitan grand plans, the settler colonial assembly, and the might of the French army all came to bear on Algerian populations through increasingly sophisticated and coordinated counter-intelligence operations and state-supported volunteer outreach alike. Social workers, teachers, aides, informal auxiliaries, associations, and nongovernmental organizations all staked claims to neutrality even while working within the colonial context that created the conditions for this social aid's necessity in the first place.[33] In the case of French Algeria at the end of empire, engaged French citizens seeking to fill the gap in colonial care still took part in the politics of empire at their peak.

Though at the time the French government in France and Algeria envisioned specialized welfare for Algerians as a weapon in a deadly colonial war, this explanation does not account for why these services persisted after the war's end. I insist upon Algerians' disproportionate visibility to French and Algerian officials, policymakers, and agents of the welfare state after 1962. Efforts to integrate the Algerian family did not end with French empire in Algeria.[34] They became even more crucial once Algerians became mostly foreigners on French soil, demanded for their labor but unwelcome because they were members of families.[35]

In other words, the framing of welfare as warfare does not capture the complexities of this particular case. I also speculate that we might find in late colonial and especially early postcolonial welfare the antecedents to neoliberal *workfare*. This term, coined in the United States in the 1980s, refers to the exchange of labor for social benefits.[36] France's bilateral treaties outlined the terms for foreign nationals' social rights while living abroad in France. Although some European citizens were guaranteed family and maternity benefits, Algerians' social rights were always in question. Over the period spanning Algerian independence to the election of Mitterrand, French policymakers attempted to curtail Algerians' access to family benefits, especially limiting maternity benefits for fear of encouraging births. Benefits were meant for the laboring Algerian worker, not his gestating wife. Though labor migration was so often rendered as masculine, it was a conjugal family affair, and, as Lauren Stokes has pointed out in the case of guest workers in West Germany, male laborers were also members of families.[37] Suggesting otherwise contributed to the myth of "cheap" migrant labor whose seasonal work patterns meant social benefits were less a question of citizenship or family dependency than a contract that was conditional as well as revocable.[38]

Undermining welfare for Algerian families could equally represent the government's attempt at neoliberal cuts to welfare.[39] Over time the French government curtailed family migration from Algeria and insisted instead upon family resettlement *only after* a head of household had migrated to France, found housing, and acquired a job. The loopholes in this language tied social benefits—and the right to live in France—to labor, which weakened the familialist model of the midcentury welfare state. While most Algerians in France officially became foreigners in 1962, successive French administrations continued to offer them social benefits in exchange for their labor. Family benefits were contingent in this new era on the head of household's measurable labor for French industry and families' own demonstrations of their deservedness—their commitment to integration. These benefits were often difficult to access, proving how the "wages of whiteness," in David Roediger's memorable phrase, acted upon non-European migrants.[40] The end of empire institutionalized specialized social aid associations for Algerians as a service apart. The economic downturn of the 1970s threw Algerian family migration into question, as blanket immigration bans and conservative social policies made funding for foreign families' benefits more uncertain. By the opening of France's neoliberal era in the 1990s, welfare access had become increasingly conditional, whether French, foreign, or caught somewhere in the morass of citizenship paperwork following the end of empire.

By unraveling the thread of the midcentury welfare state, it becomes clear that to speak of the contemporary "crisis" of the welfare state misses much earlier and critical turning points in the provisioning of social services.[41] Framing the welfare state as "in crisis" during the 1980s and 1990s presumes an earlier period of stability. But welfare was always imperiled, often in question for Algerians, whether they were subjects or citizens of France or foreign nationals living abroad. The winnowing of welfare followed a colonialist logic that viewed the Algerian migrant family as a constraint rather than an opportunity for promoting belonging. When we reframe the history of welfare along the axis of decolonization, we see there was no "golden age" of welfare for Algerians.

Thread Two: Family Migration from Algeria and the Failures of Integration

Abdelmalek Sayad famously argued that Algerian family migration only followed single worker migration, locating the former phenomenon in the 1970s.[42] Lyons and others have made clear that family migration from Algeria in fact began much earlier, following the Second World War.[43] In this book I focus on family migration from Algeria in the post-independence period.[44] In these years of increasing migration to France, French and Algerian diplomats became especially concerned with family migration for the problems they believed it presented. French diplomats weighed the cost of hosting the family relative to the labor the father provided. For their part, Algerian diplomats equated family migration with permanence and sought to prevent the "brain drain" that they believed family migration augured. This permanent relocation symbolized loss of knowledge and professional training that the Evian Accords and subsequent Franco-Algerian agreements mandated that France offer Algerian nationals working abroad. Both states converged in their understanding that family migration represented permanence and therefore introduced an imperative to *belong* alongside an ability to migrate.

As such, I trace family migration from Algeria as it grew from the years of the Algerian War even through the 1974 French temporary ban on migration. Family migration from Algeria did not become an important point of policy discussion in and of itself. Instead, in the eyes of French bureaucrats, it was crucial to harness because they linked family migration with societal disintegration.[45] Foreign workers from the European Economic Community and southern Europe received French benefits, including family allocations for Italian (and, later, Spanish and Portuguese) workers, whether their families lived in France or remained in their home countries.[46] The French negotiated these bilateral accords to compete with other European countries for workers in a tight labor market. Algerians, though, were part of a separate immigration regime negotiated at independence in 1962. According to the agreement, Algerian families were entitled to the same social rights as French citizens, including the right to family and housing subsidies as well as pensions and unemployment.[47] After independence the French hastened to restrict migration and equal access to social rights where they could.

At the crux of the issue was *integration*, a policy that, in the late years of Algerian empire had referred to the political integration of the two territories under one legal rubric, but, after independence, became a soft measure of Algerians' social and cultural belonging in France.[48] Here, I turn to Sayad, who called integration a "loaded notion" that implied "a state, a point of arrival" that was nonetheless "never total and never totally or definitively achieved." This was due in part to its colonial heritage.[49] During the colonial era politicians promoted "integration" as a set of policies that made Algeria a part of France. Integrationists such as Jacques Soustelle, the governor general of Algeria in 1955, promoted these policies to improve the standard of living in Algeria, offer full political and social rights to Algerians, and insist upon the future value of French Algeria. These rights, according to integrationists, were granted to Algerians *regardless* of religious or ethnic difference, insisting upon Algerians' inassimilability to French legal and social codes.[50]

The most important gulf between the two meanings grew from social workers' interpretation of integrationist metropolitan and colonial policy. For over a century successive French administrations, colonial officials, and European settlers participated in making Algerians different, part of a long-term and large-scale project to make "Muslim" into a racialized "sliding signifier," as Stuart Hall memorably put it.[51] And, as Judith Surkis has shown, this effort was sexualized in nature and naturalized through law. The "Muslim family" was a distinct legal entity, founded on Roman and French frameworks of plural law known as personal status law. This discriminatory regime legitimated Algerian difference by endorsing a Franco-European definition of the conjugal nuclear family. French colonialists had consistently positioned the authoritarian father, the subservient and religious mother, the absent complementarity of the couple, the unruly son, and the under-nurtured daughter as justifications for Algerians' exclusion from French citizenship.[52] Consequently, in midcentury France these archetypes all became targets of intervention in the integrationists' imagination. These underperforming familial characters—either alone or in sum—had the potential to create instability in the home and especially in France's social fabric. As the number of families from Algeria grew, they became a crucial target of social workers' and the welfare state's attention. The imagined dysfunctional family dynamic necessitated social work's integrationist efforts as a cultural imperative to assure Algerians' belonging in France.[53]

Integration was never quite attainable in the sense that it insisted upon Algerian difference as its starting point. It was thus both an imperiled project from the outset and strikingly resilient. After Algerian independence, Algerians' ability to transform or hide this difference determined their futures in France. The social and cultural mandates social workers used looked like something closer to assimilation, an older concept that historians have interpreted as the asymptotic quest to make colonial subjects into Frenchmen.[54] Algerian families could be taught to speak French, Algerian men could receive paraprofessional training to better fulfill their employers' demands, and Algerian women such as Madame K. could continue to attend housekeeping, sewing, and knitting classes. Only then could Algerian families learn to take advantage of their social rights, to navigate the welfare state as French families. Social welfare's purported failure to ease this integration served as a justification for ever more stringent border controls for families as well as forced deportation policies in the 1970s.

If, as the French children of Algerian migrants asserted in the 1980s, France had sought to erase Algerians and the Algerian War from its social fabric, this was a belated operation, achieved only in the 1970s and early 1980s.[55] By the late 1970s, I show how French politicians, many of whom had been in government since the colonial era, sought to eradicate specialized social services for Algerians that had existed since the late years of empire by mounting the case for those services' failure to integrate Algerian families. Family migration, a second durable thread connecting France's empire to its present, required the integrationist work provided by social services. It thus worked as a powerful institutional reminder of France's colonial past even as French administrators sought to undermine it.

Thread Three: Moral Neocolonialism and
the Social Work Relationship

Finally, I tease out a third thread: the intermediary role played by specialized social aid associations and individual social workers navigating between Algerian families and the midcentury welfare state.[56] I argue that colonial racism's afterlives shaped social policy for *all* foreign beneficiaries of the French welfare state. While an earlier historiography of postwar immigration to France prioritized state-led narratives of social disintegration and policy disagreements, newer studies bring the local to the fore.[57] In *Disintegrating Empire* I insist upon the presence of individual families beneath the official statistics. Social workers' interventions were rarely one-off phenomena; they encountered brothers and sisters, extended families, and entire neighborhoods through word of mouth and drop-in visits at their offices. Encounters like these—and indeed women's weekly presence in classes—should trouble how historians of welfare tend to categorize relationships of power and coercion, care work and social aid.[58] The dialectical nature of social work invites questions about how we categorize relationships of power between the state, para-state actors, and marginalized citizens and noncitizens.

This is not to say that integration as social workers interpreted it—as a form of assimilation—was a "good" or "bad" idea. Rather I pose the question: How did the dynamic relationship between specialized social workers and their Algerian clients shape their care *and* the larger history of the French welfare state? I draw from Andrea Muelhebach's argument in the Italian context that the sense of morality animating social workers' care work was both a "social palliative" and a "smokescreen," which is to say, it was both deeply felt and a veil for the state's repressive agenda. Social workers helped collapse the state-supported care network in favor of private initiatives that undermined their own positions. In my analysis, social workers functioned as moral neocolonialists—to paraphrase Muelhebach—who propped up successive colonial and, later, postcolonial administrations. They accepted the bureaucratic parameters of the colonial state and worked within—and sometimes against—it in "critical-complicit" ways.[59] My analysis of this thread shows how these relationships at the heart of social work helped tether welfare services to empire.

After Algerian independence social workers in France found themselves charged with the interpretation of French legal regimes of citizenship on the one hand and Algerian needs on the other. They made these judgments relative to other "categories" of migrants whose supposed ability to belong shifted alongside definitions of Europeanness during a period of European integration.[60] As historian Darcie Fontaine has shown, social workers were often driven to this care work out of a religious—read: Christian and often Catholic—commitment to serving the underserved.[61] They were almost always young women, many of whom, at least initially, had held postings in colonial North Africa. Many could speak either Arabic or Kabyle and were engaged in professional development to improve their interventions with Algerian and North African families. Over time, French social workers sought to recruit from among their clients, though with little evidence of success. Especially by the 1970s these associations frequently attested to the difficulty of hiring *anyone* to take on this work, finding that many new trainees lacked the expertise or will.

Those who worked with the SSFNA and other social work associations cultivated relationships with families that, in some cases, lasted years. Social workers, family home aides, and course instructors introduced themselves to Algerian communities, whether in the workplace, low-income housing, hospitals, schools, or other civic spaces. They made connections between local housing, hiring, and social service providers and newly arrived families, helped open bank accounts, brought women to the grocery store, taught them to use the subway or local public transport, and made introductions to the local school and after-school programs for children. The quotidian details of this work are often left out of the scholarly literature, which focuses on the state's instrumental and bureaucratic logic. I draw from the thousands of "family stories" recounted in social work paperwork in the Nord's archives to bring the relationships between Algerian families and social workers, the relationships at the heart of the profession, back into the narrative. I do so without losing sight of the larger mechanisms that structured social workers' decisions and possibilities.

As we see through Madame K., migrant families forged relationships with employees of social aid associations even as they navigated the fraught colonial dynamics of belonging in France. I acknowledge the often-insurmountable constraints that Algerian families faced in trying to gain an audience for their cases—how they may have confronted institutional and interpersonal racism in their attempts to access the resources the French administration made available to them. Perceptions of Algerian families were both created by and built upon the family stories told by the social aid associations at the forefront of the migration process. Even at the most idiosyncratic and personal levels reflected in these dossiers, the difficulties encountered in social work relationships came to have lives of their own.

I am also acutely aware of the constraints of my own research. I read one of every five SSFNA casework files conserved in the Lille archives as well as more casework files from other social aid associations. Given the nature of these sources, my work and these family stories unavoidably amplify some of the problems imagined by the French midcentury welfare state rather than the very real problems flagged by Algerian families. Especially detailed, thick dossiers like Madame K.'s include police reports, litigation records, correspondence between multiple French agencies contesting marriage, divorce, child placement, and other private dramas, while others who never encountered these legal and institutional structures provide little insight into the family's history at all. The selection bias of these archives is abundantly clear. While French administrators and even some social workers described Algerian migration in spectacular terms ("exodus," "anarchy," "flood"), families' quotidian realities did not necessarily make it into casework files.[62] It's mostly *not* fabric left behind in classrooms.

Yet I found these sources a necessary complement to the work I did in the central administration's archives in Paris. I studied governmental reports, which included presidential dictates down through mid-level management's interpretations to individuals' syntheses of the so-called Algerian problem. I spent much time combing through the records of the Social Action Fund, which underwrote the budgets of specialized social aid associations from the fund's creation in 1958 through my period of study. Annual reports from specialized social aid associations testified to their work, spoke to their continued need for funding, and presented a public face that in many respects glossed over internal contradictions and problems. By turning to the internal archives of the SSFNA, I consider the specialized social work apparatus as the work of individuals rather than the design of an all-seeing French state, or even successive French administrations. At no point did social workers seek to render themselves invisible: they made claims both well-meaning and self-preservationist on behalf of their clients and themselves to justify their continued efforts. Even as the memory of the Algerian War and decolonization became hazy for some in metropolitan France, social workers and families from Algeria carried this legacy with them through their institutional affiliations and family paperwork.

Threads of Decolonization Untangled

I imagine the threads I have described—the midcentury welfare state, Algerian family migration, and social work relationships—as distinct but interwoven, which help us understand the resilient shape of French welfare over the long period of decolonization. Social workers, agents of midcentury welfare, upheld welfare's institutional structure and guided the integration of families from Algeria. The disparate threads of disintegrating empire that connected France and Algeria gave both territories form and meaning over 130 years. The fabric that emerged proved durable, but not everlasting. My threads help us understand why this was so.

Narratively, these three threads undergird the chronology of this book. Without thinking through how tightly welfare and empire were tied, we cannot understand how this connection unraveled. These threads also make a nuanced reading of the social process of decolonization possible. Because decolonization occurred according to multiple timelines depending on the institution in question, I take up individual threads in different chapters to examine them in greater detail. While chapters may dwell specifically on one thread, as I make clear, they always existed in relationship with each other. The book proceeds largely but not perfectly chronologically to revisit each thread's distinct history. This is a stylistic as well as an analytical choice that illuminates the dynamic way the midcentury welfare state evolved with Algerian independence. Finally, these threads allow for multiple readings of the *same* people, organizations, and offices, showing the competing meanings these actors ascribed to their work.

Disintegrating Empire is composed of six chapters that bring the diplomatic, administrative, cultural, and political stakes of decolonization into focus. Synthetic chapters—chapters 1 and 6—bookend my story to show how the three intertwined threads at the heart of this history worked together. The other chapters focus on specific threads. In chapter 1 I argue that the familialist roots of the welfare state allowed for the emergence of a specialized social welfare network of associations for Algerian families to promote integration. The integrationist goals of this network were not beholden to Algerians' French citizenship, which allowed these services to outlast empire in Algeria. Chapter 2 focuses especially on the development of the social work profession during the Algerian War to make the case that the war profoundly shaped this work. I argue that the absence of care in the earlier colonial era served to stifle all provisioners' eventual efforts. In chapter 3 I retrace the institutional history of the midcentury welfare state from the start of the Fifth Republic in 1958 to 1966. Algerian-specific welfare, which paradoxically expanded in the 1960s, continued its mission to integrate families from Algeria though they were no longer citizens of France. Even as offices of state sought to distance themselves from their colonial past, its presence remained in personnel, mission, and state-building projects.

Chapters 4 and 5 are interconnected. In chapter 4 I explore family migration as a policy debate between France and Algeria. Between 1962 and 1973, the year of the oil shock, both countries worked to curtail the resettlement of families from Algeria in France. I show how Algerian families—and not single male workers—came to represent the post-independence "immigrant problem." Consequently, chapter 5 examines how social work organizations sought to integrate these "problem immigrants." I revisit the same period from Algerian independence to the oil shock to interrogate the nature of social work within specialized social aid associations as they reformulated integration for newly arrived Algerian migrant families who were no longer citizens of France.

In chapter 6, a final synthetic chapter, I examine the economic downturn that led to political and public debates about the place of migrants on French soil. Though France suspended worker migration in 1974, I argue that Algerian women were in fact a central policy concern. When French administrators compared them to increasingly visible working European migrant women against the backdrop of European integration, Algerian women seemed even more absent from the French workforce. The resulting restructuring of the midcentury welfare state prioritized European migrants and disassembled Algerian-specific care.

Even as the many threads frayed, the connection between France and Algeria held. Understanding their slow disintegration challenges the chronology of decolonization as a singular event. This period witnessed the winnowing of a midcentury welfare state as administrators resized and tailored it for French and European migrant populations. At first glance these services for Algerians may appear as a blip on the radar, a curious hangover from the colonial era that died off only slowly. The movement of families back and forth between France and Algeria seemed to ebb and flow according to the expansion and contraction of the so-called Thirty Glorious Years of post–World War II economic expansion.[63] Shifts of labor and family migration patterns were nonetheless refracted through deeper cultural logics of integration tied to historically, socially, and culturally contingent definitions of the family and gender roles. Growing numbers of migrating families from Algeria encountered obstacles to obtaining their benefits as well as constricted definitions of the "family" that aimed to prevent equal access. Family migration after the end of empire led to a new institutional home for specialized social aid associations. They were isolated as window dressing to the welfare state, foreshadowing later and deeper cuts to social services. Algerian families' supposed failure to integrate contributed to the fracture of their specialized social services, undermining the sprawling mosaic of the midcentury welfare state.

This is not a specifically French political problem, as welfare regimes across the Global North have positioned non-white populations as problems in need of excess support rather than equally worthy beneficiaries of services. Here I attempt to make clear the colonial politics of welfare. Since the 1980s, attacks on social services have configured welfare benefits as an "entitlement" rather than a human right. Resurgent right-wing regimes have targeted access for immigrants, citizens of color, and eventually poor white citizens. These techniques of restriction were part of earlier efforts to reconcile the history of empire with the new politics of global labor and immigration. There is no shortage of threats to welfare; here I especially underscore the failure to understand the past and the pernicious ways in which politics on the right and the left have coalesced to restrict welfare to those who need it.

1

A Greater French Family

Germaine Detrez worked on the first floor of a nineteenth-century building at 218 rue Nationale in Lille. Once at her desk, she was the first social
worker employed by the inaugural regional office of the North African
Family Social Service (SSFNA), which opened in January 1952. Since then
she had dedicated her time to helping newly arrived "Muslim"—mostly
Algerian—families acclimate to France.[1] In the first year Detrez expanded
her team to include a second social worker and a family home aide—both
French women—to help her visit over two hundred Algerian families
and one hundred "mixed" Franco-Algerian families.[2] Their task: providing
remedial services, education, and training to colonial subjects from Algeria
who had recently become citizens of France. Detrez and her coworkers
built on a long-standing tradition of benevolent care work by non- and
para-state actors and especially women.[3] Their efforts often bore fruit, not
least with the French administration, which was increasingly concerned
with broadcasting a multiracial and multiethnic greater France to its allies
abroad and its detractors in the empire.

In this chapter I build upon historians' investigations of the specialized
social services network at the end of empire to introduce my three analytic
threads and the dynamic relationship between them at the twilight of
empire.[4] Together these threads illustrate the French republic's commitment to familialism beyond metropolitan France as well as the ways that
Algerians' French citizenship allowed them to negotiate the specialized
welfare network created on their behalf.[5] Historians of France have long
established that the family served as the acculturating institution par excel-
lence.[6] Successive French administrations had prioritized the family as the

primordial political and social unit. Familialists in the Third Republic, distinct from pronatalists with whom they collaborated, were concerned with demographic growth *and* the "moral quality" of the families that ensued.[7] They helped create an infrastructure for family policy in the nascent welfare state. Families, they believed, were the "nursery of the state," the incubator through which individuals became French.[8] Architects of midcentury welfare later tailored these services so they were primarily accessible to French citizens and European migrants, now prioritized. Colonial citizens and especially Algerians had much more difficulty gaining access to their benefits, which were not only circumscribed but also differential.

I trace the French state's commitment to familialism at many levels, from its largest global postwar institution, the French Union, all the way to the inner workings of specialized social aid within the midcentury welfare state. This commitment legitimized the political integration of France with its colonies, creating a new framework for a greater French family. I show how France's migration management system and the bilateral accords that governed it established a loophole for Algerian families to migrate and access social services that were not open to families of other migrant workers or colonial citizens. Social workers mediated between their clients and the state to translate laws governing migration and access to social welfare, while also insisting that their clients conform to French definitions of normative family life. The familialism inherent in these institutions rested on the importance of growing France's metropolitan population to counterbalance the non-white populations of France and its colonies. This familialism also paradoxically contributed to a system that prioritized Algerian family migration over other colonial citizens and justified their access to social benefits.

The period immediately following the Second World War thus gave birth to a more expansive welfarist spirit of social aid and to the late colonial logic that rejected empire as such. Colonial frameworks provided additional social services to Algerian families and promoted their belonging. Both these developments required an assumption of Algerian difference and an imperative to integrate. While French politicians primarily thought of integration as a political phenomenon, one that brought together France and Europe, France and Africa, and France and Algeria, integration also had a cultural meaning.[9] Integrationist policy flipped the civilizing mission, which demanded assimilation prior to citizenship, on its head.[10] Instead, integrationists assumed Algerians would remain different, fundamentally un-French despite their French citizenship. Cultural belonging was therefore an unfinished and unachievable task. Nonetheless, specialized social services made integrating the Algerian family the core of their work, tying this project to the reimagining of French empire.

When Union Was Not Enough: Algeria and France

The reconfiguration of empire after World War II relied on what had come before, though the emphasis was now on the political integration of the colonies, including a broader conception of France and French citizenship. Algeria was always unique in French empire. Since 1848, when the Second French Republic divided colonial Algeria into three departments with equal standing to their metropolitan counterparts, Algeria was France.[11] A hundred years later, following the Second World War, European nations hastened to rid themselves of any affiliation to empire after the collapse of the Third Reich. The French Union thus emerged in 1946, integrating French territories across the globe into France proper in a manner not dissimilar from the Algerian model of the century prior. Political integration created a new geopolitical order, which remade France as a federation of the metropole and its colonies, now simply territories of a French Union.[12] As had been the case with Algeria, this disavowal did not necessarily signal a rethinking of colonial relationships.

The eventual Union included the "old colonies," many of which became overseas departments (DOM), such as Martinique and Guadeloupe, and overseas territories (TOM), as well as Indochina, which in 1949 became Vietnam, Laos, and Cambodia. It also extended to the protectorates, now associated states, Morocco and Tunisia, as well as UN trusteeships. It naturally failed to include the former French Levant, Lebanon and Syria, which had declared independence during the war. Algeria was different. While Algeria was integral to France's empire, Algerians' place in the French Union was both taken for granted and difficult to define. There was no consensus about *why* Algeria was a member of the French Union, however: Because it was a colony? Or because it was France?[13]

French Union citizenship put all residents of the Union on equal footing—at least theoretically. The Constitution of the Fourth Republic recognized that the political integration created by the French Union included peoples and territories with differing demands, which created difficulties from the start. It promised citizens of France and the French Union "sacred and inalienable" rights regardless of "race, religion, or creed."[14] To wit, constitutional articles 80 and 81 granted French Union citizenship to all members of the French Union while allowing for potential limitations on the exercise of those rights.[15] Algerians were, like all other former colonial subjects, French Union citizens.

If this federated government created new legal possibilities for other colonies and colonial subjects, Algeria's place was simply reinforced. They, like all other colonial subjects, were extended the "quality of the citizen."[16] As Muriam Haleh Davis has put it, a "racial regime of religion" had denied Algerians French citizenship in the colonial past and into the postwar moment.[17] The 1865 *sénatus-consulte* made Algerians nationals without any of the rights of citizens. Citizenship (and the rights therein) was limited to those Algerian men who surrendered their right to be tried under "personal status law" or, in other words, renounced Islam. The gradual extension of citizenship to European migrants living in Algeria and Algerian Jews only verified the supposed impossibility of being both a French citizen and Muslim.[18] The postwar period represented a remarkable break with the past because of the legal ramifications of the Union. As Todd Shepard has explained, this citizenship erased the old legal distinction between "personal status law," which governed colonial subjects separately under Muslim religious law (or the French interpretation of it), and the French civil code, which was reserved for settlers and metropolitan French.[19] The Constitution of the Fourth Republic conceded once and for all that one could be both Muslim *and* French.

But even in this case, the Constitution still stipulated that there remain "particular laws in overseas territories."[20] The result was a piecemeal legal strategy that upheld inequality. French Union and metropolitan citizenship federated a greater France while maintaining separate laws and institutions in the Union territories and overseas departments that protected the colonial status quo. The subsequent 1947 *loi organique* on Algeria selected which rights would be conferred. To restrict Algerians' access to the benefits of French citizenship, it only guaranteed Algerians' citizenship rights when living in the metropole.[21] Promising political rights was one thing; enforcing them through the settler-majority Algerian Assembly invested in protecting their separate and unequal society was another.[22] The concern was not only political but also financial; benefits for Algerian families were expensive. Limiting the "rights" of citizenship to the metropole or stratifying access was a cost-saving measure.[23]

The Constitution of the Fourth Republic that created French Union citizenship theoretically promised once and for all that Algerians' citizenship did not depend—as France had so long argued—on assimilation to the French legal regime. The personal status law that governed Algerian Muslims apart in matters of marriage, divorce, inheritance, and property no longer justified Algerians' disenfranchisement. Instead, French officials acknowledged that while the territories of France and Algeria were indivisible, the people were in fact quite distinct, and this "local character" was acceptable, a central integrationist script. The flip side of this admission was the easy way French officials could undermine their own pretenses to equality by stating that it was not the law that distinguished, but "culture." According to this thinking, the local character of "French Muslims of Algeria"—as they were now legally called—justified the unequal implementation of the law in metropolitan France and Algeria and the eventual welfare framework that arose to address it.[24] Citizenship was a symbolic cultural aspiration whose rights were continually deferred.

Governing Migration without Algerians

The French Union and the 1947 *loi organique* also gave rise to new mechanisms for colonial citizens' migration to the metropole, according to which Algeria was once again unique. Though they were French Union citizens, Algerians derived their ability to migrate (technically only internally, across the Mediterranean) from the *loi organique* rather than from the legal framework of the French Union. Indeed, as Amelia Lyons has shown, the *loi organique* unintentionally encouraged Algerian family migration.[25] Algerian families received social security and family and maternity benefits on par with metropolitan levels only when in France. By failing to enact full social rights in Algeria, the French administration accidentally incentivized family relocation and undermined French claims to beneficence.

According first to a 1944 ordinance established in the wake of the war, French Muslims in Algeria had the same rights as French settlers. The 1947 *loi organique* established equality between Algeria and the metropole but limited certain benefits of citizenship to the metropole. These competing legal regimes created murky political waters for Algerian migration across the Mediterranean, especially because French administrators themselves could not agree on what they would allow. If the letter of the law established free circulation between France and Algeria, migration often depended on the most recent circular—or internal migration guidance—which painted a different picture. Algerians did not need work contracts or visas to move to metropolitan France in this period, but government officials in the Ministry of Population worked to change this fact by advocating for more regulation and requiring employment paperwork or a certificate of good health. The Ministry of the Interior, which administered Algeria, pushed back. Restrictions, they believed, would work against national security interests in Algeria; they saw migration to metropolitan France as a way to mitigate Algeria's social and political unrest.[26]

Algerian migration did not occur in a vacuum, however. After the war, France rethought migration generally to cultivate the migrating populations of European refugees and labor migrants from southern Europe. A November 1945 ordinance created a general immigration protocol controlled by the new National Immigration Office (ONI) that offered the possibility of movement across the French border to all potential workers from outside of France including—after its creation—French Union citizens.[27] This was, as Herrick Chapman notes, the government's most direct oversight of France's labor migration yet, replacing individual firms and the interwar business-directed General Immigration Society (SGI).[28] The ordinance extended civil and social rights to migrants in France and fostered a guest worker program including European countries but not Algeria. The National Immigration Office used bilateral treaties to create priority regional offices in cities across Germany, Italy, Spain, and Portugal to recruit European workers. Though the ordinance and French politicians loudly proclaimed their commitment to fostering migration from all countries and territories, these local agencies introduced a de facto selection bias for selecting Europeans judged "close" to French civilization.[29]

Xenophobic ideas about the supposed superiority of the European labor force compared to France's colonial populations guided the office's selection criteria.[30] To attract European workers the French administration tried to recruit entire families. Parents who had arrived in France at the age of thirty-five or younger and had remained in France for at least three years were eligible for a "privileged" residency card, renewable every ten years (compared to the usual one to three years). Further, foreigners married to a French citizen were eligible for this benefit after one year, as well as foreigners who were parents to French children. Immigration officials also sweetened the pot for these workers and families, offering enhanced family allowances as part of their recruitment pitches. The French midcentury welfare state competed with West Germany and Switzerland for European migrants, though they often lost out.[31]

Member states of the French Union could use the National Immigration Office as well. When Laos, Cambodia, and Vietnam gained nominal independence in 1949, nationals retained their citizenship in the French Union and, therefore, the ability to move to and around metropolitan France.[32] Colonial subjects in Morocco and Tunisia were technically eligible for—if ordinarily excluded from—labor recruitment through the National Immigration Office. The Moroccan administration, for example, worked directly with the office to advocate for work contracts and quotas for Moroccan workers to travel to France, but their numbers remained small: only 2,258 workers in 1947.[33] Tunisians and Moroccans may have encountered greater difficulty procuring work contracts because of French xenophobia toward Algerians, especially as they were often simply called "North Africans."[34] French reticence to work with Tunisia and Morocco arguably contravened their stated interest in managing migration. The National Immigration Office had greater control over migration, and prioritizing bilateral relationships with Tunisia and Morocco could have proven a powerful example. But as it stood, France primarily received Algerian workers whose free circulation evaded migration controls.

As Patrick Weil observed of this period, "Juridically, immigration was Italian, Spanish, Polish, or Portuguese. Politically, then socially, it was Algerian."[35] In other words, while Algerian workers and their families only sometimes figured as part of these discussions, they were central to labor migration. Officially outside of the purview of the National Immigration Office since they were not really crossing a border, Algerian workers and their families arrived more frequently in France than other North African and colonial populations thanks to the *loi organique*. As French citizens,

Algerians could theoretically circulate freely between France and Algeria and within metropolitan France. If France organized labor and family migration through the National Immigration Office to take control of the process from businesses and prioritize the selection of European migrant families, they could not apply this same selection to Algerians. Thus French policy officials became increasingly fixated on Algerians' status as French citizens. Algerians' ability to move around greater France made social benefits and remedial social services even more important not least because French officials believed Algerians required them.

Familialism, Demography, and Welfare at Odds

The "global France" created by the French Union and expansive immigration was not one whose borders were readily known or easily traversed. The National Immigration Office created a structure for migration and guaranteed social rights for migrants, at least in theory opening the door to family migration. Under the rubric of political integration guaranteed by the *loi organique*, Algerians had the right to migrate as well as social rights once in the metropole; by virtue of this integration, French officials also expected that Algerians *be* integrated. As a result, integration also served as a metaphor for citizenship-as-process: only by adhering to the social values of citizens would Algerians find full belonging. Yet the welfare services charged with this mission also envisioned Algerian families as a problem, a cultural fortress to scale and remake from the inside for them to truly take advantage of the promises of French citizenship. As more colonial citizens—and especially Algerian families—found themselves on French soil, the limits of that promise became apparent.

The midcentury welfare state heightened the stakes of the migration question and the terms by which Algerians could arrive in metropolitan France. Social benefits for families—wives and children—were an especial point of contention. The 1932 introduction of pronatalist family benefits included bonuses to workers with large families. Family codes and family law established over the course of the Third Republic, during Vichy, and then after its fall developed further protections for families as "deferred wages." Under these laws, families saw bonuses for new births and for stay-at-home mothers, protections for prenatal care, housing subsidies, and various tax and inheritance incentives for large families. Social security itself built upon its architect Pierre Laroque's solidaristic view of society; he saw this policy as a way to "empower the working class" and as an instrument of social integration.[36] The political integration of France and Algeria forced an early reckoning with welfare: were Algerians—entire families—guaranteed the same benefits by virtue of their French citizenship?

In Charles de Gaulle's now famous speech asking the nation for "twelve million beautiful babies," he also proposed repopulation through immigration and, specifically, the "introduction of good immigrant elements."[37] For de Gaulle and his senior ministers, immigration policy was integral to family policy. In the interwar period as after the Second World War, noted familialists were concerned with the quantity and quality of immigrant families, seeking to introduce only those who were readily assimilable—European and Christian, if not Catholic—to life in France.[38] The postwar institutions supporting immigration protected and promoted this desire. In particular the High Committee on Population and Family, a shadow of the interwar High Committee on Population and the Vichy-era Committee on the Family, weighed in on the French state's immigration and demographic policies.[39] Georges Mauco, infamous eugenicist and esteemed member of the committee, argued for selection based on national background. As Elisa Camiscioli has shown for the interwar period, Mauco had pushed for "Nordic" immigration instead of Algerian.[40] Mauco's hierarchy of immigrant desirability led to "scientific" studies of culture that consistently found "North Africans" to be a problem population.

Founded in 1945, the National Institute for Demographic Study (INED) provided a postwar institutional home for Mauco and a mouthpiece for his policies.[41] Indeed, many studies supported by INED in this period justified policies disincentivizing Algerian migration.[42] To this end, the institute's journal *Population* published research in the early postwar period attesting to the hurdles Algerian families faced in metropolitan France. Sociologists Alain Girard and Jean Stoetzel positioned the "immigrant" as a person between two lands whose adaptation became more difficult the greater the "mental and psychological" distance between a person's home and the host country.[43] Distance was not just geographic; it was also cultural. The closer the cultures, the easier path to integration.

Weighing the costs and benefits of family migration led to disagreement. Researchers at INED and members of the High Committee on Population and Family, often one and the same, hoped to attract (European) families in their entirety to France, while economists tended to prefer single workers who could adapt to the needs of the market. Once the High Committee on Population and Family took control of the immigration plan, however, families became the desirable unit of migration, not least because the migration of women and children could assuage the administration's fear of miscegenation when only single Algerian male migrants were concerned.[44] Though Mauco wanted to prevent Algerian migration, another member of the committee argued that "migration from Algeria to France could be considered internal migration" and therefore difficult to prevent.[45] Members of the European settler administration in Algeria concurred with this latter reading for political reasons: Family resettlement could alleviate the poverty faced by Algerian families in light of demographic growth and systemic underinvestment in infrastructure. Further, it might break up the anticolonial movements gaining momentum in the colony.[46]

Families were also havens for cultural difference, however, and therefore potential obstacles to integration. Single workers could migrate temporarily to the metropole and adopt French customs and practices through the workplace, and their children could adapt through the time-honored tradition of French schooling. Algerian women, whom the researchers believed remained "isolated" in the home, had no such educational framework.[47] Girard and Stoetzel conflated "Algerian" with "Muslim" in their analysis. The supposed centrality of Islam to family life—and the religious justification for women's isolation, the researchers argued—created an automatic "opposition to Western culture."[48] The metropolitan "dissociation" between "civil and religious life" was foreign to Muslim families, they argued, whose embodied experience of religion compelled a boundary between home and outside world.[49] Thus administrators' and social scientists' concerns about Algerian women were tied up in the French logic of Islam, a force that supposedly conditioned the possibility of women's (but not necessarily men's) acceptance of French culture. Islam, according to this belief, was static and all-encompassing, the source of the distinction between migrating to and belonging in France. Wives' cultural and religious conservatism would prevent them from making a home in France, destabilizing the family.[50]

Far from consistent on this question, researchers also suggested that women and mothers could normalize the family's existence in the metropole. Family migration guaranteed a more stable workforce with fewer social problems, they believed. Wives could bring order to an otherwise abnormal social situation created by husbands' separation from their families. Assertions about the stabilizing nature of families were not unique to Algerians or to the postwar moment; familialists, following Frédéric LePlay, had long made this case.[51] More recently fascist political leaders had also built upon these principles in Italy, Germany, and Vichy France.[52] Far from discrediting this idea, the recent past helped shape the midcentury welfare state's commitment to family policy.[53]

Ambivalence about the Algerian family was rooted in the French administration's social obligations to these citizens. In 1950 family allocations spending was about the same in France and Algeria, though France paid out support on behalf of far more children in Algeria than in France (French, Algerian, or foreign).[54] Some 130,000 families in Algeria, including 90,000 "Muslim families" and 240,000 "Muslim children," received benefits.[55] This was not even a full accounting. The number of births in Algeria outstripped the number of registered children receiving benefits due to under-administration and Algerians' mistrust of the colonial government.

France paid out family benefits at a lower rate to families whose heads of household went to France while they remained in Algeria. French demographers estimated that between 1948 and 1953 the number of Algerians in France roughly doubled from 120,000 to 240,000 but included only around 5,000 women and 15,000 children.[56] Benefits also depended on the labor sector. Only industrial workers in Algeria were eligible for family allowances, not agricultural workers (a sector that often hired Algerians).[57] Government officials explained away these differences. Family allowances would always remain different because of the "natural" distinctions between the "European" and "Muslim" populations. As they put it: "A part of the population—because of its origin, its religion—has noticeably different behavior than the other part."[58] These benefits existed by virtue of Algerians' citizenship status as French citizens. If the results of these benefits were uneven, this was not the fault of the legal system, provisioners argued, which guaranteed citizens equal access. It was instead the fault of those making use of them. "Difference" enabled proponents of integration to stand for equality but settle for discriminatory access.

There were other biopolitical considerations. French demographers were concerned with Algerian population growth.[59] Mauco's committee reported that European birthrates in Algeria were declining while the "Muslim" community had increased to the point of overpopulation.[60] The most recent postwar Algerian census had counted 1,788,000 Algerian families, of which a third had four or more children.[61] Members of the High Committee on Population and Family argued against the extension of equal benefits to Algerians in Algeria in no uncertain terms.[62] Fernand Bovérat, who had been an interwar-era president of the familialist and xenophobic National Alliance for the Growth of the French Population, became a postwar member of the committee.[63] Despite his commitment to population growth, the revanchist Bovérat argued staunchly against benefits for Algerians out of the fear that colonial societies' population growth outpaced more "industrialized" Europeans' birthrates: "If family benefits on the order of magnitude of those that already exist in France were extended to the Algerian population, they would cause a considerable increase in the birth rate at the same time that they would encourage many heads of household to work as little as possible."[64] Apart from this assertion that Algerian families would drain the welfare state, administering benefits for Algerians was also made prohibitively difficult because of the colonial legal regimes Algerians straddled in Algeria and France.[65]

Yet this unequal application of the law had the perverse incentive of encouraging Algerian families to resettle in metropolitan France to gain access to the entirety of their promised benefits. Algerian wage workers whose families remained in Algeria already contributed a disproportionate percentage of their salary to social services that they did not receive.[66] In theory the "difference" between what Algerian workers paid into social security and the benefits their families at home received was funneled into the Social and Sanitary Action Fund (FASS), a special fund charged with constructing housing for Algerian workers and providing social support.[67] France also asked Algeria to pay for additional social services to "prevent any appearance that the metropolitan budget subsidized welfare for Algerian migrants."[68]

Politically, demographically, economically, and socially, Algerian families had reasons to relocate. The *loi organique* made traversing the Mediterranean possible—if not straightforward—for Algerians as citizens of France.

Families' perceived social qualities and demographic growth tempered access to the benefits of citizenship, however; they were often inequitably distributed. The consequences of this inequality created a new problem. The midcentury welfare system bolstered French claims to integration: Algerian families were included, and the welfare state celebrated its accommodation of difference. And yet, when the social services of the midcentury welfare state took up their work on behalf of Algerian families in the metropole, they found "integration" as a program insufficient for remedying inequality.

The Midcentury Welfare State

The midcentury welfare state was an agglomeration of institutions, bureaucracy, and—crucially—specialized services, associations tailored to serve Algerian families. This "network state," as Pierre Rosanvallon might put it, came into being in response to the supposed holes in traditional welfare, but it nonetheless also bore the imprint of French familialism.[69] If, as Hegel and the French civil code have suggested, the family is the "ethical root" of the state, then these associations also sought to emulate this model.[70] They would mold discrete individuals into worthy citizens by giving them the tools to thrive in French society. Families and associations alike were envisioned as integrationist bodies, imparting civic values through education. During the final years of empire, these associations became a central part of social aid provisioning and the scaffolding of the welfare state, which made their removal after empire much more difficult.

These associational services functioned as a "civilizing mission in the metropole,"[71] but here I focus on how these welfare providers—from the moment of their construction—advanced policies and philosophies not so easily pulled apart after the civilizing mission and empire in Algeria withered. Integrationists' familialism underwrote the reproduction of Franco-European heterosexual families, and the ideology flourished as the welfare state grew across decolonization. Algerian families—as the most visible symbol of the colonial subaltern living in France—stood in for the potential trans-Mediterranean greater French family *and* the pitfalls of too perilous a bridge across the sea. Algerians' French citizenship had a natural legal consequence: promoting their social rights under the guise of fuller integration. This integrationist mission was qualifiedly distinct from the past: it accepted Algerians' citizenship as a fait accompli and instead organized remedial care on the premise of Algerians' inequality of access and deficient abilities. In this case integration was a cultural mandate.

Social services existed for many populations of migrants, building from mutual aid and charity organizations of the interwar period and capitalizing on their success. Take the Social Service for Aid to Emigrants (SSAE), founded in 1926. While migrants from Italy (the largest migrant community) or Poland or Spain (other well-represented populations) were not French citizens, their status as migrants welcomed through the National Immigration Office after 1945 reflected a French investment in promoting their labor and family migration.[72] Bilateral treaties with these countries established, for example, family benefits for Italian workers, whether their families remained at home or migrated alongside them.[73] Even before the 1957 Treaty of Rome and the creation of the European Economic Community, France competed with other European countries for migrant labor and sought to attract European migrants to aid in reconstruction projects. Thus, the SSAE took on many of the social service responsibilities guaranteed to European migrants under the National Immigration Office's ordinance, including advocating for family resettlement and family benefits in addition to services for workers.[74] Yet the French welfare state did not offer European migrants individualized associational support as they did for Algerians.

There was an equally rich history for such associations for North Africans and Algerians in particular. The Aid Commission for North Africans in the Metropole (CANAM) opened in 1927 to treat Algerian colonial subjects in sanatoria there. The association moved across the Mediterranean in 1950 under the presidency of Guy de Serres-Justiniac, who later became a fixture in the administration of the Fifth Republic.[75] CANAM provided an important example for others: their specialized social aid association worked especially on behalf of North Africans—by which they mostly meant Algerians—to offer courses in French language and job training for men, home economics and child rearing for women, and get-togethers and home visits for new families. CANAM eventually established offices across the Meurthe and Moselle in northeastern France as well as Paris.[76]

CANAM modeled the kind of integrationist work that France had undertaken with other foreign laborers but tailored it to Algerians. Integrationist social work for Algerians borrowed considerably from earlier iterations of assimilationism promised to migrating families in the interwar period. Mauco himself defined assimilation as "the definitive *integration* of foreigners in a national collectivity." While this assimilation sometimes "implied" "nationalist propaganda," he also stressed the promise of equality, the guarantee of "free entry into a collectivity."[77] With southern European families in mind, Mauco argued, "just as we do not change a tree or a plant without surrounding its roots with a certain number of precautions that allow it to withstand the terrain, so the transplanted human being adapts better in a family environment."[78] Integration through familialism was older and broader than colonial politics yet colonial politics nonetheless shaped it.

Building upon the experience of religious and lay activists, colonial functionaries, and social workers who had lived in North Africa, more Algerian-specific associations opened their doors after the Second World War to offer services for and knowledge about Algerian families. French missionary Jacques Ghys was central to the creation of the network. In 1945 he created Moral Assistance for North Africans (AMANA) to provide job training and instruction to Algerians in the metropole.[79] Then, in 1951, he worked alongside the Ministry of the Interior to found the North African Family Social Service (SSFNA), which became the premier association for Algerian families in France.[80] It established its first office—Detrez's office in Lille—in 1952 with the financial and administrative support of the Ministries of Public Health and Interior. Between 1950 and 1951, governmental funds supporting specialized associations for North Africans quadrupled from 35 million francs to 130 million francs.[81] These new associations worked in concert with French ministries to establish a paradigm for welfare for newly arrived families.

The specialized welfare network's response reflected French familialism. Ghys's third association, North African Social Studies (ESNA), published a sociological journal known as the *Cahiers Nord Africains*, which made the Algerian family central to social work. The ethnology of colonial Algerians that the *Cahiers* produced suggested more evidence of the incommensurability of "Algerianness" with Frenchness through a focus on the family form.[82] There was a continuum rather than essential difference between "North African" and French families: the patriarchal North African family was an earlier iteration of the now-industrialized "individualist" French family. French familialist thought in the nineteenth and early twentieth centuries consistently reiterated the potential dangers of industrialization and modern individualism and anomie.[83] Similarly, if an Algerian father left his family in Algeria, the mother and children moved back to her father's house, the journal explained. Modern French families received support from the state through family benefits to shoulder the burden of this economic and social dislocation.[84] However, when Algerian men arrived in France, specialized aid associations followed quite logically as a replacement for the kinship networks to which these migrants were supposedly accustomed. Social aid filled in the holes left by the absent families to promote integration.

The "traditional" model of the family—with a male breadwinner and female homemaker—also reflected integrationist fantasies of a conjugal, nuclear family that aligned with the midcentury welfare state's structure.[85] Social aid associations emphasized that working toward this family model was a goal of integration for two reasons: it overlapped with the existing policies, and it reflected their belief that "Muslim" families would already be predisposed to these traditional gender dynamics. Social workers impressed upon Algerian women the importance of becoming modernized house-wives who nurtured their families and aided in their transition to life in France. They argued against patriarchal despotism without upsetting the supposed complementary function of the couple in the heterosexual family. Well-integrated families included fathers who supported the evolution of the family toward French culture. The father's work outside the home was meant to pave his way toward an understanding of French language and society; likewise, he ought not stand in the way of his wife and children's development as residents of France.

Social aid organizations such as the SSFNA drew on the experience of its staff in French North Africa as they conceived of their offerings. Renée Bley became the first head social worker for the association. Born in 1911, Bley held a degree in social work and had trained in nursing to work at a mutual aid society, the Entr'aide des Français, in Algiers from 1945 to 1950. She returned to France and participated in the creation of the SSFNA.[86] Alongside Ghys and the first director of the organization, Pierre Racine, Bley shaped the SSFNA's approach to care. She and the SSFNA believed in the midcentury welfare state's ability to provide remedial aid to those whose needs fell beyond the purview of traditional welfare services. She hired specially trained social workers who had lived or worked in North Africa with knowledge of Arabic to aid North African families. These predominantly female teams established the usual battery of courses and offerings: French language and job-training courses for men, in-home economics and child-rearing courses for women, and home visits for new families, drop-in hours for administrative issues, and public and governmental outreach.

While social workers ordinarily navigated workplaces, schools, or hospitals, the ssfna focused on families as a unit. Bley orchestrated a strict division of labor between social workers, who led teams and coordinated care among social workers employed by the local prefectures, schools, and private enterprises; the family home aides (*travailleuses familiales*), who acted as ssfna "missionaries of the household"; and the teachers (*monitrices*), who led group classes. Private charity organizations had long mobilized young women to homes in working-class neighborhoods to educate families.[87] Family home aides were different—recipients of a newly created special diploma and recently introduced into the constellation of official social aid.[88] With the emergence of homemaking as a matter of technical expertise in the postwar period, the family home aide became the much-needed companion to struggling mothers. Aides hired by the ssfna had an additional level of training in language and the history and culture of Algeria. These aides introduced themselves to newly arrived families and worked through networks of friendship and families in predominantly North African neighborhoods in Paris, Metz, Lyon, and cities across the Nord.[89]

This network of care providers came to their professions from a variety of backgrounds with diverse experience in France's colonies and with diverging specialties. Despite these differences, however, the midcentury welfare state had a shared assumption: Algerians were citizens of France but were not, in essence, French. This clear reading of Frenchness as an obtainable set of skills, given the correct education, clearly referenced earlier civilizing missions. But the mandate had flipped. Algerians were guaranteed these services because of their citizenship, though the classwork assumed that Algerians did not fundamentally belong. Read through one optimistic prism, this surprising project reveals a moment of potential for Algerians in France. Yet life in France was more difficult.

The Social Lives of Algerian Families of the Nord

Germaine Detrez's social work at the SSFNA's first office bolstered the Nord's reputation as the "primordial land of paternalism."[90] Local businessowners had helped inaugurate the modern family benefits scheme of which the specialized social aid network was now a part. The Nord was also the site of industrial expansion and regrowth after the Second World War and, therefore, an important destination for North Africans. The SSFNA offices in Lille, Tourcoing, and Roubaix all played important roles in establishing the national practices for the association and shaping the policies promoting integration. Social workers and organizers at the Nord's SSFNA offices assumed that "integration" was a cultural mandate for assimilation. While the SSFNA was aware that Algerians' French citizenship underwrote their access to social welfare, the association had another justification for their work. Algerian families adapted unequally to metropolitan life, they believed. Incomplete acculturation or the acculturation of the husband and not the wife created an obstacle to social cohesion. Only specialized welfare could support this transformation, which still often failed. The specialized social welfare network provided Algerian families with their best option, social workers believed, even as they reflected on the holes in their vision.

As French citizens, Algerians worked with social workers such as Germaine Detrez to negotiate with local authorities. At Detrez's Lille office in 1953, 91 individual families—20 percent of their clients—solicited her help receiving their family benefits or registering for social security.[91] Completing this task was arduous, involving filling in missing paperwork, tracking down official documents, needling reticent employers, or following up with departmental authorities. Departmental social services asked specialized social workers to advise on social security for Algerians or provide general advice for departmental employees who were already struggling to complete the necessary paperwork for Algerian workers and families. The SSFNA organized day-long orientations for hospital and departmental social workers to inform them of the usual procedures for Algerians in the region but found their colleagues' ignorant of the bureaucratic hoops Algerians faced.[92]

The sheer volume of interventions relating to benefits is illuminating. Algerians made use of the SSFNA offices to protest the difficulties they faced receiving their promised benefits. Family benefits, the pride of the French welfare state, required paperwork by the pile. The local office of the Family Allowance Fund (CAF) asked for birth certificates for each member of the family, a marriage certificate for the spouses, and proof of employment in France. Depending on their original birthplace, a family might find those documents difficult to supply. Families from large cities— Algiers, Bône, Constantine—lived closer to local mayors' offices where they could register new births, but many families arriving in the Nord often came from rural areas in Algeria where colonial administration was sparse. Births went unregistered, and marriages performed as a religious rather than civil ceremony meant a missing certificate. Chronic underfunding of governmental offices in Algeria also made it difficult to request new copies or to track down missing records. In other cases colonial citizens avoided the French administration.[93] These compounding snares had the unsurprising consequence of making it easier to deny benefits.

Apart from family benefits, the SSFNA also spent considerable time fielding housing requests. Whether in Marseille, Lyon, Paris, Lille, or beyond, Algerians found insufficient housing and an especial lack of suitable housing for families. Employers in the Nord, who had historically offered housing and benefits to their workers, often failed to deliver on the promised apartments. Some employees of the famous firms of the region—metallurgy, automobile manufacturing, mining—put employees on waiting lists that were over two years long before they could move them into permanent housing. When the local SSFNA was called, they often found families living in poorly ventilated temporary housing, barracks, or shantytowns, without enough space or windows.[94] To resolve housing insecurity, however, SSFNA social workers could only act as advocates to private and public landlords and rarely resolved requests.

Given the constraints on space, availability, and cleanliness, social workers did what they could to intervene on behalf of families seeking housing. They were more effective at intervening *in* family's homes, however. From its earliest days, the SSFNA confronted the problem of integrating the family unit. Family migration was desirable to promote family stability and discourage reliance on social aid, or so the thinking went. Allowing the family to be together helped with the "adaptation of all the family members to

French life." Yet integrating women proved most difficult, as they joined a world in which their husbands were allegedly already "at ease," while they felt "unhappy, far from home, isolated from [their] family."[95] The SSFNA in the Nord usually found itself remedying "uneven" integration.

Many wives joined husbands who had already found work and established homes in the metropole. Take one family story from Roubaix in which a wife and her six children joined the father. While he held down a steady job, his salary was low and only provided for a small two-room home. Without the intervention of the SSFNA, he had been unable to access family benefits. His wife was nice enough, the SSFNA reported, but she struggled to organize her home. A family home aide "won their trust" and pitched sewing and home economics courses to the husband, who eagerly enrolled his wife. By the time they were finished, they reported that the family was "perfectly adapted to metropolitan life."[96]

The SSFNA's focus was on the wife, whom they saw as the linchpin to adaptation to life in the metropole. The family home aide acted as an emissary to the newly arrived mother: she worked slowly and with caution and offered to help take care of urgent needs with care not to upset the balance in the home between husband and wife. The SSFNA recommended that the aide make slow inroads to the family through concrete tasks, such as sewing or knitting, whose completion helped the woman feel accomplished and improved her confidence.[97] Little by little, the aide made more and more suggestions to help the family adapt: the SSFNA focused especially on the external markers of non-adaptation, such as dirty laundry hanging outside windows of low-income housing and women continuing to dress in Algerian *haïks* and veils.

As the family home aide earned the trust of the family, the SSFNA suggested home economics courses for women or guided outings with social workers as chaperones. At least initially the SSFNA was successful in its attempts, but they worried about husbands' reactions: "Most of the time [social workers] are stopped by husbands who don't accept their work and don't want the emancipation of their spouse."[98] In these cases social workers attested to two facts: First, they claimed that the children clearly benefited from social work, so the husband's concern was not for the family, but for his position vis-à-vis his spouse. Second, social workers argued that heads of families were "progressively accept[ing] this menace of emancipation" when faced with demonstrated improvement: acculturation to metropolitan life made everyone's life easier and smoothed over marital discord resulting from culture shock.[99]

Despite these potential pitfalls, deep-seated familialism and conjugal logic supported the resettlement of Algerian families in their entirety. Rather than encourage only the temporary migration of fathers and of-age sons—ready-made workers—social workers advocated for the entire family unit. One social worker from the Nord completed a six-week internship in Algiers and returned home convinced of the importance of family migration. On her rounds in Algiers, she saw the homes and household dramas of families of Algerian workers who were abroad in France. She advocated for social workers to do what they could to reunify families. In her reading, the "abnormality" of the situation of divided families drove social problems.[100]

This relocation of the family as a unit also ideally prevented what social workers called "mixed unions," relationships—formal or otherwise—between metropolitan women and North African men. Concerns about miscegenation were long-standing, and after the war, the SSFNA tried to promote family migration as a solution.[101] To support their argument, the SSFNA tracked "mixed" unions year after year, calling them "a constant source of worry."[102] Roughly half of the families they followed were "mixed unions," two hundred in Lille compared to two hundred "pure Muslim" families in 1953.[103] Social workers rarely commented on the potential benefits of this union; they did not posit metropolitan women's "civilizing" capacity for Algerian men. Social workers found instead that metropolitan women were unreliable, and they related anecdotes to discourage these relationships not only for the families' sake but also for the impact on social services. A metropolitan French woman, Lucienne M., for example, left her two children with public assistance in 1954, and her Algerian boyfriend and the father of the younger child could not assume custody of them because he was already married in Algeria. The couple did not work, the SSFNA went on, so Lucienne made a living through sex work.[104] Both Lucienne and her boyfriend represented drains on the SSFNA in particular and welfare in general, social workers argued. Lucienne's income—not work, in their eyes—supported the couple but could not extend to the family, who became indebted to social assistance.

The Algerian partner was also culpable in the failure of these unions, according to SSFNA social workers. They generally applauded Algerian fathers' "patriarchal" tendency because it led them to provide for their children. But these marriages rarely succeeded for "cultural" reasons, in the SSFNA's analysis. Algerian partners did not have "the respect for women that twentieth century Christian tradition has taught to Westerners."[105] The French conception of the family mattered to their analysis of Algerian families: patriarchy was not in itself a problem. It was the supposed domination of wives by their husbands—encouraged by the SSFNA's reading of Islamic law—that sustained the critique. Despite giving lip service to these colonial tropes, social workers seemed equally concerned about French family law in the case of divorce or separation, which offered few protections for mothers. Similarly, they feared for metropolitan women who had no recourse to French family law in the case that the lawful father brought the couple's children back to Algeria.[106] Mixed unions seemed decidedly undesirable from these perspectives and further incentivized the resettlement of entire Algerian families.

Again and again social workers voiced a contradictory understanding of the role of the Algerian family as a stabilizing feature or as a potential third force in France. The husband was both capable of adapting to life in France through his work in factories and contact with the French population and a brake on his family's adaptation if he feared for his traditional authority. In contrast, women provided a safe, clean, and "normal" home for their husbands when they arrived in the metropole, but they were also isolated by their lives as homemakers, which prevented the family from fully assimilating into life in France. Only the children could be trusted to fully adapt to their new lives in France and act as cultural transmitters for their slower-to-assimilate parents.[107] Regardless of the perceived "problem" or the member of the family causing it, the Algerian family unit was the target of social aid in this period in extraordinary ways. As more and more Algerian families arrived as "French citizens" through the *loi organique*, social workers were optimistic but realistic about their ability to bring Algerian families into French society.

The files of social work at the local level burst with examples of the dynamic relationship between social workers, their clients, and the mid-century welfare state. The familialism that shaped welfare equally infused individual interactions between provider and client. The political impulses that made this work possible trickled down from the highest levels of geopolitical governance and supra-territorial structures. Nonetheless, if the law strategically deigned to acknowledge Algerian difference, social work still tried to erase it, seeing it as the source of continued inequality within the family unit. Benefits, social equality, economic resources, and political rights all meant nothing if the family unit was out of balance. In this sense, and at the most local levels, integration was a policy indebted to familialism, emphasizing unity through difference.

Although Algerians were full citizens of France, their social rights were always imperiled. As French politicians debated what rights they owed to Algerians, and as they extended specialized services to Algerian families, Algerians' place in the metropolitan fabric shifted. They were not just laborers; they became potential neighbors, classmates, and *concitoyens*. Algerian families' presence on metropolitan shores in increasing numbers forced the issue of how and for whom the midcentury welfare state functioned. Algerian families resettling in metropolitan France had greater access to the benefits of the welfare state, but also—according to French policymakers and employees of the social services—required greater care from it.

Family was a powerful political metaphor. It legitimated France's role in Algeria, rhetorically fashioning family ties that bound colony to metropole. More to the point, metropolitan France's social infrastructure from the welfare state to immigration depended on a singular model of the nuclear family as a reproductive unit to repopulate the nation and as an incubator of values, a decidedly French familialism. The reconstruction of the midcentury welfare state hinged on this definition of the family including a male breadwinner and a female homemaker; it was through the family unit that one accessed France's regime of benefits. The socializing role this institution played introduced new possibilities for families in need.

Integration was thus a familialist project. What began in the 1940s as a set of related policy proposals redefining the place of the colonies in France became a cultural imperative as well. This project gained strength after the start of the Algerian War (1954–62). Beginning with his 1955 speech on reforms to Algeria's status, Minister of the Interior François Mitterrand promised to protect the rights—political, legal, and social—that the French government had promised Algerian citizens in its earlier declarations.[108] These mandates doubled down on welfare for Algerians whether in France or in Algeria, extending specialized social aid across the Mediterranean. The three threads I follow—midcentury welfare, family migration, and the dynamic social work relationships thereby engendered—were braided together at the twilight of empire to promote Algerians' full political and social integration into the greater French family. In the next chapter I retell the history of the Algerian War through the development of social work and social work relationships, the book's third thread.

2

The War over Social Work

In 1969, seven years after the end of the Algerian War (1954–62), ethnologist and activist Germaine Tillion sent a letter to a former colleague reminiscing about their shared work in the social centers of Algeria.[1] Sites of education, training, and camaraderie between French and Algerian men and women, the social centers had been a showpiece of the French colonial government's integrationist campaign to preserve French Algeria in the early years of the revolution. But Tillion had never considered herself part of this political project: she was a researcher who had conducted decades of fieldwork in the Algerian mountains of the Aurès. She had deliberately worked along-side pro-colonial proponents of French Algeria and engaged in talks with National Liberation Front (FLN) freedom fighters to avoid the appearance of bias. Tillion designed the social centers' infrastructure, organized a sub-vention from the metropolitan Ministry of Education rather than from the colonial governor general of Algeria, and crafted the mission to preserve the centers' independence. So deep was her belief in the project, she "opened her doors" to researchers interested in the social centers after independence to allow them access to her archives. Yet she wrote that she "could not summon the dedication" to read the resulting work. As she wrote to her colleague, "everything about the social centers continues to hurt me, morally."[2]

It is easy to understand Tillion's heartache, and many historians have investigated the gray moral space that the social centers inhabited, some-where between complicity with and co-optation into the colonial project.[3] Employees of the social centers—especially Algerians but also French men and women—faced violent retribution for advocating for Franco-Muslim solidarity through social welfare. Tillion also reflected on the troubling reception of the social centers' work. The social aid they provided was inadvertently but undoubtedly part of a broader governmental strategy to "modernize" Algerians and broadcast a positive view of empire to the international community.[4] Tillion always insisted that the social centers were not instruments of the colonial government; rather, they were concerned with providing for human need. Yet the fact remained: they had been part of the government's attempt to preserve French Algeria.

In this chapter I revisit the debate about the politicization of social work from a different angle.[5] Rather than focusing on social work as "good" or "bad," "collaborationist" or "emancipatory," I disaggregate the kinds of social *works* occurring in Algeria during the war, which were only loosely affiliated. I follow the threads of social work to understand how social workers filled roles within and without the colonial government in Algeria. An acute lack of service providers in Algeria encouraged many other forms of benevolent aid. As social workers attempted to define their purview, well-meaning volunteers, army officers, and employees of the social centers all offered "social aid" and claimed to be doing "social work" in Algeria while performing very different roles. The proliferation of social aid with various (and sometimes nefarious) goals during the Algerian War reveals the tension between the professionalization of social workers on the one hand and the politicization of loosely defined social action on the other.

Credentialed social workers defended their profession over and against what they saw as the corrupting power of politics. This politicized moment made the importance of care work for all beneficiaries clear, especially in the most under-resourced communities in colonial Algeria. I do not mean to suggest that social work was the "pure" or "better" form of aid, somehow immune from colonialist politicking. Nor do I mean to simply unveil this supposed neutrality as politically motivated. Rather, social workers' fight against the politics of war that threatened their profession also masked an important truth, a truth that likely troubled Tillion for the rest of her life: social work was inherently politically motivated. By examining the multiplicity of social *works* in this period, I argue that social work and social work relationships, my third thread, became tightly wound up with the moral colonialism of the war, tethering future social work to the fabric of French empire.[6]

"A Delicate Training"

Social work existed in a hazy social space with indeterminate occupational boundaries in colonial Algeria. The lack of credentialed personnel led greater numbers of volunteers and hastily trained French laypeople to become involved as the Algerian War broke out. Framed as a moral or religious calling, this aid was especially possible on the basis of shared sex.[7] White women nearly exclusively made appeals about the importance of providing aid and sometimes "emancipation" to Algerian women across what one historian has called a "chasm of difference."[8] Social aid purveyors obscured race, ethnicity, religion, and class in favor of a broad-based solidarity between women that often prioritized the demands of the French war effort over the needs of their clients.[9]

Social work became a vocation in France during the interwar period. A 1932 law established a diploma for the profession, prescribing schooling and on-the-job training for all new social workers.[10] In 1946 new legislation ensured that only social work professionals with diplomas in hand could call themselves "social workers."[11] Yet the government offered no job description (what did social workers do?) nor a legally binding code of ethics (how did social workers behave?). The multivalent nature of social work as well as a lack of administrative oversight left the door open for many other uncredentialed amateurs to perform social aid without the diploma. Older forms of benevolent aid and charity work were difficult to disband, especially in the colonies, where under-administration meant an absence of care. Women volunteers had a long history of engagement in Algeria, especially to correct the inequalities they perceived between the sexes, and which they attributed to Islam.[12] Yet the growing cadre of social workers coming of age after the Second World War aimed to legitimate their profession by denying the legitimacy of the others. In 1944 they created the National Association of Social Workers (ANAS) to codify the laws and ethics of the profession out of a belief that only licensed social workers could uphold these principles. The organization—and licensed social workers more generally—saw themselves as the standard-bearers for care and as the only ones capable of protecting their profession from the corrupting power of politics.

The association set to work defining a code of ethics. This code would distinguish professionals from the larger corps of social service auxiliaries and volunteers to preserve social workers' preeminence. The laws of 1932 and 1946 established a hierarchy of the social aid professions with social workers at the top. Family home aides, family instructors, and social auxiliaries were all licensed members of the social work corps but with less rigorous training and education. Despite these new regulations, paid and unpaid "benevolent" social work offered by unlicensed women persisted as part of the tapestry of the social services.[13] Well-meaning volunteers posed a problem for social workers, who saw in these providers specters of nefarious motives and unintended consequences. Without proper training, how could they assure the best and most appropriate care to their clients? "After the [Second World] war," the High Court, the Conseil d'État, recognized that social workers "needed to meet growing and increasingly complex needs by making sure there was a tried and true professional," who could prevent the role from "being invaded by people who were insufficiently prepared for the role of social worker, a delicate training."[14]

When members of ANAS drafted a code of ethics, they attempted to buffer social work from politics and insulate the profession from politically motivated outsiders. For social workers it shored up the integrity of their profession "in crisis."[15] The code of ethics defined social work proper from social aid and cautioned against the "general eruption of pseudo assistants."[16] It outlined the obligations of licensed social workers toward their clients, employers, and each other. Social workers were duty bound to serve their clients on the clients' own terms with respect for their autonomy and human dignity. Social workers vowed to consider the repercussions of their interventions and to avoid proselytizing or discriminating based on difference of "philosophical, political, or religious opinion."[17] Social workers were not organs of the state, but aid providers who vowed to put aside their personal views to win the trust of the clients receiving their help.

In social workers' minds, the code of ethics was crucial to their own professionalization. As doctors had the Hippocratic oath, social workers invoked their own ethics. Yet the French state had little appetite for policing the disciplinary boundaries of social aid professionals. When the members of ANAS attempted to receive recognition for their code of ethics from the Ministry of Public Health, the ministry declined.[18] It likely had one overriding reason: a problem of supply. Very few social workers were employed in poorly administered colonial territories. French metropolitan and colonial administrations had failed to institute adequate medical care in most colonies, and there were never enough social workers to go around. In 1944 a school for social workers opened in Algeria, but most social workers came from settler families and worked with the "European" population. In 1952 in Algeria there were just over 150 social workers serving a population of ten million, though these social workers generally confined their work to outreach in hospitals on behalf of settlers.[19] Allowing for looser professional standards served a practical purpose. More people could receive "social aid" even in the absence of licensed social workers.

At the Brazzaville Conference of 1944, France had pledged to create social services for all populations in France's colonies as part of a broader goal of reforming French colonialism. Yet, as historian Jennifer Johnson has shown, these international developments did not democratize health care or social work in Algeria, an integral part of France since 1848.[20] To address the continuing shortage, in 1946 the colonial government created a "Medico-Social Service of Algeria" under the direction of the local Public Health and Family department. This service had its own training and diploma distinct from metropolitan social work.[21] Supervised by social workers, these new employees often performed many of the same tasks.[22] Yet these workers all existed outside the formal boundaries of the profession outlined in the 1932 and 1946 laws, and certainly beyond the consideration of the metropolitan social workers' code of ethics. In the government's absence as under its oversight, forms of social aid beyond official social work flourished.

Since few licensed social workers were employed in Algeria and even fewer worked with Algerians, these novel ad hoc auxiliaries filled the gap. The Red Cross and other international organizations staffed by religious orders arrived in Algeria. Credentialed social worker Marie-Renée Chéné created the first social center for Algerians—then called the "Arab" or "Muslim" population—in Boubsila, a bidonville or shantytown in Algiers, in 1953.[23] About seven kilometers from downtown in the southwest of Algiers, the dispensary was difficult to access. There were only cobbled or dirt roads, and the nearest bus station was nearly two kilometers away.[24] Chéné, a Catholic, was recruited by the influential left-leaning priest Jean Scotto of a parish in Hussein Dey.[25] She and Scotto set the tone for a sect of engaged, progressive Catholics in Algiers, learning Arabic, preaching rec-

onciliation between the Christian and Muslim communities, and addressing the poverty and underdevelopment of urban Algerian neighborhoods.
Their work sat upon a sturdy foundation: Catholics and Protestants had a
long history of volunteerism and missionary work in North Africa, but as
part of the Mission de France. Scotto saw himself as distinct, a radical in
colonial Algeria advocating for Franco-Muslim cooperation. In the same
vein, Chéné's social center in Boubsila functioned as a facility for medical
aid, a staging point for distributing water in the bidonvilles where there
was no access, and an educational center that included men, women, teens,
and children.[26]

Yet this social action was not enough for Chéné. Education, she believed,
was crucial to solving the long-term problems of the community. In particular, she wrote that she was "persuaded that the evolution of the Muslim
world will be accomplished thanks to the woman, our efforts to recruit
educational aides—as many from the 'evolved' Muslim world of Algiers
as amongst European students—will not cease."[27] In the beginning she
used a French Scouts building to organize a school for young Algerian
girls, including two classes of forty girls each. The courses included sewing
and darning. It gradually opened to boys and then adult women as well
by 1954. She admitted that though the work had only just begun, this
social aid emanated from a desire to address both immediate needs and
long-term "evolution." Eventually she hoped that Algerians could take
over this education.[28]

Chéné hired two European settler social workers, Emma Serra and
Simone Gallice, who later took part in Germaine Tillion's social centers.
Like many social workers in Algeria, Serra had initially worked exclusively
with the settler population, but she transitioned to outreach on behalf of
Algerians, stating she wanted to "do more than give out bread" to counter-
act the inequality of care.[29] Serra and Gallice opened a supporting social
center in the bidonville of Hussein Dey and founded a new organization,
the Association of Social Workers, in 1952 to bring together Christians
and Muslims through social work. At the Hussein Dey social center, Serra
employed one Algerian nurse and midwife, Baya Sadoun. Through the
association's efforts, training programs began to educate Algerians as social
work "auxiliaries" to support the licensed social work staff.[30] As engaged
social worker Andrée Doré-Audibert has written, in Algeria there were

essentially two diverging interpretations of the social workers' code of ethics, which broke down along political lines: were social workers only beholden to the settler population, or were they trained to give care to *all* who needed it?[31] Serra and Gallice certainly embraced the latter, using their roles as social workers to address the absence of social support for Algerian families, taking seriously the code of ethics' insistence on providing aid for all who needed it.

The hodgepodge of services that existed for Algerians addressed the lack of care without fundamentally reconceiving of family and individual benefits, which guaranteed continued unequal access to health services, social welfare facilities, or the social security system. For example, the newly created metropolitan National Union of Family Associations (UNAF) established Algerian offices to address social inequities. The Algerian wing, the Algerian Center for Documentation and Familial Action (CADAF) hoped to serve as a kind of integrationist escalator to social and economic parity with the metropole until the time when "it will be possible for Algeria to fall under metropolitan legislation."[32] The CADAF provided social services to rectify gaps in the existing welfare network. Despite the efforts of social workers, volunteer organizations, and do-gooders on the ground, inequalities of care persisted. In this sense social aid in Algeria shared some congenital similarities with the specialized welfare network in France. Namely, it served to fill a hole through extraordinary means and regardless of best practice. This patchwork of services implicitly recognized the inadequacy of colonial-era social aid and sought to remedy it through short-term fixes.

The Politics of Intervention

When the Algerian War broke out in November 1954, social work became embroiled in the politics of French Algeria. Because social workers were mostly part of the settler population, provisioning care to Algerians was a political decision. To those in support of French Algeria, caring for the local population was a traitorous act, while, in the view of social workers engaged with the indigenous populations, refusing to provide services was failing to live up to their code of ethics. For Emma Serra, the choice was a false one: to help a nationalist was not the same as being "anti-French." She wrote, "My code of ethics requires me to care for and help those who need it, without choosing the person, and I would be very embarrassed to try to determine who is more French than the other."[33] Professionalism, Serra believed, protected her from taking part in the politics of the war. Political motives were moot for social workers.

Of course, social work had a political agenda regardless of the individual goals of social workers. As Judith Surkis has argued, an individualist "ethics of ambiguity" permeated the Algerian War. This existentialist idea underscored individual actors' inability to foresee the outcomes of their actions in the face of the immoveable force of French colonialism.[34] The very nature of guerilla warfare as a series of discrete acts of violence fell in line with this interpretation. The FLN was organized into different *wilaya*— sectors—with section leaders and small cells reporting to them to prevent the early decapitation of the movement. This ethics maps equally well onto the politics of social work: the individuated spirit of social work, so clear in Serra's testimony, encouraged social workers in Algeria to see themselves as interventionists engaged with grassroots care among communities in need. As the code of ethics suggested in 1949, care did not hinge on any one political, philosophical, or religious project, but rather the humanity of the client.

Even if this depoliticized approach to care existed in theory, the Algerian War posed immediate threats to its practice. During the early years of the war, the politics of the insurrection divided the capital city of Algiers. Increased colonial police and military presence in the capital centered their efforts on undermining the rebellion from the inside out: finding and imprisoning individual "terrorists" in FLN cells and undermining local networks for gunrunning and resource provisioning. Social workers also took on—or were forced to take on—this policing mentality. In May 1956 eighty social workers from the Departmental Direction of Health in Algiers were roped into a police operation in the Algerian-majority Casbah.[35] On May 25 the director of social services in Algiers summoned the district's social workers and demanded their addresses and whereabouts day and night. In the early morning of May 27, police rounded up social workers to participate in a raid. As police officers, members of the military, and special police forces searched the Casbah, a predominantly Algerian neighborhood, for FLN militants, district social workers were directed to search Algerian women suspected of harboring or indeed *being* FLN militants.

Frantz Fanon famously theorized the mystique of the Algerian veil—the haïk. A shield against the colonizers, protection from members of the French military, and a vehicle for liberation, the haïk became an important instrument of defense during the Algerian War.[36] That morning French soldiers wanted to avoid publicly unveiling Algerian women and so relied on the almost exclusively female social worker corps.[37] Through this unveiling, social workers helped the French army maintain the charade of cultural respect. As the appointed unveilers of Algerian women, social workers provided reconnaissance to the military and collaborated in counterinsurgency. Very few social workers refused this duty, according to Marie-Renée Chéné's letter relating the events of the day to the president of the National Association of Social Workers, Agnès de Laage. Chéné testified that the prefect and the departmental director of health *required* social workers in Algiers to round up potential nationalists. Of the social workers involved, only the eight social workers in Chéné's van refused to take part.[38] The others, perhaps fearing for their careers or their safety, participated. The eight abstainers were locked in a police van for over eighteen hours.[39]

After receiving Chéné's letter de Laage flew to Algiers to protest the misuse of credentialed social workers for police operations. She demanded an audience with Robert Lacoste, the governor general. Incensed, de Laage reminded Lacoste that these social workers were *known* to the community they were coerced into unveiling. By helping the police and military enter Algerian homes, by taking part in the raid, social workers became a part of the war effort, which compromised their code of ethics.[40] Lacoste promised de Laage that licensed social workers would never again be asked to take part in police raids, yet de Laage remained concerned. In the July issue of the association's newsletter, she wrote: "To make . . . social workers force entry into homes, especially with the goals of a police operation, is to irredeemably ruin the reputation of a profession whose essential goal is to bring aid to individuals and families independent of overall ends. It is to violate one of the fundamental principles of social services, which can only exercise so long is there is mutual respect and trust."[41]

The ANAS called the code of ethics the "first stone laid at the base of the structure of our profession."[42] De Laage argued that social workers who took part in the raid aligned themselves with the forces of order, raising suspicions about the goals of social work. Even those who claimed it was their professional duty to bear witness or to "humanize" the police search appeared to take an anti-nationalist stance.[43] Others who collaborated claimed it was their political duty to follow the requests of the police. For de Laage, the police's co-optation of social workers' services called into question the profession's ethics of neutrality and raised "juridical issues" about social workers' position in the colonial and metropolitan chain of administrative command. De Laage's quick condemnation of the operation also divided the social work field in two: those who had taken part found themselves alienated from the metropolitan body organizing social work professionals. The police operation opened up many questions. As functionaries of the state, what was social workers' duty? To whom did social workers report in Algeria? And what were their responsibilities toward the community they served?

The social workers' code of ethics was, after all, only a guideline for best practices, a nonbinding agreement. It could not be expected to dictate individuals' responses in the face of a war. Yet this code of ethics also represented the social work degree that demarcated the profession and was a symbol of its authority. This relatively new profession still struggled to outline the boundaries of the role and especially its relationship to the French imperial nation-state.[44] The stakes of the war in Algeria brought to light the frailty of ethics framed as personal choice, even as social workers continuously appealed to this framework. The fragility of the social work profession in the colonial context made space for the creation of other sorts of social aid work that did not shy away from the more political aspects of the war.

Wartime Integration: The Social Center and the Army

Social work was—or at least could be—a potent tool of the state, especially as new colonial institutions appeared during the war to obfuscate which social aid provisioners were credentialed and thus putatively "neutral" and who collaborated with the army. In the early days of the war, French metropolitan and colonial administrations worked in concert to weaponize care and "integrate" Algeria into France. As I explain at the end of chapter 1, in 1955 Minister of the Interior François Mitterrand announced a new plan to extend legal, political, and social rights to Algerian Muslims under the rubric of integration. This policy became part of the government's war strategy.[45] The 1947 *loi organique* on Algeria had established rights for Algerians living in France, sharpening the distinction between metropole and colony rather than erasing it. Through his integrationist policies, Mitterrand promised to promote Algerians to positions within the government and guaranteed belated access to social security and other social protections, such as unemployment, and benefits for families.

When Jacques Soustelle, ethnologist and colleague of Germaine Tillion, became the new governor general of Algeria in 1955, he, too, promised to integrate Algerians into the French social fabric. Soustelle, like Tillion, came to integrationist governmental work from academia and at that time saw these policies as a way of promoting equality in Algeria in partnership with France. The two feared that without France, Algeria would remain—in Tillion's words—"pauperized."[46] Integration, in Soustelle's view, would elevate the quality of life of the Algerian population to defuse the political power of the National Liberation Front.[47] In war-torn Algeria, the most emblematic example of underdevelopment was the "illiterate Muslim woman." Integration programs thus focused with particular intensity on women's social improvement. Here, too, the controversy over social work played an important role.

As governor general, Soustelle had two integrationist services to promote: the social centers and the Specialized Administrative Section. Both represented French acculturating institutions, education and the military. Together they worked toward improving the education and health of Algerians in cities and rural areas that colonial governments had ignored. The social centers would provide education, community, and instruction for men, women, and children based on the model of the dispensaries and schools established by Chéné, Serra, and Scotto in Hussein-Dey.[48] Soustelle brought Germaine Tillion on board to oversee the new social centers and lend them credibility. Her years of fieldwork in the Aurès mountains of Algeria had made her a valuable resource on Algerian colonial society, and her moral authority as a former Resistant and engaged Christian democrat brought gravitas to the mission.

Tillion hired licensed social workers to promote neutrality and humanitarian aid in the centers' care. She relied on the expertise of those with experience providing social work in Algeria, hiring Emma Serra to direct an early social center. Tillion tried to recruit Chéné as well, but Chéné reportedly refused.[49] At the end of 1955, Tillion had opened 6 centers across

Algiers, followed by 25 more across the country in the next year.[50] By 1962 there were 125.[51] Each social center employed a handful of people: a director, an assistant director, a nurse, a social worker, a home economics instructor, a pre-professional training instructor, a literacy instructor, and, in rural areas, an agricultural instructor (*moniteur*).[52] Staffing each center could sometimes prove difficult, with staff members doubling up on instruction.

Social workers lent credibility to the social centers in the early years. Serra and others with a reputation of working toward Franco-Muslim solidarity made the social centers a more welcoming place for Algerian employees and clients. Algerian employees were difficult to recruit in colonial society. The classroom monitor positions needed to have passed the *brevet*, which some Algerian men had completed but few young women.[53] In keeping with the modernization theory of the mainstream social sciences, Tillion and her employees argued that many Algerians had never received a fundamental education (*éducation de base*), so the first task of the social center must be the fight against illiteracy to improve quality of life and to create an indigenous Algerian workforce.[54] The social centers chose the Laubach literacy method for adult learners, a method that required no special training of social workers to help their clients learn to read and write French, provided they could already speak it.[55] Social workers also organized special training for young Muslim men heading to the metropole to give them the necessary education to understand French society just as the social centers insisted upon young metropolitans learning Arabic and the ethics of "contact."[56]

Professional social workers were at the heart of the social centers, yet this cadre of public employees were still targets of suspicion and mistrust. Initially the French military was interested in recruiting members of the social centers to the fight for French Algeria. Yet everywhere from official newsletters to private correspondence, social center employees rejected the overtures. In their internal bulletin they wrote about the army's attempts to replicate social centers' educational work: "We must try to avoid this duplication. . . . We must demonstrate the interest that exists for each to remain independent and to safeguard the educational character of the social center."[57] Social workers and other employees of the social centers insisted on their neutrality in the fight against underdevelopment, yet no organization promoting Franco-Muslim unity could escape the politics of the Algerian War. During this period Emma Serra noted, "When one is a social worker who doesn't do politics and limits oneself to doing social work for Muslims, we are still suspected by all sides, forced out by the French, boycotted by the FLN, we are always suspect since neither of them has understood our conscience as social workers."[58]

As the police and the military received special powers during the urban guerilla Battle of Algiers (1956–57), social workers at the social centers became increasingly aware of being followed and, in some cases, detained, tortured, or expelled from Algeria. Social workers and employees of the social centers were also targets of reprisal. Historians have documented the trial of sixteen social center employees following their support of an FLN-led boycott during the battle.[59] These employees were both European and Algerian and were only the first of many members of the social centers persecuted for their work.

Social center professionals proved largely unwilling to take part in social services outside of the social centers for fear of muddying the political waters. Protecting social work proper from cobbled-together colonial services emerging under the auspices of integration became quite difficult—to the extent that it was ever possible. Could any social aid possibly be construed as neutral when it was part of a government project for the integration of France and Algeria? Could Franco-Muslim solidarity as organized through the social centers and as espoused by French colonial administrators, social workers, and independent-Algeria sympathizers really be apolitical? The social centers themselves were lightning rods for controversy during the Algerian War because of the very premises of colonial social work itself. There could be no care for colonial subjects when none had previously existed without confronting the politics of the war.

Soustelle's other integrationist project came to fruition through the army. In 1955, the same year as the social centers appeared, he created the Specialized Administrative Sections (SAS) and the Urban Administrative Sections (SAU) to bring the army into the colonial government's integration efforts. These units provided outreach to the rural and urban populations of Algeria, respectively, harkening back to an earlier army operation, the Arab Bureau of the nineteenth century, which gathered information under the guise of community support.[60] The dual role of these units as both on-the-ground surveillance and social services complicated the nature of their social action. The sas helped build infrastructure, including roads and schools, and alleviate the poverty of communities at the periphery of the colonial administration. Bringing much-needed support to populations in need after years of neglect, the sas had potentially great influence among Algerians. This aid came at a price: the second, larger goal of the units was to weaken nationalist influence through these appeals to "hearts and minds." While the new specialized army units brought real weight to Soustelle's promises of integration—improving the "level of civilization" of Algeria—these integrationist projects also created new categories of care that primarily served the army rather than their clients. Social aid in the service of war and social work more generally were thus mutually implicated.

As historian Jennifer Johnson has shown, despite some of the do-good intentions of the sas, its primary directive was political: to stop the spread of the nationalist movement. Both the sas and sau worked under the Fifth Bureau, which included the psychological warfare branch of the French army. They brought the military into contact with the civilian population to "monitor" the nationalist movement.[61] Indeed, the sas officers were drawn from active duty and reserve military, those who served in Indochina, as well as those (civilian or military) with a background in Arabic or medical training.[62] These specialists had knowledge of colonial war and, sometimes, the Algerian population. No matter their assigned task—constructing schools, playing games, building roads, or providing medical care—the military was careful to document it for international distribution and for posterity.

The sas was particularly concerned with recruiting Algerians as ambassadors for their services, and no one served as a better ambassador in their minds than "Muslim" women. sas offices looked to recruit Algerians with medical training, but as in the social centers, segregation and lack of educational opportunities created difficulties.[63] The recruitment of women was most difficult of all. In 1957 the sas created roving teams in charge of serving Algerian women, known as the emsi. The emsi—the Itinerant Medico-Social Teams—were made up of one doctor, one European woman assistant, and two "Muslim" women assistants. The emsi, like the sas, were civilian-military teams devoted to promoting French Algeria propaganda among women under the guise of social aid.[64] Together, the teams worked in rural parts of Algeria to win trust and offer social, educational, and medical assistance.[65] New recruits received a month of training, which included nursing, midwifery, childcare, Arabic, and the "history and sociology of Muslim society" and Muslim law.

EMSI interventions had two main goals. The roving teams first spread French Algeria propaganda, which, second, served as a recruitment tool. The EMSI tried to hire those they had previously helped. The army designated the European and Algerian female support members of the EMSI teams as social and sanitary rural auxiliary assistants/interpreters or ASSRAS. Civilian ASSRAS provided social education or medical assistance under the supervision of doctors of the SAS (who had various levels of training). All women—metropolitan, settler, or Algerian—were welcome to apply. The military was primarily interested in finding women who had completed primary school, had "good morality," and were malleable and in good enough shape to work in roving groups. ASSRAS were offered six hundred new francs a month, a good wage for Algerian women, who were mostly excluded from work in the colonial administration.[66] After basic training they were tasked with the "psychological work" of "emancipating" other Algerian women, which they did under the aegis of social aid. The psychological campaign sought to recruit other Algerian women to "turn them against the rebellion and encourage them to become auxiliaries of our propaganda."[67] Within two years the French army had 85 EMSI teams including 213 ASSRAS composed of French metropolitan, European settler, and Algerian women.[68]

Social aid provided by the EMSI and the SAS proliferated, blurring the lines between what social workers saw as their "professional" mandate and the propagandistic uses of care. The National Association of Social Workers vehemently protested the French army's social aid programs. Already in 1956 the association became aware of army pilot programs of female "social auxiliaries" through the metropolitan press. According to reporting, the social auxiliaries would take part in a three-week training in Algiers before joining the national defense—likely the SAS and SAU—to "help doctors and French officers charged with pacification."[69] The ANAS quickly responded to the news item by pointing out that these "social auxiliaries" did not have the proper diplomas—at least two years of work—to be hired in the field, and protested the creation of these new posts to the Ministry of National Defense.[70] Rather than respond to the content of the critique, the ministry responded by denying the provenance of the news story and saying that they had "not even been consulted on the article."[71]

The kinds of female "social aid" workers the French military employed multiplied. In February 1958 the SAS circulated a memo publicizing the creation of "attachées féminines des affaires algériennes."[72] The attachées would form a kind of social vanguard, using the SAS bases as points of departure to advance into the countryside, where they would meet new families beyond the lines of battle. These attachées were virtually indistinguishable from the already circulating EMSI teams and ASSRAS, especially for Algerians in the *bled* (countryside), who had only rare contact with colonial officials. According to the memo, the attachées would "fulfill a mission of training and education. By using elementary concerns, giving advice on hygiene and childrearing, . . . by facilitating the solutions to certain social problems, they will essentially fulfill their activities in the family setting, bringing out in women a need to evolve in their daily habits."[73] The role of the attachée clearly mirrored that of the social worker in the dispensary or in the bidonville before and during the war, yet in this case the army called this work "emancipation." They tied this social action strategy to the future of French Algeria. If the French army won the support of Algerian women, they believed that they could win the war.

As historians have argued, competing with the FLN for women's support was the crucial social battle of the war.[74] The emancipation campaign saw colonial women as the primary constituency in turning the tide of the war. Women's roles as homemakers and child-rearers supposedly made them uniquely susceptible to propaganda that promised care under the auspices of integration. This propaganda equated the state of women and families with the ability of the governing body—whether colonial or nationalist—to provide for the population and its future. In a leaflet circulated by SAS, a mother drawn in black-and-white holds her emaciated child in the image of a pietà (see figure 1). Addressing Algerian villagers, the leaflet provocatively asked: "What will you eat this winter? Do you believe that the *fellaghas* ['bandits,' pejorative for 'nationalists'] will be capable of refueling your village and feeding your children?"[75]

In a clear response, the FLN also began employing and promoting women within the nationalist organization.[76] The FLN recruited young women with medical training or backgrounds (in short supply) to join roving

Habitants des Douars : Que mangerez-vous cet hiver ?

Croyez-vous que les fellaghas seront capables de ravitailler votre douar...

... et de nourrir vos enfants ?

1. "Inhabitants of the villages: What will you eat this winter? Do you believe that the *fellaghas* will be capable of refueling your village and feeding your children?" Archives nationales d'Outre-Mer, 932 89.

FLN groups providing care to militants and Algerians in need.[77] Their goal was also anti-colonial and pro-nationalist. The goal of the FLN social worker, they wrote, was to "awake in the client a national instinct to bring them to sacrifice everything for the independence cause."[78] Yet the means sound familiar: improving moral and material conditions, bringing comfort, providing supplies, guiding women in the household, educating children. They recruited young women from the families of nationalist fighters and widows of war to serve the revolution.

This is not to create a false equivalence between the social aid work of the FLN and the French army nor to suggest that social work was politically pure while other purveyors of social action were compromised. Instead I want to suggest that social action of all kinds, including social work proper, were politicized by the war and *already* political within the context of colonial society. Social action, no matter the purported neutrality of the provider, carried within it a commitment to modernizing "primitive" societies and, therefore, a kernel of both the support it received from French authorities and the mistrust evinced by the FLN. Women were targets in this battle, as clients, students, and potential recruits. The conflicts over *who* could provide social work, with what authority, and on whose behalf, all contributed to the growing conflict over care. Social work developed as a profession through this conflict and was permanently marked by it.

Burning the Veil

The French army and colonial administration's "emancipation" campaigns are perhaps the most notorious social aid mission of the war. They began before the fall of the Fourth Republic but gained prominence in May 1958, when members of the army's Fifth Bureau, the propaganda office, orchestrated public demonstrations to put Franco-Algerian "solidarity" on display to assuage concerns about France's treatment of Algerians in the midst of the colonial war.[79] The infamous demonstrations, well documented by international newspapers at the time and historians in the years since, rounded up Algerian women who agreed to throw their haïks into a fire in the central Forum of Algiers.[80] "Until then," Nafissa Sid Cara, the first Muslim woman to become part of a French president's cabinet, reflected that she and other Algerian women "had lived as if excluded from real life." From that moment "the veil, the barrier that separates them from the world . . . fell." For Sid Cara—as for the propagandists who organized the demonstration—"burning the veil" represented the end of the division that allegedly separated Algerian women from the public sphere.[81] For the French army, it also proved France's central role in emancipating colonial women and legitimizing France's claim to the colony.

The French army's coordinated outreach mobilized "Muslim women": the EMSI trucked women to the demonstrations.[82] In a *New York Times* report, one member of an EMSI team proudly related how she was able to win the trust of rural women over several days, until "the fourth day they took rides in our truck and sang, '*kif-kif la française*' [We love French women!]."[83] The army's network of women's social aid made the participation of rural and urban women in the unveiling possible. These "emancipation" campaigns tied social action on behalf of Algerian women to the outcomes of the Algerian War. In their view only the army's emancipation campaign could ensure the future of French Algeria. If French care could reach enough Algerian women, the logic went, then women's new resources and education would inevitably allow them to see the benefits of French colonial rule. This "silent" constituency of French colonialism would then become vocal, enfranchised, and mobilized toward French Algeria. Through this strategy, they drew upon the modernizing logic already inherent in social work and bent it toward colonial ends.

Uncredentialed social services mushroomed under the new French Fifth Republic that emerged in 1958, especially with the help of the newly created Women's Solidarity Movement (MSF). The MSF was organized by the wives of army officers Raoul Salan and Jacques Massu. Lucienne Salan became the new president of the organization, though she had little outreach experience, while Suzanne Massu, a licensed social worker with years of experience in the colonial context, most recently in French Indochina, became the head of the first regional circle in Algiers. The MSF promoted French Algeria by appealing to Algerian women as the symbolic link between Algerian families and the French nation. As the association wrote, the movement's purpose was "friendship and humane contact and to help Muslim women learn their civic responsibilities, their social rights, and their educational duties."[84]

These goals went beyond political enfranchisement—though that was the first order of business—to include shaping Algerian women into French citizens.[85] Salan and Massu built upon the already existing propaganda effort to provide social services to Algerian women and attract them to the French cause. The MSF began by establishing "women's circles" across Algeria built exclusively for Algerian women, referencing the structure of the social centers. By the early summer of 1958, the MSF had already created five hundred "circles" across Algeria to offer classes on child-rearing, hygiene, and the importance of maintaining a modern household.[86] Headed by the wife of the local commanding officer with the help of some *"évoluées"*— emancipated members of the colonial population—the courses had the clear goal of offering material aid to the Algerian population and introducing "modern" domestic practices into the Algerian home. One officer wrote with news of the MSF in Batna in eastern Algeria, inviting "all civil and military functionaries to sign up their wives" and arguing: "Everyone knows the influence of the wife in her home. She can be the artisan of rallying hearts since friendship and trust are worth more than all the propaganda."[87] While the MSF was clearly influenced by contemporary social work practices, especially given Massu's training, its work was also made possible by the army's infrastructure.

As a founder of the movement and the head of the Algiers section of the MSF, Suzanne Massu worked primarily with Algerian women living in the bidonvilles and low-income housing of the Casbah. In 1957 she established the Association for the Training of Children in Algiers, an organization financed by the French army with the goal of "providing aid, protection, security, and professional and moral education to the youth" of Algeria.[88] Earlier, during the Battle of Algiers, Suzanne Massu organized sewing and knitting circles for women whose husbands disappeared or were rounded up to teach them to knit sweaters to sell. General Massu himself opened up a showroom at the Grands Magasins du Louvre in Paris to showcase the women's goods.[89] Massu's history of "do-gooder" politics was criticized within the MSF: the second president of the association and Gaullist minister Nafissa Sid Cara commented disparagingly, "The creation of carpets or embroidery are extras, but we have to pay attention since, if there are not cultural exchanges, these women [clients] 'hang out' and that changes nothing at all."[90]

The French army and the delegué général—the Fifth Republic's new central administrator in Algiers—sponsored the MSF's work, which in addition to classes included the production of journals, *Femmes Nouvelles* (New Women) and later *Miroir* (Mirror), as well as weekly radio shows aimed at attracting Algerian women to the French cause. The MSF worked alongside the French army's social teams, the SAS, the EMSI, and the ASSRAS to promote emancipation in the countryside by reaching out to children and families through aid, cultural programming, and athletics. Indeed, the MSF sometimes used the women instructors—attachées, ASSRAS, and other auxiliaries—employed by the SAS. Madame Massu reminded the board of the MSF that these instructors were "entirely at the disposition of the president of the committee," though, of course, these subcontracted workers were also beholden to their first employers, the French army.[91] These initiatives, when taken together, formed a sophisticated propaganda effort to bolster support for French Algeria by adopting and exploiting the language of social aid.

Social workers with metropolitan and international aid organizations immediately noted the deliberate adoption of the language and means of social work as a tool of war. Even before the creation of the MSF, Emma Serra commented with suspicion about Suzanne Massu's intentions: "She seemed to want to help me, but I understood before long that any beneficial action for us would be blocked, without ever knowing exactly by whom." Instead, Serra said, it always seemed as though their social action came from opposite poles, Serra versus Massu. Employees of the social centers eyed Massu and later the MSF with suspicion, much as they held the SAS and SAU at arm's length. This mutual distrust was confirmed by a friend who played tennis with General Massu, who in Serra's retelling complained: "Mademoiselle Serra is a smooth talker [*belles paroles*], but she's always getting in the way of our work."[92]

The birth of the Fifth Republic embedded strands of social action within the French army and governmental initiatives. By 1958 it was difficult for observers—and especially potential clients—to disambiguate the social aid and social work offered by members of the military, the French colonial state, and the government of the Fifth Republic. This confusion could also represent the lack of distinction between intent and outcome. Social workers and socially engaged volunteers came to their work with a variety of purposes. These intents mattered individually. Yet the content of the work—whatever its ideology—was remarkably similar across groups, particularly regarding social action on behalf of women. This was no accident, of course, as the army knowingly drew from grassroots organizations' strategies and professional social workers' toolbox. The outcomes shaped the response: propagandizing through social aid had exactly the outcome that professional social workers had feared early in the war. It served to discredit the work as a whole and had the unintended consequence of allowing professional social workers to avoid thinking more seriously about their profession's role in colonial ideology and reform.

"Social Works in the Broadest Sense of the Word"

Confusion about social aid did not just stem from the French army, and propagandizing was not simply a product of the colonial government. The metropolitan government under President Charles de Gaulle was an equal partner in wedding integration to social aid and sowing confusion about social work. De Gaulle announced a new future for Algeria in his 1958 Constantine Plan, which included integrationist social action, affirmative action hiring policies, and an attempt to include Algeria in France's "modern civilization" by addressing the "well-being and dignity" of all Algerians.[93] The plan included construction in cities, agricultural improvements, and vocational training for Algerians. The Constantine Plan spanned the Mediterranean: it included social action and reform both in Algeria and in metropolitan France.[94] The metropolitan government thus became yet another axis for care and social action during the war, in addition to volunteers with international organizations, the Education Ministry–sponsored social centers, and the French army's multiple initiatives, including volunteers, military, and civilians.

The metropolitan government's increased presence and oversight in Algeria after the creation of the Fifth Republic extended to social work initiatives. In January 1960, the "Week of the Barricades," French settlers and army officers seized major governmental buildings in Algeria to demand de Gaulle's resignation. That same week the colonial government welcomed a metropolitan social worker writing a report on the social services in Algeria. The délégué général, Paul Delouvrier, asked Cécile Braquehais, the principal inspector of Population and Social Aid and technical adviser for the metropolitan Ministry of Public Health and Population, to explore the state of services in Algeria: how could the colonial administration better integrate colonial social work within metropolitan norms?[95] This visit as much as any metropolitan government–led plan aimed to promote integration of the social services.

Braquehais was a prominent metropolitan social worker and administrator. At the Ministry of Public Health and Population, she had overseen the development of social work in the metropole since the end of the Second World War. As a special inspector in Algeria, she had similar goals. Over the course of her two-week trip, she met with social workers and social aid employees of varying degrees of professionalism across sectors: international organizations, local volunteer groups, the social centers, army-led initiatives such as the MSF, EMSI, and the ASSRAS, as well as credentialed settler social workers. Her findings were revelatory: even the most organized of social action in Algeria diverged substantially from the recruitment, training, and promotion of social workers in the metropole. Despite several decrees passed under the Fifth Republic, there was still a gulf between what constituted a "metropolitan" social worker and those providing social aid in Algeria.[96]

Braquehais was quick to distinguish between credentialed social workers—of which there were 414 employed in Algeria in 1960, half in Algiers—and the ever-increasing number of uncredentialed employees of the French army throughout Algeria.[97] Trained social workers, she noted, were in short supply, and their morale was low. They were paid poorly, suffered from overwork, and lacked administrative support. Even though they ought to be governed by the same statutes as the metropole, they found themselves taking on more and more tasks. Some whom Braquehais interviewed could not pay rent despite taking on risky jobs in cities in the midst of war.[98] Clumped as they were in city centers, moreover, representatives of the social work profession were almost completely absent in the rural areas. This absence created the conditions that allowed the army's monopoly on social aid in the *bled*.

According to metropolitan legislation, social workers should have been supported by uncredentialed social auxiliaries, who could work under the supervision of a trained social worker. There were plenty of people who could have functioned as these social auxiliaries in Algeria, but they were mostly engaged in other roles. They performed instead what Braquehais called "social works in the broadest sense of the word," or politically motivated outreach like that provided by the MSF. She took note of the army's "para-social" organisms and framed them as organizations that "do work that looks like and sometimes is confused with social services."[99] Her report included interviews with officers in the Fifth Bureau, the propaganda wing of the army that oversaw the EMSI teams (composed of individual ASSRAS) as well as the SAS and SAU.

In her view, the problem was as much that the ASSRAS were unqualified as that social work in Algeria was decentralized enough that these positions could take root in the first place. The sheer number of "European" civilian women, such as wives of army officers, as well as "Muslim" women and "harkiettes" (Algerian women working for the French army) hired by these para-social services, were proof of the need for increased social services in Algeria, and Braquehais took note of the army's strategy. "In principle," she wrote, the ASSRAS "are not doing social work but we cannot deny that they are participating in a certain social action to reach Muslim women. Without professional qualities, they do as much good as harm without any technical training, performing tasks that usually require social workers, home help instructors, and nurses."[100] The women that the army targeted had little educational background, and the ASSRAS mostly functioned as outreach to Algerian women in the pacification campaign. Braquehais's concern was less political than technical: the personnel simply did not have the necessary skills.

The promotion of "Muslim women" was not in itself a problem in Braquehais's view. Education was a cornerstone of social work. Yet the young Algerian women hired as ASSRAS were set up for failure without training; this was not true social promotion.[101] Indeed, social work's commitment to its clients' "evolution" was evident across the many sectors of social action that Braquehais investigated in her report, yet she policed social work's boundaries vigilantly. Braquehais ultimately endorsed the integration of some Algerian social auxiliaries into the metropolitan framework, but not the army's EMSI or ASSRA programs. Above all else, Braquehais had parochial fears: the devaluing of the social work diploma.[102] As was the case across integrationist programs during the Fourth and Fifth Republics, administrators wanted to elevate Algerian services to the metropolitan level without considering the years of disparity and systemic underfunding that had created these gaps in the first place.

Braquehais's report demonstrated the failure of integration in the field of social work. Her two-week study revealed just how far Algeria had to go to achieve parity of services and personnel with France. Braquehais carefully delineated social work from the array of social action currently available in Algeria but provided few plans for filling the vacuum of care that existed. The lack of administrative and political will meant social action in Algeria could only be sufficiently provisioned by alternative means. For licensed social workers, the outcome was disillusioning; their profession devalued, they retreated to drawing boundaries around what they saw as "true" social work compared with politically motivated social action. This was a distinction without a difference for the population who was the target of this care. Social work and the broader field of social action was suspect, at best.

Braquehais's report did not have the impact she might have hoped. The army continued its support for the EMSI. The teams grew to their largest size in 1961, even as de Gaulle opened negotiations with the FLN for a ceasefire. The army continued to employ 315 ASSRAS and 223 EMSI teams through 1961.[103] Despite the metropolitan government's political shift toward Algerian self-determination, the army seemed to remain optimistic (at least in written reports) about the EMSI's ability to attract and convert Algerian women. However, the turnover of ASSRAS was high throughout the war, and especially as de Gaulle's commitment to independence became clear. Algerian ASSRAS were concerned about FLN propaganda against the EMSI, a fact that attested to the EMSI's successes and made Algerian ASSRAS particular subjects of reprisal.[104] They were far more susceptible to retribution in independent Algeria. Retention was shaky.[105]

The army was aware of the predominating political winds, however. They showed much less faith in the MSF circles organized across Algeria. As early as 1960, the SAS officers overseeing MSF operations questioned their efficacy in quarterly reports. One relayed that it was "practically impossible to create and support" an MSF circle in Batna; courses for women had completely failed there.[106] Another complained: "The movements in Batna make progress, but with such difficulty. This is due to the fact that the women who participate in these movements are already evolved or come to meetings with the goal of getting free things, not with the goal of evolution."[107] The MSF's popularity varied from region to region, but many chapters of the MSF faced the same fundamental problem: their links to the army made gaining the trust of the population difficult, especially among women who were not already "evolved." MSF organization and retention became practically impossible as the army wives in charge of the local movements packed up and left rural areas alongside the French army.[108]

The para-social aid organizations that had caused so much concern about the future of social work withered with the end of the Algerian War. The army dissolved the EMSI in March 1962 as the Evian Accords, which declared the plan for Algerian self-determination, were signed. The MSF initiatives disappeared with the retreat of the French army. In May 1962 a remaining local MSF leader, Madame Morel, wrote of the current status of the Oran region's centers: the army had entirely emptied some offices, while one had been burned to the ground.[109] Morel attempted to organize the Algerian offices, but the MSF offices had moved to Paris as Algeria declared independence in July 1962. After independence many of the Algiers centers closed with few plans in place for continuing their work.[110]

As a French future for Algeria slipped away, the question of social aid and solidarity in a time of great human need remained. The social centers faced violent retribution from the pro-French Algeria paramilitary group, the Secret Army Organization (OAS), for their part in providing care. The centers had become so emblematic of the spoiled potential of Franco-Algerian solidarity that their staff—especially Algerians—faced grave danger. Just before the Evian Accords were signed in March 1962, the OAS ambushed and murdered six directors of the social centers. Of the six, three were Algerians: Mouloud Feraoun, Ali Hammoutene, and Salah Ould Aoudia.[111]

The war had lasting impact on social work and licensed social workers. The experiences of the war, including danger, torture, and even death, made the political stakes of colonial social aid clear. Even those who championed integration and the promise of the social centers continued to sit with the complicity of social work in French Algeria. This was the "moral trouble" that Germaine Tillion referenced in her letter to her colleague in 1969. Social work's deep connection to the politics of war made it impossible to simply provide care. Instead, all choices to engage in Algeria were shot through with the dynamics of colonial rule, wartime violence, and postcolonial reckoning. Those dynamics did not disappear simply because French rule in Algeria did.

The social worker's ethics of care was also a victim of empire. The profession never accounted for its involvement in a colonial war, which divided its efforts and its proponents during a crucial period of professional formation. After independence social work's credibility with the former colonial population was imperiled, though social workers rarely reflected on this outcome. More commonly they espoused the belief that social workers were not political pawns but engaged individuals motivated by a shared commitment to equal access to care. The proliferation of many forms of social action alongside social work proper contributed to confusion over the politics of care. The relationship between social worker and client at the heart of this work, my book's third thread, thus suffered a blow. Social workers' vision for an apolitical and humanitarian aid met its match in the messy quotidian politics of care as even the social services became tools of war and a thwarted instrument of Franco-Algerian unity.

3

The Double Bind of Specificity

Monsieur Abdelkader T., an Algerian man living in northern France in Roubaix, died at the age of forty-three after an unknown illness on the twelfth of May 1967. In the months leading up to his death, Monsieur T.'s social worker tried in vain to help him gain access to benefits that would help him recoup the costs of his recurring hospital stays. As a self-employed owner of a local café, Monsieur T. did not contribute—as many Algerian workers did—to the local mutual or insurance. A father to one and husband to three, Monsieur T. was well known to the social workers at the North African Family Social Service (SSFNA) office in the Nord. Since the family's arrival with Algerian independence in 1962, the SSFNA had contemplated Monsieur T.'s plural marriage with suspicion, though over time they began to speak positively of the relationship between his wives. Upon his death the family's social worker helped his wives transfer management of the café to Monsieur T.'s father and inquire about—but fail to receive—Monsieur T.'s life insurance, which he had canceled, and his death benefit, for which they were ineligible because he had never contributed to social security. Despite an absence of contributions, ten days after Monsieur T.'s death, the family received word that the Office of Social Aid would cover the cost of the hospitalization, but not his medical costs or prescriptions.[1]

There are several intriguing aspects to this family story, but I am primarily interested in the claims that Monsieur T. and his family made for benefits during his illness and after his death. Algeria had declared independence in 1962, and Monsieur T. was Algerian, not French. Nevertheless, the French midcentury welfare state preserved its specialized services as well as its benefits structure for laboring Algerians in the former metropole, the first thread I unravel. The extant services as well as Algerians' demands for benefits are salient reminders of the institutional continuity of empire after independence. Historians have argued that Algerian independence led France to reposition its welfare offices to erase its imperial past.[2] Yet in the post-independence period, these services and benefits did not continue to exist to keep Algeria French. Instead, the specialized social services that fortified the midcentury welfare state worked on behalf of Algerian migrants abroad in France, tying the Fifth Republic to its former empire through the 1960s.[3] This chapter begins with the creation of the Fifth Republic in the fourth year of the Algerian War, spans independence as many services for Algerians did, and ends in 1966 with the reorganization of these services under new direction. I follow this thread to show the resilience of empire within the midcentury welfare state, especially as this network grew alongside Algerian migration.

Beyond tracing continuity, however, I also argue that the "Thirty Glorious Years" of economic expansion and redoubling of the welfare state were glorious only for those covered by accident of birth.[4] While welfare funding bodies may have attempted to restrict funding to Algerian-specific aid offices, the internal papers of specialized social aid associations reveal how they made arguments for growth, though they remained embattled. These papers also allow us to see that care providers' colonial assumptions were not solely responsible for undermining their work (though they did clear damage). Instead, I focus on the organization of offices that made up the midcentury welfare state to expose the colonial infrastructure undergirding the system. With these facts in mind, we must at least question abstractions about the robust midcentury welfare state.[5] To speak of the European welfare state's expansion or rise in the postwar period is to miss that it was never at an apex when Algerians were the clients.

French offices premised migrants' social services on a specific exchange: labor for benefits. This exchange was not new or exclusive. Since the interwar period, European migrants had taken part. As Nimisha Barton has shown for an earlier period, European migrant women could leverage their "reproductive citizenship" to insist on their ability to assimilate and access welfare.[6] Yet after Algerian independence Algerian families represented a threat. Their imagined fecundity as well as the understanding that benefits were an inducement to immigration led administrators of midcentury welfare to question Algerians' worthiness. I therefore contrast Algerians' access to social benefits in France with that of other foreign nationals. Administrators sought to ensure that only able-bodied workers could take part in this social services exchange, in which assimilation and benefits were market mechanisms. The very existence of the specialized social services that facilitated access to benefits reveals what I call the double bind of specificity. Algerian migrants used these associations, which allowed French administrators to politicize and pathologize Algerians as a population with extraordinary need.[7] Administrators prioritized white or European beneficiaries (imagined as one and the same), slowly unraveling Algerians' place in the midcentury welfare state, the book's first thread. This choice institutionalized Algerians' precarity, which ultimately undermined specialized welfare more broadly.

An "Unlocatable Institution": Social Services for Algerians across Independence

In the middle of the Algerian War, the foundation of the Fifth Republic fostered the growth of the midcentury welfare state to include even more services for Algerians, now officially and at long last beneficiaries of the rights of citizenship whether living in France or Algeria.[8] Rather than integrate Algerians into French welfare services completely, however, the French government constructed metropolitan and colonial offices to oversee these colonial citizens living on both sides of the Mediterranean. As a result, social welfare offices for Algerians did not report to the traditional offices of welfare, such as Public Health and Population. Instead, Algerian-specific offices worked in ad hoc arrangements, sometimes reporting to the Ministry of the Interior, which oversaw the civilian administration in Algeria under empire, while others had no official ministerial home and reported directly to de Gaulle's prime minister Michel Debré or even to de Gaulle himself. The new organizational chart of social welfare made it easier to overlook the existence of these specialized social services because it effectively hid the services, scattering them in the nooks and crannies of the administration.[9] Maintaining separate services for Algerians prolonged their longevity as they were essentially hidden within the structure of the state.

Take the diverging fates of two Fifth Republic offices for Algerians: the Service for Muslim Affairs and Social Action, known as SAMAS, and the Social Action Fund for Algerian workers and their families, or FAS. Founded in April 1958, SAMAS worked within the Ministry of the Interior to provide services to Algerians living in France and Algeria while also serving an anti-nationalist surveillance mission. The department built upon a network of oversight and social action that connected the central administration to the regional and departmental police and prefectures. Above all, it operated as a tool against FLN nationalism.[10] Twenty-five technical advisers for Muslim affairs (CTAM) worked with inspectors general across the metropole to gather intelligence on the population of French Muslims of Algeria living in France.[11] The advisers coordinated with national and local private associations such as the North African Family Social Service (SSFNA) and the Aid Commission for North Africans in the Metropole (CANAM) to supervise aid.

SAMAS attempted to extend its efforts after Algerian independence in July 1962. After this date Algerians could still live and work in France and receive benefits. As Algerians were (mostly) no longer citizens, France quickly narrowed Algerians' ability to access the benefits of citizens and to reorganize them bureaucratically and symbolically as no different than any other group of migrants.[12] The Ministry of the Interior had administered French Algeria prior to independence; after 1962 it had little reason to support its former French Algeria offices such as SAMAS. To respond to this change, SAMAS established new priorities to reorient its outreach: housing, remedial schooling, and vocational training, all areas of dire need considering growing migration from Algeria.[13] Despite these new directions, others within the administration questioned the utility of the Ministry of the Interior's actions on behalf of Algerians, urging the ministry to pass off its past work to another "competent" service.[14] In 1965 the office belatedly changed its name to the Liaison Service for Migrant Support (SLPM) to promote the image that specialized social aid was now available to migrants of all nationalities.[15]

The Social Action Fund for Algerian workers and their families (FAS) drew a different lot. This metropolitan office, also created in 1958, was responsible for funding social services for Algerians.[16] FAS promised to bring much needed support and social services to Algerian workers and families in metropolitan France and Algeria. It was not connected to the Ministry of the Interior, which oversaw Algeria, and was also distinct from the metropolitan Ministry of Public Health and Population. Within the first year of its creation, members of the FAS Board of Directors elected to extend the work of the organization to Algeria. The organization divided its funding across the Mediterranean, with one-third of its efforts directed at Algerians in the metropole and two-thirds directed at constructing housing in Algeria.[17]

Michel Massenet, technocrat, Gaullist, and, after 1958, key architect of social services for Algerians, was indispensable to the Social Action Fund from the start. Born in 1926, Massenet considered himself a man of the republican tradition. Before the start of the Algerian War, he had earned degrees in political science and law and attended the government's feeder institution, the National School of Administration (ENA). He became an inspector general for the administration (IGAME), an office created after World War II as a regional helpmate to the central administration's fight against communism and anticolonial nationalism.[18] During the Algerian War Massenet was appointed the first delegate for social action for French Muslims of Algeria in the metropole. Massenet was powerful because his office existed outside of the traditional ministerial homes. He reported directly to René Brouillet, de Gaulle's new secretary general of Algerian affairs, itself a position meant to circumvent the power of the Ministry of the Interior to coordinate France's action in Algeria from Paris.[19] This new chain of command gave Massenet a direct line to Prime Minister Michel Debré, an ardent supporter of French Algeria. This unusual administrative structure provided Massenet with privileged access to de Gaulle but also had the benefit of separating de Gaulle's "social action" from any of the lines of power historically connected to strategy in Algeria—the Ministry of the Interior, the colonial administration, and the army. These new offices, structures, and chains of command solidified de Gaulle's authority over Algeria. There was another ramification for welfare: this organizational chart funneled aid for Algerians through FAS and cut off this structure from the rest of the welfare state.

This administrative orphaning was not necessarily an unwelcome outcome. The Social Action Fund went to great lengths to protect its autonomy, which included a defense of familialist ideology as well as organizational flexibility. This independence served the office well later. The board of FAS, handpicked by Prime Minister Debré, was a "who's who" of midcentury welfare, populationism, and colonial administration. Jacques Doublet, member of the High Committee on Population, became president. Doublet was also the author of the French family benefit programs, which he had pitched as an inducement to rectify the "problems of the family."[20] Guy de Serres-Justiniac, a former high-ranking member of the colonial administration and president of the specialized aid association CANAM, became FAS's first director general.[21] The rest of the board was composed of representatives from the government (Ministries of the Interior, Public Health and Population, and others) as well as specialized social aid associations. Massenet managed day-to-day operations, protected the funding board's autonomy, and asserted his prerogative over social aid.

Massenet's vision for the Social Action Fund was especially important because he organized the budget to prioritize his favorite projects: Algerian-specific social aid associations large and small as well as public-private partnerships for housing construction. In the first year of FAS's existence, it allocated two billion of its three-billion-franc budget to projects in Algeria. In France the office spent most of its funds on constructing single male and family housing (58 percent), with the remaining funds allocated to job training (20 percent), education (11 percent), youth outreach (9 percent) and, finally, the SSFNA itself (2 percent).[22] Through these actions FAS could contribute to the livelihoods of Algerian families arriving in France while also building structures of care that showcased the generosity of the midcentury welfare state. Each year the Social Action Fund grew, so too did this insistence, which kept pace with the increasing number of family arrivals as well.[23] The administrative might of the French government situated itself squarely behind social action for Algerian workers and families during the war.

The Social Action Fund fared better than SAMAS after independence in 1962. Massenet had long promoted the idea that social aid for Algerians should be separate from the Ministry of the Interior's goals within SAMAS of rooting out Algerian nationalism and working with local police. He helped shepherd FAS's social action, which he felt represented "the final crossing point, the final link" between the French and Algerian populations.[24] In Massenet's view social aid associations transformed migration from a public policy problem into a private affair, resolved in the individual Algerian home through specialized welfare. As long as France relied on

Algerian labor, Massenet argued, training, education, and housing were crucial administrative tasks undertaken and underwritten by the Social Action Fund.[25] To this end, when SAMAS transformed its mission, it passed its funding responsibilities over to FAS, which then underwrote specialized social aid associations nearly entirely.

After independence, administrators struggled to agree on the future of Algerian-specific social aid, though they knew something must remain. The secretary general of Algerian affairs and Massenet's direct supervisor, Louis Joxe, made it clear that Algerian migration risked "creating a closed world in French society."[26] While Joxe's Algerian Affairs office dissolved after independence, he nonetheless advocated for the Social Action Fund: "The work of the Social Action Fund has been propped up by experience over four years: it is not trying to replace ordinary social organisms' interventions but to develop marginal operations defined to help Algerian migrants to benefit from the action. No one else can replace the Social Action Fund."[27] He positioned specialized associations as a necessary helpmate, echoing colonial-era arguments for their importance. FAS supported the social aid associations that scaffolded the midcentury welfare state. In this analysis the Social Action Fund and the services they underwrote were both indispensable and inconvenient. As Joxe understood it, the fact of Algerians' presence in France necessitated FAS's continued existence. Its utility outweighed the symbolic and geopolitical significance of Algerian independence.

After 1962 the Social Action Fund ended financial support for any work contracted in Algeria but expanded work in France.[28] In a decree passed in July 1964, the government retracted FAS's prior mission as specifically for Algerian workers and families. It became the Social Action Fund for Foreign Workers.[29] Unlike SAMAS, however, this change only allowed it to grow. Between 1962 and 1967, the budget for the Social Action Fund increased from 33.5 million francs to over 101 million francs.[30] Housing subsidies made up much of the budget, though the funds never satisfied the demand. Educational programming and social promotion were a small but crucial part of FAS's budget. This spending doubled from 6.33 million francs in 1962, to over 13 million francs in 1967.[31] Educational programming and social promotion—together "social assistance"—subsidized specialized social aid associations to support their courses and pay their staff.

While FAS's mission expanded on paper, the substance of its work remained focused on provisioning aid and services to Algerians, now foreign nationals in France. This consistency came in part from FAS's institutional positioning, stranded between ministries and generally without administrative oversight. Yet the opposite was also true. Without a formal home within a traditional welfare ministry, the Social Action Fund could also appear redundant or extraneous to welfarist missions, rendering it an "unlocatable institution," in the words of one later FAS director.[32] The infrastructural sleight of hand sidelined specialized social welfare in pockets outside the welfare state, which—eventually though not immediately— endangered the future of Algerian-specific welfare.

The Double Bind of Specificity

Specialized social aid associations for Algerians fought for subsidies from the Social Action Fund and their place in the midcentury welfare state. Their expertise, they argued, was central to Algerians' success in France. Even in the early days of the Fifth Republic during the Algerian War, they reflected on their own longevity: if Algeria became independent, what would be their role? These administrative institutions of the midcentury welfare state transformed certainly, but not to the extent that they abandoned their past work. Their continued outreach made Algerian migrants especially visible as recipients of specialized social aid. As these services grew and doubled down on their expertise, they continued to target Algerian communities that they deemed at risk. This work had profound ramifications for services' reputations, which were tethered to their Algerian War–era work on behalf of Algerian migrants, single men, women, families, and children alike. While Algerians were only part of a broader tapestry of migration, this additional support created a double bind of specificity. It led French administrators to judge Algerians as less capable of integrating and more expensive to host.

This double bind of specificity had roots in the colonial era. Early in the Fifth Republic in January 1959, social workers met to study the "social problems" accompanying Algerian family migration and to consider their specialized roles. Renée Bley, the chief social worker for the SSFNA, Louis Belpeer of the prominent Marseille-based Association for Aid to Overseas Workers (ATOM), and others agreed that specialized associations—and the

French funding bodies that supported them—needed to focus especially on the needs of mothers and children to manage the steep growth in numbers of Algerian families in the metropole (from an estimated five thousand Muslim families in 1952 to fifteen thousand in 1958).[33] This "delicate task," they argued, should fall to social workers and home help who were already engaged in this work over the course of the 1950s.[34]

The "expertise" model had important consequences. First, deference to specialized social aid associations' expertise allowed the prevailing colonial coursework, outreach, and interventions they established to persevere.[35] These associations also drew from a reservoir of strategies that equally informed the military's social action campaigns as I suggest in chapter 2.[36] Second, this deference also assured that private associations for Algerians would remain distinct from the rest of welfare provisioning. Even the recognition that specialized services were better equipped to support migrating Algerian families meant that families were referred away from generalist social workers at local mayors' offices, hospitals, and businesses.

Third, and relatedly, social workers were cautious about their administrative orphaning. Were specialized social service providers *always* required to take on Algerians' cases? For whom did the traditional welfare network exist? Madame Berthelot, the chief social worker for CANAM, argued: "North Africans don't suffer except from the fact that they are unadapted. Social services are made for unadapted people."[37] She went on: "We will go completely against what we want to do for North Africans if we do not absolutely reestablish the notion that France's services are made for North Africans. We [specialized services] were made to help those services take care of them."[38] Berthelot boldly argued that specialized social services were redundant to the welfare state at best, discriminatory at worst. In her estimation specialized services were truly auxiliary, created as helpmates to the wider welfare network as support but not replacements. In the words of Louis Belpeer, "We cannot substitute ourselves for the larger apparatus that normally exists."[39]

Clients indicated a preference for these specialized services, however. In the 1958–59 SSFNA Lille office report, the organization boasted that their courses for women were so popular that they outgrew their classrooms. One female student reportedly asked, "Where would we go if we couldn't come here?"[40] Specialized services' expertise and their unique design were intrinsic to their philosophy, both of which led them to prioritize Algerian women. Their clients' appreciation lent credence to the continued need for their services. Algerian families made demands on the French welfare state as part of their acculturation to metropolitan life by choosing or being sent to these associations. Yet CANAM's Madame Berthelot was right: the existence of specialized social aid fortified the belief that traditional services were not for Algerians. Even the expanded parameters of the midcentury welfare state set specialized services apart, segregating services for Algerians. Rather than provide support for the welfare state's existing programming, specialized services for Algerians restaged the welfare state's offerings for their clients, lending credence to the assertion that Algerian families represented an additional burden.

These problems persisted in the period after Algerian independence, just as these social workers had predicted they would. While the Social Action Fund expanded its budget and scope in 1964 to reflect its broader mandate on behalf of all migrant workers and families, specialized social aid associations maintained their focus on Algerians, justified by their own expertise as well as the recent colonial past. In an annual request for funding, president of the SSFNA Pierre Racine quite pointedly argued, "The government has decided on a politics of the whole [*politique d'ensemble*] for the social welcome of foreign labor and the families of these workers; while part of this whole, Algerian workers require very specific competencies and social action interventions."[41] Racine and other leaders of specialized social aid associations found themselves trapped in this double bind: Algerians were a population in need of specific support when it came time to justify the importance of their work, and yet Algerians found themselves maligned by the additional attention (and cost) associated with these services.

Take, for example, CANAM, which continued to serve "North Africans," by whom they mostly meant Algerians. They referred to the "Muslims, migrants, or repatriates," who "[called] on us rather than other administrations of consular services."[42] CANAM's established reputation and substantial reach into Algerian communities contributed to their continued focus. Algerians outnumbered naturalized French Muslims (born in Algeria who adopted French citizenship), Tunisians, or Moroccans in the Moselle, the home of CANAM's largest regional offices. The Ministry of the Interior counted 168 Tunisians and 954 Moroccans in the Moselle in 1967.[43] In contrast, CANAM reported 350 naturalized French Muslim families (with over 1,100 children) as well as 554 naturalized French workers living in the Moselle. This is to say nothing of the number of Algerians who did *not* adopt French citizenship living there.[44] To wit, CANAM's president, M. Nicola, reiterated in his address to the rest of CANAM's organizing committee that the specialized association "contributes largely, wherever it is found, to a better cohabitation between French and Algerian populations." Without it, he went on, "the void that it would leave would quickly create a state of things that the public powers would be obligated to remedy."[45]

Despite repeated requests, reminders, and even threats of withheld funding from the Social Action Fund, CANAM dedicated itself to its Algerian clientele. In 1964 de Serres, the deputy director of FAS, used CANAM's quarterly funding update to remind the board that the administration had asked CANAM to reorient its work toward the general migrant population in the wake of Algerian independence.[46] The association had an ally in Massenet, however, who was still well positioned within FAS. Massenet argued for CANAM's public utility to the reticent funding board.[47] In a meeting with the board of directors of CANAM, including many members of the government, the chair of the meeting thanked Massenet for "his interest in the association" and his "precious support."[48] In 1966 and 1967 CANAM's work remained focused on Algerians. In their 1966 request for subsidies for its general functioning and its social activities, CANAM was careful to avoid requesting funds for their foyer, which housed mostly North Africans, or their work with the Muslim repatriate community, funded by a private organization. Their strategy was successful: FAS pledged the same 250,000 new francs in support that they had offered the previous year.[49]

This double bind of specificity even led the Social Action Fund to obfuscate about the extent to which their subsidies predominantly served Algerians after independence. In its annual report for 1966, FAS noted that one of its primary goals was to develop "educational action for migrants *other* than Maghrebis," a signal that the directors of FAS had not yet successfully pivoted away from the funding body's previous specialization.[50] Social workers also ruminated on the shifting priorities of the funding body but did not always follow suit. When the Ministry of the Interior ended SAMAS's Algerian-exclusive mission, specialized social workers for the SSFNA were undeterred; they had never even been consulted. As a result, they asserted, "The consequence to be drawn from this for us is that nothing has changed with regard to previous skills: everything concerning social service in the departments, the coordination of social services, social action, is still relevant."[51] When the SSFNA could no longer petition both agencies for subsidies, they shifted their proposals for funding from SAMAS to the Social Action Fund, but their work remained consistent.

The Social Action Fund's use of national and ethnic descriptors also complicated whether or to what extent services simply continued their work. While in 1966 FAS made its desire to pivot away from "Maghrebis" clear, who exactly did they mean? Morocco gained independence in 1956 but did not establish a bilateral migration treaty with France until the summer of 1963.[52] Moroccan workers could then access France through the general immigration protocol established by the National Immigration Office in 1945. After that date Moroccan worker migration grew from nearly 4,000 in 1961 to 11,000 in 1963 to 17,502 in 1964. Tunisia also signed a bilateral migration treaty with France that summer, but on-the-books Tunisian labor migration was low.[53] France reported 93 Tunisian entries in 1963, though that number grew to 5,776 in 1965.[54] In the same years, however, Algerian migration grew from 133,210 entries in 1961 to 269,543 in 1964.[55] Specialized social aid associations for Algerians certainly helped Moroccans and Tunisians in the 1960s, but Algerians were far and away the largest North African migrant body.

Emergency systems established at the start of the Fifth Republic were expeditious ways to extend social welfare without increasing oversight or building these supplemental services a permanent home. Even from the beginning of the Fifth Republic, social aid providers self-consciously reflected on the perception that the services they provided to Algerians were auxiliary and separate. The infrastructure provided by the Social Action Fund nurtured this perception. FAS's floating administrative structure made this continuity of action achievable. There was no easy solution for FAS's board nor for the various ministries of the French state charged with winding down funding for specialized social services for Algerians after independence. Need was great. As a result, FAS and its proponents attempted to thread the needle. If these services needed to exist, they should petition FAS as best they could without referring to the extent to which their work remained primarily focused on the Algerian population and remained much the same in content as during the colonial period. With Massenet steering the mission, the Social Action Fund functioned as a kind of closed loop, where most of the decisions came from administrators who had built their careers on providing specialized care for Algerians and who were equally invested in continuing this cycle.

The Housing Conundrum

If social workers and specialized social aid associations believed their work could remain the same, housing agencies—which received the majority of the Social Action Fund's annual budget—received clear directives that prevented them from pursuing the colonial-era status quo.[56] During the latter part of the Algerian War, the Social Action Fund allocated most of the housing funding to buildings and units that would accommodate families alongside workers. After the war and despite pressing need, this was no longer the case.[57] By December 1965 Seine Prefect of Police Maurice Papon attested to the presence of over two hundred thousand migrants from North Africa and "French Africa" in the Parisian region. He was not motivated by concern. Cramped quarters did not stop Paris and other cities from continuously attempting to raze bidonvilles and rehouse their inhabitants, creating a cycle of precarity and homelessness. Algerian migration in particular had become, in the prefect of police's words, "an infiltration," a "peaceful invasion of floaters and itinerants" overstaying their welcome in France.[58]

Funds for housing construction came from the French administration, including the Ministry of Housing and Rebuilding and the Ministry of Public Works, but the Social Action Fund also contributed to France's housing budget to support migrant families. The largest colonial-era association for housing construction, the National Society for the Construction of Housing for Algerian Workers (SONACOTRAL), changed its name and orientation from construction projects for Algerians to housing projects for all migrant workers in 1963. Now known as SONACOTRA (National Society for the Construction of Housing for Workers), the association managed five regional affiliates to which it allocated funds for the upkeep of existing low-income housing and *cités de transit* (transit housing) as well as the creation of new units. The affiliates typically received guidance as to which *kinds* of housing to construct as well, with priority placed at different times and for different political reasons on housing for single workers or housing for workers and families.

French administrators' attitudes toward funding for Algerian families in particular had shifted. In 1963, for example, Michel Massenet noted the importance of social action to adapting Algerians to life in the metropole, an especially pressing matter for families. He called the "adaptation of the wife to metropolitan life" an "essential transitional stage." He went on to argue that the number of families and children arriving in France, often in precarious conditions and with little social support, was quickly rising.[59] Massenet made clear that Algeria remained an important "reservoir" for labor that would serve France's needs, so social action ought to remain protected.[60] In his mind the flow of immigration was tied not just to demand for foreign workers but also to the French ability to house them and their families.

Yet by 1967 the Social Action Fund reallocated its funding, so housing for single male workers was its "absolute priority."[61] FAS set aside 58 million francs for new single-worker housing while allocating only 6 million to educational programming and 6 million to social promotion, which funded specialized social aid, and which usually supported families. The next year, single-worker housing construction projects received 60.5 million francs, while educational action and social promotion remained stagnant. By 1971 nearly 100 million francs went to housing (both single workers and families), while social assistance received about 10 million francs, and only 2 million francs went to specialized social aid associations.[62] During these years FAS increasingly redirected funding toward housing for single workers rather than the social assistance and programming that especially helped migrant families in general and Algerian families in particular.

The choice to underfund family housing construction hit Algerian families particularly hard. As the number of Algerians in France grew after independence, so too did the housing problem. In 1965 the SSFNA office in Lille reported that they had received over two hundred requests for housing from newly arrived unhoused fathers of families. The report drew especially from the case of the M. family, who had arrived in France at the end of the previous year to join Monsieur M. While they had initially stayed with family, they tried and failed to find their own place to live. Even with the help of the SSFNA, the M. family could only procure an unheated attic, where they lived with their five children. They sent their youngest, a baby, to child services so that he would not freeze to death.[63] This family story, as the SSFNA told it, also proved an argument: the entire housing system was stacked against Algerians. Family after family failed to find suitable housing. Some tried repeatedly to find a unit in a low-income housing building while living with their parents as newlyweds, while others *had* found suitable housing "five or six years ago, but the number of children grew one by one each year and the walls are not extendable."[64]

Each bureaucratic hoop compounded the problem. While the Social Action Fund could theoretically subsidize the creation of new housing whether for families or single workers, heads of household could not necessarily afford it. As the SSFNA wrote, "When the father of the family received a 500-franc monthly salary, it is impossible for him to spend 250 francs on rent, even if the housing subsidy covers a part." In 1965 the housing offices in the Nord were hardly able to satisfy 10 percent of the demand. Lower-cost options, such as renovated buildings, would be one solution, but the housing affiliates were rarely able to pay the asking price for these older buildings as well as the renovations they would require.[65]

As a result, Algerian families often found themselves in temporary housing or makeshift shantytowns known as *bidonvilles*. Regional construction offices put up cités de transit, modest prefabricated facilities, as an interim solution. As historian Minayo Nasiali has explained, after Algerian independence, SONACOTRA had an elaborate social engineering schema built into the framework of housing possibilities. Some migrant families from Portugal or Spain could go directly from a bidonville to available HLMs (low-income housing), while others—notably Algerians—"required" socialization in the transit housing.[66] Local welfare associations testified to this need as well: "The stay [in a cité de transit] is justified because the stay is not simply an intermediary situation, a waiting room," one regional director argued. "It should be, in fact, a school for promotion."[67] If this intermediary stage was necessary in the eyes of social aid provisioners, Algerian authorities made the case that there were simply not enough HLM apartments or cités de transit available for those in need. Without a national welcome service, Algerians had to rely "on their own safety net," the general consul for Algeria in Paris argued, which led them to gravitate toward bidonvilles, where they would find fellow Algerians.[68]

Bidonvilles provided makeshift homes, but they were rarely permanent as French authorities continued to "liquidate" them. Housing associations benefited twice from this effort: eradication created more land on which to establish housing developments while demolition of homes in bidonvilles increased the number of families who needed a place to live.[69] A representative from the High Committee on Population and Family, Philippe Serre, attested to the segregation created by the bidonvilles, which isolated and alienated not just Algerians but other migrants as well, thereby limiting their ability to integrate. In 1966 he wrote, "It is incorrect to say these migrants are inassimilable except if we keep them in a state of material and social inferiority."[70] Instead, he argued, France needed to commit more money and effort to the creation of new, cheap housing units to rehouse the four thousand families currently living in bidonvilles in Paris. At the current rate this construction would not be completed for six or seven years.[71]

Algerian families rarely succeeded in winning rare HLM housing either by design or out of administrators' fear of creating Algerian-dominated housing units. They also had difficulty getting on lists for relocation to cités de transit and low-income apartments. Once on lists, they were overlooked as tenants in favor of French citizens or European migrants. HLMs limited their units to only about 15 to 20 percent Algerian occupancy per building.[72] When Algerian families found housing, they faced more harassment and received fewer protections.[73] The lottery for housing perpetuated the existence of bidonvilles in different locales, impermanent structures meant to house permanent family migration. Housing units served an administrative bottom line that favored European migrants, who were imagined as more easily assimilable. The move from family to worker housing represented France's desire to host European—and not Algerian—migration.

Whether organizations paid heed to administrative pressure to pivot away from their original Algerian clients, as did the housing association SONACOTRA, or if they held fast to their client base, as in the case of CANAM, presidents of these associations found themselves in a double bind. To prioritize Algerians was to single them out, to acknowledge their particular trajectory, and to open themselves up to the argument that Algerians presented a unique problem. To accept a more general migrant body, on the other hand, meant that Algerians did not receive the aid they needed, contributing yet again to the perception of Algerians as a unique problem. The symbolic place Algeria and Algerians held in the French administrative memory and in its very infrastructure made this fraught decision into a self-fulfilling prophecy. With or without specialized social aid for Algerians, the need for these services—and the perception that it was only *through* these services that these needs could be met—persisted.

Working for Welfare

The continued existence of specialized social aid and the structures of funding that supported it were one important wing of care for Algerians in France after independence. But other guaranteed benefits—"social rights"—promised in the ceasefire agreement, the Evian Accords, were also a contentious issue.[74] France's welfare state ran according to a male bread-winner model, which meant that all migrants—and not just Algerians—were entitled to housing, work, and family benefits. In practice this meant that family allocations from child bonuses to maternity benefits to tax incentives became potentially available to migrant families through the laboring head of household's wage labor, that is to say, all migrant heads of households with recognized employment in France. Yet these benefits were unevenly granted and sometimes difficult to access. Even if Algerians did not encounter *legal* prohibitions to their family benefits, the process of navigating the welfare state after independence presented obstacle after obstacle to accessing benefits, as the family of the prematurely deceased Monsieur T., with whom I opened the chapter, learned.

Foreign nationals, Algerians and Europeans alike, had access to health insurance by virtue of their residence in France and worker benefits and social security through their employment contracts. Family allocations were possible but negotiated bilaterally. Countries in the European Economic Community, which at that point included France, West Germany, Italy, the Netherlands, Belgium, and Luxembourg, could send their workers to France with a labor contract, giving them access to French social security, retirement, unemployment benefits, and family allocations. Bilateral agreements concluded with Spain, Portugal, Morocco, Tunisia, and new states in French West and Central Africa in the early 1960s all testified to the terms of their foreign nationals' ability to work and resettle in France.[75] Most of these treaties required a labor contract for migration and a visa for official resettlement. While these treaties were specifically about labor, here too France's midcentury welfare state tied labor to benefits, upping the stakes for adhering to France's terms.

French officials had long suspected that the country's benefits acted as an accidental incentive for foreign family migration. This was not necessarily an unwelcome outcome. During the Third Republic, foreign mothers—or at least foreign *European* mothers—leveraged their "reproductive citizenship" to gain benefits and belonging in France.[76] During and after the Second World War, however, the tide clearly turned, especially depending on the foreign national population. For French administrators, family migration from the European Economic Community posed no insurmountable problems. France competed with West Germany and Switzerland in particular for foreign workers and offered family resettlement as an inducement to choose France.[77] Outside the Common Market, Portugal negotiated family resettlement terms in their 1963 bilateral negotiation with France, which I explain in greater detail in chapter 4. This European labor, which was now—but not always—coded as "white," seemed especially desirable when counterposed with the other possibilities.

As the largest North African—and indeed African—migrant population in France in the early 1960s and because of the possibility of family benefits, Algerians' arrival posed an outsized problem. Algerian workers had a right to social security benefits. According to the postwar Social Security Code, families remaining in Algeria received welfare benefits at a lower rate than if they emigrated to France alongside workers.[78] This differential access created an incentive to immigrate, an unintended consequence of the separate-and-unequal colonial regime. After independence Prime Minister Georges Pompidou created a commission to settle the question of benefits for Algerian families to eliminate these "perverse incentives," but the commission found itself limited by established law and the Evian Accords. According to Evian, families were entitled to the same "social rights" as French citizens but not political rights.[79] Algerian migrant families in France had the right to family and housing subsidies as well as pensions, unemployment, and disability and medical leave. Nonetheless, the commission argued that maternity benefits were "demographic" in nature, intended to bolster France's postwar birthrate. While the commission conceded that maternity benefits were a social right, it asserted that one needed to have "political rights" to receive them.[80] This decision excluded Algerians from maternity benefits unless they adopted French citizenship and gained political rights. The commission wrote, "We could ask ourselves if we should encourage the development of the Algerian population on French soil when there are already 100,000 Algerian children here who create considerable social problems."[81]

The panic around Algerians' supposed fecundity was not new or even necessarily specific. During the interwar period administrators ranked foreign births by order of desirability.[82] Persistent fears about Islam especially shaped the emphasis on delimiting Algerians' benefits, however. Polygamy in Monsieur T.'s household is a case in point. Although polygamy as a practice had been in decline for nearly a century, French demographers linked population growth in the colonies to unrestrained births and, incorrectly, to polygamist families.[83] The arrival of Algerians in France had threatened familialist visions of the family, as I have shown. Monsieur T.'s family situation meant *something*, but the interpretation was fluid. His family's polygamy was often only an incidental part of their social workers' case notes. The social workers who followed the family made repeated remarks about his wives, differentiated among them, and tracked their relationships. They noted more than once that despite his three wives, Monsieur T. had only one child, a young daughter.[84] Further, the family's case eventually resolved with a refusal to pay out many of the benefits Algerian workers might have expected. As the T.'s family story made its way through case notes into year-end associational accounting and, eventually, into official statistics, it could have held symbolic resonance. The T. family had the power to haunt administrators' conversations, acting as a "distorting mirror" of French demographic concerns, as Judith Surkis has suggested, despite the facts of the case.[85]

In the final months of his life, Monsieur T. and his social workers labored to fulfill the bureaucratic red tape required to have his health-care costs covered as his condition worsened. One intern for the SSFNA reported six separate trips between Monsieur T.'s home and the Bureau for Social Aid to collect the paperwork necessary to compile his request.[86] Though Monsieur T. did not pay into social security or insurance, he was still entitled to public aid by virtue of his status as a foreign worker in France. The demands he made on the state with the help of the SSFNA attest to tireless work to gain access to promised social rights. Services such as the

SSFNA were created to serve—and in the late 1960s still largely served—Algerians whose welfare was especially politicized. Even though the system shouldn't have worked, even though the T. family encountered roadblock after roadblock, his family still received some compensation after his death.

The SSFNA issued a note of caution, which equally addresses the historian of social work: "Social workers may be tempted by their observations to move from the particular to the general, to build a migration policy on individual cases."[87] This would be imprudent, they believed. Facing an imperiled Social Action Fund, a recalcitrant administration, and the prevailing interpretation that Algerian migrants presented a specific problem *by virtue of* their social rights, social workers felt that drawing too much attention to the SSFNA's work in this case would be a mistake. Algerians' success or failure in accessing benefits was often circumstantial, haphazard, and a matter of pure luck. Instead, I highlight the conditions of possibility that made those benefits even available to Monsieur T., the colonial circumstances that underwrote their existence and directed their use in the first place.

The French administration was less cautious in drawing conclusions, however. Reacting to the growth of migrant populations in France, the Pompidou administration sought to define which migrants were worthy of benefits. In 1966, Pompidou created a new office, the Bureau of Population and Migrations, and appointed Michel Massenet as its first director.[88] The office took responsibility for the Social Action Fund and specialized associations, clumping them together under the Ministry of Social Affairs.[89] This administrative reshuffling brought social aid and welfare offices, previously scattered across ministries, under Massenet's control. The new bureau definitively cordoned off specialized social services from the broader midcentury welfare state, tying these associations not to welfare but to migration.

Massenet took ownership of the policies and procedures for managing migration and administering social welfare.[90] His goals for social action for migrants represented an important if incomplete shift in the administration's concerns about workers and families from Algeria. As part of an effort to make clear that the only acceptable migration was labor migration, the Bureau of Population and Migrations posed migration in terms of quality and not just quantity. In an internal memo, the office pointedly asked: "Should we base this politics [of migration] on economic needs and demographic needs and not pay attention to the ethnic composition of immigration? Put differently, should we only be worried about quantitative short-term problems and ignore the future?"[91] The bureau was always at least implicitly as concerned with the quality, the presumed assimilability, of migrants as the quantity admitted to or born in France each year. Massenet's office pursued policies that sought to limit—rather than simply organize—migration.

Under Massenet's direction, the Social Action Fund also followed suit. In 1967 it discovered that much of its social action budget went to only two associations, the SSFNA and CANAM, "two services with a Maghrebi vocation," justified by the fact of the "particular problems posed by certain categories of migrants."[92] FAS administrators also hastened to note that this need was immediate: "North Africans" made up nearly eleven thousand of the estimated twenty-one thousand students in the classes, more than double the "Africans" who attended, and over five times the number of Portuguese funded through this social action.[93] The facts and figures seemed to underscore that North Africans, and Algerians in particular, seemed to require greater intervention and costlier social programming than European migrants. The specialized social aid associations that advocated for Algerians were window dressing for a bigger problem. Classwork, office hours, and professional training all still existed, yet even the savviest of social workers could not negotiate benefits for an unemployed or underemployed Algerian seeking their help. Their labor was the necessary tribute to the French market that opened the doors of the welfare state. Algerian men were compelled to work to earn social security and family benefits; if they did not, the entire web of welfare disappeared from their grasp.

While migrant workers—Algerian or otherwise—were promised the same social rights as French workers, it was much more difficult to see those rights fulfilled. The immigrant aid organization FASTI (Federation of Associations in Solidarity with All Immigrants) documented the ways these rights were ignored or abused. Families were permitted to migrate to France to join heads of household, provided they had housing. Housing was often only guaranteed *if* a family had already arrived; fathers could get family benefits but only if their families were in the country; otherwise they were paid out at lower rates.[94] In other cases family benefits were denied to families in cités de transit because of alleged overcrowding, a product of France's decision to limit construction of adequate housing for the migrant workers they recruited.[95] This logic worked both ways. Those who were out of work (or lacked paperwork attesting to their employment) were socially excluded because they lacked access to benefits. Moreover, those who were employed yet unintegrated were proof of the administration's magnanimity and evidence of social services' failure.

Benefits for Algerians existed at the very small center of a nebulous Venn diagram of recognized labor, adequate housing and integration, and bureaucratic negotiation. Algerian families were dependent in the bureaucratic sense of the word: wives and children who did not provide on-the-books work outside the home required a male head of household to access their family benefits. In an about-face with the past, without a link to the husband's or father's labor, families' arguments for state support were challenged. These complications were no less true for male workers seeking family support. Even when they were gainfully employed, as Monsieur T. was, receiving benefits was not a fait accompli. His own lapsed or declined coverage points to the importance of specialized social aid associations for Algerians. These associations found homes outside the traditional offices of the French midcentury welfare state and received state support and funding outside and in addition to these regularly existing programs.

The shape and meaning of the Thirty Glorious Years shift when non-Europeans in Europe become the subjects. The changing politics of funding and administrative infrastructure reflected the fates of Algerians in France. While the early post-independence years had seen little change in terms of material and administrative support for specialized social aid for Algerians, as the years went on, this support wavered. An emphasis on single male workers' migration meant fostering the migration of employable men while drying up social support for their families, and especially the Algerian families who made up the majority of the services' clientele. Market logic undercut the specialized services for Algerians within the midcentury welfare state.

In a 1968 interview given a decade after the birth of the Fifth Republic, Massenet flippantly commented, "Racism did not exist in France, but too much immigration necessarily provoked it."[96] Guided by a commitment to race-blind republicanism, Massenet papered over hundreds of years of racism endured by French colonial subjects across the globe, the recently concluded Algerian War, and even his own efforts to restrict social services and welfare benefits to Algerians as the director of the Bureau of Population and Migrations.[97] While Massenet framed racism as a social consequence of migration, in this chapter I have shown how the institutional continuities that kept the midcentury welfare state afloat despite Algerian independence nurtured racism at the heart of the Republic.

As France decolonized across the 1962 divide, the midcentury welfare state appeared to expand in competence and special services for Algerians and other migrants of empire. Yet this growing capacity to house, educate, and administer to Algerians equally revealed a conservative vision of how welfare services could be allocated: as part of an agglomeration of specialized services apart from the infrastructure of the welfare state itself. Even as specialized social aid associations remained in communication with the midcentury welfare network—the departmental public health offices, local schools, hospitals, and businesses—they drew funding and support from the central administration to spin off on their own.

During decolonization, the French midcentury welfare state, like all states, taxonomized. This impulse allowed the midcentury welfare state to sustain the services required by the conditions of empire well beyond Algerian independence. Historians of the welfare state in the postwar period—historians of what we might in this context only apocryphally call the thirty glorious years—must now understand this period not as the height of the welfare state and everything that came after as the fall. At first glance this story could represent the obstacles faced by any number of migrant workers from outside France upon their arrival in the country, but I insist on the specific obstacles Algerians encountered. As I have shown in this chapter and develop further in the next chapter, iterative revisions of migration protocols between France and Algeria served as a test case in limiting family migration from Algeria, my second thread. By limiting Algerians' ability to migrate as a family unit and prioritizing a process through which fathers and heads of household migrated first to find work and housing, French migration protocols effectively limited

Algerian families' access to the social rights they were owed. The unraveling of these two threads, midcentury welfare and migration from Algeria, meant that work alone justified Algerians' social benefits in France. These early experiments in regulating and restricting family migration targeted Algerians especially. When only a labor contract created the framework for family resettlement, France effectively restricted Algerians' access to the welfare they were due.

4

Foreign Relations

If, as novelist Zora Neale Hurston wrote, "there are years that ask questions and years that answer," then 1962 was the former.[1] Who was French?
Who was Algerian? What would be the fate of the thousands of people
now moving across the Mediterranean? Waiting to board ships, they faced
the unknown. Many passengers making their journey that summer were
European settlers, known informally as *pieds noirs* and legally as repatriates. French officials had expected this migration. They were accompanied
by others: the population that would become known as "French Muslims," those who left Algeria seeking French citizenship in the former
metropole.[2] Complicating matters, Algerian men, women, and children
moved alongside these resettling populations with various motives ranging
from work to opportunity. There was also an opposing migration *to* the
newly independent country: those Algerians traveling to take part in the
celebrations brought about by independence. The relatively fluid boundary
of the Mediterranean, however, served as a contrast to the strengthened
policies and practices meant to deter migration in this new era.[3]

I argue that families from Algeria occupied center stage in the minds of
French and Algerian administrators after independence. Both parties were
trepidatious about migration between the two countries. Early scholarly literature of this period focused on migrating men, led by Abdelmalek Sayad,
who observed the "three ages" of Algerian migration beginning with single
male workers followed only later by families in the 1970s.[4] Yet as Amelia
Lyons has shown, families from Algeria arrived in France from the years
following World War II through the Algerian War.[5] After Algerian independence migration officials positioned entire families more consistently

as a "problem" to resolve rather than as a solution to the imagined dangers posed by single men. It is not so easy to distinguish workers from family members, however.[6] As Sayad postulated: "When a worker is a progenitor, his status as a benefit is transformed: the labor power he supplies is no longer enough; he is a cost."[7] French officials positioned families from Algeria as marginal to the formal and informal economies of labor and capital. They became the focus of concerns about public health and sanitation, the shortage of suitable affordable housing, and the capabilities of the "overburdened" welfare network. These families were symbolic barriers to integration, while male labor was considered temporary, helpful, and disposable. Taken in sum, the family was imagined by French administrators as dependent, a symbolic drain on the welfare state.

Here I unravel the book's second thread, family migration from Algeria, to contextualize how Franco-Algerian diplomatic discussions came to assume that family migration was a problem. During the Algerian War, administrators offered Algerian families a conditional welcome and created specialized care structures within the midcentury welfare state to assist them. After independence, we might expect a clear diplomatic rupture, an attempt to excise Algerians from France. Yet French and Algerian diplomats engaged in negotiations to manage family migration.[8] Family migration was a symbol that stood in for French administrators' racialized fears about the future of the population. In the post-independence period, the Algerian family was delimited to only nuclear family members and more consistently defined as undesirable. The debate over the size and scope of family migration was a proxy for the central issues of decolonization: what did France owe Algeria and Algerians after the end of empire?

These diplomatic discussions may have occurred in a new geopolitical reality, but power relations between France and Algeria still favored France.[9] During the first decade after independence, France continued to exploit its former colonial relationship to prioritize the migration it desired while demonizing that which it judged unproductive. By making the family a problem, administrators paved the way to restructure access to their benefits. France tailored bilateral discussions convened first at Evian and then in 1964, 1968, and 1972—the principal negotiations I cover here—toward this end. These negotiations defined the productive worker as able-bodied and male, restricted the members of the family who could migrate to France, and limited the movement of family members to "resettlement," which could only occur after the arrival of the head of household and his successful job and housing search. These conditions hampered families' ability to come to France and petition for social rights pending their successful navigation of this process. I connect migration and social policy because French officials did; family migration was a question of paying for benefits. Without the proper paperwork, predicated on migrating through the proper channels, families could not access the care they were due.

The Right to Migration?

As European countries decolonized, they conjured a new population problem. Migrants from former colonies relocated to the metropole to flee instability or poverty created by decades of extractive colonialism. Whether in France, Great Britain, the Netherlands, or even Germany and Italy, European officials escalated their rhetoric about migrants arriving within their borders recruited under the auspices of postwar economic boom conditions and low unemployment. Indians and Pakistanis arrived in the industrial capitals of London, Manchester, and Birmingham, as Moluccans and Indonesians arrived in Amsterdam, prompted and even encouraged by housing construction and reindustrialization.[10] Global independence movements did not create these conditions, yet decolonization provided a ready-made metaphor for this experience: colonization in reverse.[11] Former and still-existing colonial powers shared the perception that empire was "coming home" or that formal colonial subjects were "swamping" the former metropole.[12] This perception led metropoles to limit or attempt to withhold previously guaranteed social rights to new foreign nationals.

The Algerian case was specific. In 1962 de Gaulle negotiated a peace agreement, the Evian Accords, with the members of the Provisional Government of the Algerian Republic (GPRA) to formally excise Algeria from the French national territory. What had once been proudly French—at least rhetorically—was now independent. As the two delegations convened for peace negotiations in the town of Evian beginning in 1961, they debated future cooperation, natural gas and oil ownership, and citizenship rights over the course of the next year. But attention to these issues overlooked the larger social concern that came into view in the summer of 1962.[13]

The Franco-Algerian agreement ultimately placed greater emphasis on the safe passage and social rights of French settlers than of Algerians. French officials had foreseen the exodus of French settlers, designated as "repatriates," and ensured that they automatically retained their French citizenship. While the accords promised continued "freedom of circulation" across the Mediterranean to all French and Algerian nationals, French officials were especially concerned with protecting the passage of the settler community.[14] According to some statistics, the number who left Algeria reached five hundred thousand between January and August 1962.[15] Other clauses in Evian protected minority rights for Europeans in Algeria.[16] French negotiators ensured that the settlers who wished to remain in Algeria were granted the same civil and social rights as Algerian nationals.[17] Officials had made no such provisions for former colonial citizens fleeing Algeria and seeking French citizenship status in the metropole. Many in this population had served as administrators in the colonial government or recruits in the French army and feared retribution in independent Algeria. Once in France they petitioned to become, once again, "French Muslims."[18]

Technically, Algerians had the right to free circulation as well.[19] Evian automatically conferred Algerian citizenship on any colonial citizen who had previously been known as a "French Muslim of Algeria" or "French with North African roots" upon independence.[20] They became foreigners in France. Algerians' protections in France were buried deep in the Evian Accords. As article seven of the Declaration of Principles Concerning Economic and Financial Cooperation stated: "Algerian nationals residing in France, particularly workers, will have the same rights as French nationals with the exception of political rights," the right to vote.[21] Social and civil rights—the right to benefits and employment as well as the right to a fair trial, and so on—were extended to workers as well as their families. The arrival of families from Algeria weighed particularly heavily on French and Algerian diplomats' minds as they sought to promote worker migration but prevent the arrival of families.

Nationals from countries in the European Economic Community enjoyed free circulation as tourists. Once nationals of West Germany, Italy, the Netherlands, Belgium, or Luxembourg signed a labor contract, they were free to live and work in France. Migrants from Italy had the right to *any* job after four years in France, regardless of their original contract, while others had less generous terms.[22] Europeans from outside the common market, such as Portugal or Spain, could still migrate to France through the 1945 general immigration protocol, provided they had procured a visa for settlement and a job contract through the National Immigration Office (ONI). French administrators prioritized these mechanisms of migration because they tied the ability to migrate to employment status.

Yet Algerians negotiated "at will" migration, a right offered only sparingly to other former colonial subjects. Colonial subjects from French Indochina, part of the French Union created in 1946, were guaranteed free circulation. When Laos, Cambodia, and Vietnam gained nominal independence in 1949, nationals retained their "citizenship" in the French Union and, therefore, the ability to move to and around metropolitan France.[23] When the Geneva Accords were signed in 1954, this freedom remained much the same, though the countries later signed their own bilateral agreements with France. The case for former protectorates, such as Morocco and Tunisia, was slightly different. Colonial subjects in these territories did not have freedom of circulation during the colonial period. Moroccans and Tunisians migrated instead through the general immigration protocol created in 1945 and governed by the National Immigration Office.[24] Though Tunisia later demanded the same benefits offered to Algerians during the 1960s, French delegates succeeded in pushing Tunisians into the ONI by 1969.[25] During the early postcolonial period, the French fostered a long-term goal of integrating all foreign nationals into the general immigration protocol to establish one unified office that bound the right to migrate to France's need for foreign labor.

The 1960 law governing Sub-Saharan African migration directly informed the Algerian case. Both Algeria and parts of France's Sub-Saharan African colonies such as Senegal remained home to sizable populations of "French" citizens or, in Algeria, those classified as "repatriates."[26] In the 1960 law, which applied to the new countries of the former French West Africa and French Equatorial Africa as well as Madagascar, "metropolitan French" citizens automatically retained their citizenship, while "Africans" in the former colonies could apply for citizenship at any point. "Africans" who were living and working in France at the time of independence automatically received French citizenship. In this case labor and permanent standing in the metropole conferred the rights of citizenship. In contrast, any person from

French West or Equatorial Africa—French or foreign—could enter France with an identity card following independence *only if* they were tourists. Those who arrived after seeking employment needed a medical exam and a work contract through the Ministry of Labor.[27] This legislation guaranteed "free circulation" to tourists but not workers from Sub-Saharan Africa. Nonetheless, according to historian Gregory Mann, the French government had little interest in organizing controls on the population of Sub-Saharan laborers entering France.[28] Only the (small) population of Sub-Saharan Africans living in France at independence had all the rights of citizens.[29]

The Evian Accords did not extend such broad citizenship guarantees, though the agreement did offer free circulation for tourists and workers alike. The authors wrote, "Barring a court ruling, any Algerian holding an identity card shall have freedom of movement [*libre de circuler*] between Algeria and France."[30] Algerians seeking work in the former metropole had potentially straightforward access to France, while those who wanted to permanently migrate and adopt French citizenship faced greater difficulty. French diplomats imposed a strict window within which migrating families needed to apply for citizenship and restricted their ability to gain it.[31] While Evian granted special rights to Algerians including exceptional status for entry to France, access to French citizenship and the rights therein conferred remained restricted. The agreement promised access to temporary workers but was more circumspect about any migration perceived as permanent.

Nearly from the moment of independence, then, French and Algerian officials alike began wringing their hands over the "anarchic" Algerian migration, and particularly the migration of Algerian women and children. The promised freedom of movement never did quite materialize. From independence onward, France offered only conditional freedom of circulation to migrants from Algeria. The Evian Accords and the bilateral negotiations that came afterward succeeded in separating welcome temporary or worker—male—migration from potentially threatening family migration. Limiting families' access to benefits to the head of household's remunerated labor was at the heart of these efforts.

Freedom of Circulation or Freedom of Resettlement?
After signing, French officials immediately set to work eroding Evian's "freedom of circulation" clause, insisting that it applied only to tourists, not

permanent migrants. French minister of the Interior and former Algerian colonial administrator Roger Frey provocatively argued that a liberal reading of the freedom of circulation clause as the right to resettle (*établissement*) would make migration too desirable an option for Algerian workers and families.[32] In his reading, freedom of resettlement could encourage the "wrong" kind of migrants—women and children—who were economically less useful to French industry in the long term.[33] Frey underscored the tension between the ability to cross borders and the permission to remain in France, a loophole French policymakers could exploit under the right conditions. Was freedom of resettlement implicit in the Evian Accords? For how long could Algerian nationals remain on French soil? Could France limit migrants to workers?

The slippage between freedom of circulation and freedom of resettlement maps onto French administrators' distinction between workers and their families. French industries relied on workers to take advantage of freedom of circulation *as* resettlement, at least as they fulfilled their labor contracts. Algerian migrant workers with or without the correct papers were an important part of the French economy following World War II. After 1962 officials drew a connection between labor and social services, cautioning against potential dependents' unfettered access to France. A French technical adviser for Muslim affairs (CTAM) urged officials to limit the "anarchic acceleration of migratory movement" to prevent "a mass of unemployed men, sick men, homeless or asocial men on the metropolitan territory." The adviser drew attention to supposedly disabled men who would require additional social supports and who were allegedly arriving in France following Algerian independence. His implicit concern was migrants' inability to perform labor: the infirm, malingerers, and those without labor contracts could function as drains on the social services that had previously served Algerians.[34]

Families compounded these fears. French administrators worried that if they granted families freedom of circulation, they would remain indefinitely in France, depleting the welfare state. This presence would give them access to the same social benefits as workers without providing any of the workers' labor. According to a study in the journal *Population*, there were 57,000 women from Algeria living in France by the end of 1962, roughly 17 percent of the Algerian migrants living abroad (see table 1).[35] During that year,

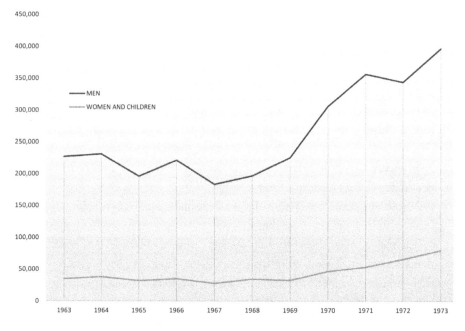

450,000

400,000

350,000

──── MEN

300,000   ──── WOMEN AND CHILDREN

250,000

200,000

150,000

100,000

50,000

0

1963   1964   1965   1966   1967   1968   1969   1970   1971   1972   1973

2. Algerian arrivals (total). Data compiled from Tapinos, "Chronique
de l'immigration: L'immigration étrangère en France en 1968,"
Population 24, no. 6 (1969): 1169–86; Gokalp, "Chronique de
l'immigration," *Population* 27, no. 6 (1972): 1119–26; Gokalp, "Chronique
de l'immigration," *Population* 29, no. 4–5 (1974): 899–907.

25,000 more migrants from Algeria arrived in France than left, including
5,907 women and children.[36] The net migration of women and children
jumped to 7,700 in 1963 and over 10,500 in 1964.[37] Similarly, as the gross
number of male migrant entries increased (from 278,000 to 368,000), so
too did the number of women and children (see figure 2).[38] French officials
pointed especially to the total entries, which included resident Algerians
and passport holders and did not necessarily reflect *new* migration. As
historians have pointed out, French administrators often miscounted or
even misrepresented the number of Algerians living in France.[39] Nonetheless, the graph told an undeniable story: the number of Algerians—men
and women, adults and children—crossing the Mediterranean grew after
Algerian independence following the provisions outlined in Evian.

French policymakers performed a cost-benefit analysis of labor against social rights. For workers themselves, relatively open access to France was a worthwhile tradeoff, but for their families, and especially the Algerian family, imagined as large and superfluous, the balance sheet reversed. Arguing as Roger Frey did that freedom of circulation did *not* include freedom of resettlement would make it harder for families to come to France without (and sometimes even *with*) a laboring head of household.

The war for independence also shifted the labor pool of Algerians who could come to France. Under empire the French had favorably stereotyped the mobile, able-bodied "Kabyle" migrant from Algeria against other Algerian populations believed to be less suited to metropolitan life.[40] During the war the French army had forcibly relocated as many as two million Algerians into concentration camps as part of a counterinsurgency strategy, uprooting entire villages and communities.[41] As families relocated from camps to port cities such as Algiers and Constantine in search of housing and employment after the war, they rarely found either.[42] Consequently these two cities became two of the largest ports of departure for France following independence.[43] Many Algerians who arrived in France after the war therefore had fewer ties to the metropole and less familiarity with urban life, having only recently arrived in Algiers or Constantine. French officials saw complications instead of opportunity, noting that these newer migrant families suffered from two forms of culture shock: the shock of life in a city and the shock of life in France.

Colonialist demography and the changing labor market led French administrators to propose an addendum to the Evian Accords that would regulate the movement of workers to keep pace with the availability of both jobs and housing. This suggested change especially affected families whose resettlement depended on suitable housing. French officials excluded Algerian diplomats from interdepartmental meetings aiming to curtail Evian protections in the fall of 1962, and without Algerian representation no official changes could take place. Representatives from the French Labor and Public Health ministries argued in favor of hardline immigration policies, while French diplomatic offices balanced a desire to limit Algerian migration with the need to protect French nationals living abroad in Algeria as well as other strategic interests.[44] They agreed upon a proposal, which mandated a medical exam for Algerian workers and families before arriving in France. The French Embassy in Algeria would facilitate the exams provided by French doctors. After the medical exam, according to the addendum, the French National Immigration Office would pay workers' way to France, a well-established practice, as an incentive to motivate single men to emigrate for work.

The French delegation also proposed the creation of a "certificate of resettlement" (*attestation d'établissement*) for single men and families. This certificate relied on the stricter reading of Evian outlined by Frey: freedom of circulation was not freedom of resettlement. According to this proposal, certificates of resettlement would be difficult to receive. They required proof of housing, which was in short supply, and proof of employment (salaried and on the books). These certificates would be valid for ten years and could only be denied for reasons of public safety.[45] This proposal served two purposes. First, it linked freedom of resettlement to employment, prioritizing labor. Second, it undercut families' ability to move temporarily or indefinitely to France. The certificate of resettlement masqueraded as a public health and safety measure that functionally proposed to impede family migration.

Without the Algerian delegation's input or participation, these proposals held no legal weight. They could not take effect, at least not immediately. However, they did constitute an outline of demands to come, a punch list that the French delegation would eventually tick off. The bilateral accords that would follow in 1964, 1968, and 1972 all followed in the footsteps of this template: prioritizing labor migration while preventing families from accompanying it.

The Bilateral "Family Problem" and the Nekkache-Grandval Accord

For its part the Algerian government was equally committed to stemming the flow of migration. They too encouraged temporary worker migration and discouraged family resettlement. In their view temporary worker migration developed the skills of the Algerian workforce and alleviated pressure on the overburdened Algerian labor market. These problems, negotiators added, were an outgrowth of the colonial economy.[46] In October 1962 the new Algerian government created the Algerian National Office of Labor

(ONAMO) to preempt any French attempt to establish their own immigration office in Algeria, as they had done in other capital cities across Europe and former colonies.[47] French immigration offices already existed in Morocco, and negotiations were currently underway in Tunisia. Algerian minister of labor and social affairs Bachir Boumaza promoted ONAMO as a tool in the "struggle against under-employment" that could encourage the movement of fit Algerian men throughout the country and abroad.[48]

In the wake of independence, over 90 percent of European settlers repatriated to France, leaving their posts as doctors, engineers, managers, teachers, technicians, and administrators, which had been reserved for them in the segregated colonial employment marketplace. Upon independence the Algerian government could not fill these vacancies. Because the infrastructure required to train workers for these positions disappeared with the end of empire, they struggled to train or even employ the population of workers, which topped 2.58 million in 1966.[49] Algerian-managed migration through ONAMO served the practical purpose of sending Algerian workers abroad for professional training they could not yet get in Algeria. These skills were important for success in the Algerian job market, though relying on temporary migration created the risk of brain drain and capital flight if temporary workers and families resettled.

As the Algerian ambassador to France Redha Malek argued, Algerian migration was a "structural consequence of the colonial economy," an economy that favored development in France and underdevelopment and extraction of resources from Algeria.[50] Even after Algerian independence, France remained dependent on Algerian labor, and Algeria depended on the French economy. Malek pointed out the inefficiencies and paradoxes built into France's migration schema. He denounced what historian Mary Dewhurst Lewis has called France's "circular reasoning," which stymied migrant workers.[51] According to various circulars—internal memos—"the unemployed must have a 'job seeker' card. . . . But some job offices refuse to give this card to new arrivals for various reasons: no social security number, never had a job in France, no right to this card."[52] Malek contended that Algerian employees faced bureaucratic dead ends by design as well as French industry's xenophobic reticence to hire them. Further, French firms threatened foreign employees with termination if they filed for workers' compensation when injured on the job.[53] Employment conditioned the terms of Algerians' stay in France: money, paperwork, benefits, and eventually family resettlement all hinged on it.

When Franco-Algerian talks began anew in 1963, the French delegation brought their initial proposal linking free circulation to employment. They sought to answer the questions provoked by free circulation: For whom was free circulation a right? Did free circulation include workers? Did it exclude dependents? The Algerian delegation sought to preserve Algeria's special status promised by Evian. In their minds, eroding the right of free circulation for Algerian workers meant revoking Algeria's preferential treatment outlined in Evian. The Algerian delegation therefore rejected the French proposal for a certificate of resettlement for workers on the grounds that it might become an instrument of selection, rather than a guarantee of Algerian workers' right to basic comforts. This, in turn, could undermine Algeria's ability to place workers abroad in France.[54]

Yet the delegations found common ground when discussing family migration. Malek conceded: "The arrival of families should only be allowed depending on the availability of housing."[55] This admission was the de facto end of freedom of circulation. As I discuss in chapter 3, there was not enough suitable family housing in and around major French cities. Bidonvilles—shantytowns—were expressly excluded from the registry of acceptable housing, responding to Algerians' concerns about France's ability to welcome families and French concerns about public health and crime that they attributed to bidonvilles' existence. Limiting family migration seemed like the solution. It assuaged French and Algerian worries about permanent relocation and protected labor migration.

The resulting 1964 agreement, the Nekkache-Grandval Accord, so named for the Algerian and French ministers of labor who signed it, preserved worker migration but limited family migration. The French won the right to establish a quarterly quota system for workers, regulated according to the demands of the labor market. The Algerian delegation agreed to curtail free circulation primarily to stop the mass migration of families. The governments agreed upon a certificate of resettlement for families, but not for workers. The certificate required that the head of household have a stable job and "sufficient" housing for his family. The accord put in place a joint commission that would meet quarterly to oversee migration between the two countries, meetings that eventually served to intensify officials' focus on Algerian families.[56]

The Nekkache-Grandval Accord had two major consequences. First, the French government ended the promise of free circulation set forth in Evian by creating the certificate of resettlement for families. Second, the diplomats ushered in a period of migration restriction for families by creating procedures that made women and children structurally dependent on worker visas. The logic of the certificate of resettlement nearly guaranteed that for family migration to be legal, it would have to occur as family *reunification*, which is to say, after the fact and pending government permission. The head of household needed to precede his family to France to find work and housing and gain the necessary permissions. This agreement became the template for controlling postcolonial migration.[57] With Algerian families at its center, labor migration management became about the family.

Street-Level Bureaucracy at Work

The resettlement procedure for families from Algeria required the cooperation of local, departmental, and national French governmental offices. To obtain a certificate of resettlement, an Algerian worker needed proof of employment and housing. His housing needed to be inspected by a local agent of the Departmental Office for Sanitary and Social Affairs (DDASS). These inspectors, often subcontracted social workers from specialized social aid associations, judged the unit's suitability for the worker's family using a state-supplied form, which asked the inspector to weigh rent against salary and square footage and condition against family size.

The number of migrating families from Algeria and elsewhere overwhelmed the capacities of French cities. Rising rents in low-income housing as well as racist application procedures compounded Algerians' difficulties finding suitable housing whether as single men or as families.[58] The bidonvilles were a response to these difficulties. Setting up a home in the bidonvilles created logistical problems. Homes had no permanent foundation, for example, and were not recognized by the local post office. The address did not exist, administratively, a problem for families registering with the local prefecture, petitioning for benefits, and signing children up for school. Beyond these concerns French administrators called attention to the poor sanitary conditions. Families shared the few water spigots that provided clean water, and there were rarely sewage or wastewater pipes. Life in bidonvilles could exacerbate health problems. Standing water and shared outhouses acted as conduits for disease, and social workers spoke regularly of the risk of tuberculosis spread from person to person in these close quarters.[59] Yet bidonvilles were also a response to French policy decisions. Lack of housing and disease outbreak were consequences of French negligence. French officials nonetheless disingenuously spun these consequences to claim that Algerian families *chose* to live in these "insalubrious" conditions.

Bidonvilles were not acceptable housing for the purposes of the resettlement certificate, and housing "suitability" functioned as a selection instrument. Nonetheless, petitioning migrant fathers could sometimes negotiate the process to their own benefit. Some inspections revealed that the family had already arrived in France on tourist visas and were hoping to retroactively receive permission for resettlement.[60] Social workers scrutinized housing size and quality relative to the number of family members present or expected. They inquired about salary, rent, and expenses before rendering an opinion on resettlement. One social worker with the Paris office of the North African Families Social Service (SSFNA) privately reported conducting a housing inspection of the same apartment at least three times for three different families. Men "borrowed" the apartment for an inspection to earn permission for resettlement, though they did not intend to live there. The social worker was aware of the practice but did not include it in her report. She instead cited the professional code of ethics that prevented her from divulging information about a client.[61]

Such was the burden of individual discretion. The undefined characteristics of "normal" housing conditions allowed local governments to arbitrarily sign off on or reject family resettlement. According to one family story in the SSFNA archives, the head social worker, Madame Detrez, issued a favorable opinion of the family's potential home.[62] The father, Monsieur A., had lived in the country since 1955. Twelve years later, in 1967, he requested permission to resettle his wife and four children. Detrez's housing inspection revealed nothing out of the ordinary.[63] The two-story house included a kitchen, a living room, a bedroom, and an extra room in the attic. The rent was 100 francs a month, which she judged appropriate, relative to Monsieur A.'s 650-franc monthly salary. Detrez noted that the housing was "not very comfortable, but it seems acceptable," before approving the request.[64]

Despite this review, the prefecture refused Monsieur A.'s petition and gave no further explanation for its decision. Rejections sometimes resulted from local fears of overpopulation of Algerians in certain neighborhoods or even departments. Indeed, by 1975 mayors across the Nord had issued unilateral decisions to stop accepting new resettlement petitions from Algerians. One such petition stated: "Request rejected: the mayor's office no longer desires the arrival of Algerian families in his commune."[65] The undefined elements of the instrument of selection—housing suitability and a normative description of conditions—gave way to precisely the form of discrimination the Algerian delegation had feared. Though the prefecture denied Monsieur A.'s resettlement request, in this period between 70 and 75 percent of families who petitioned for certificates of establishment in the Nord received them.[66]

Despite the regular flow of migrants to Algeria, numbers—no matter how inexact—were always cause for alarm. This was due in large part to a caveat in Nekkache-Grandval that escaped administrative control: the tourist visa. Under the agreement Algerian tourists could spend up to ninety days in France as long as they produced a return ticket at passport control. However, the tourist visa quickly became a loophole for migrating Algerians, who purchased but did not use their return tickets to overstay their visas as they sought employment and housing. In 1966, for example, 31,711 women and children were approved to come to France, as were 28,000 ONAMO workers; however, 256,000 Algerians entered that year, primarily through unsanctioned channels such as the tourist visa.[67] As a result, French ministries issued more unilateral circulars to establish controls to stem the flow of these "fake tourists."[68] They increased the sum of money required of tourists from 200 to 500 francs and capped the number of tourists admitted to 200 per week.[69] Algerians' reliance on the tourist visa was a consequence of the bureaucratic hoop jumping created by the resettlement certificate. In this light Monsieur A.'s rejected petition to resettle his wife and children is unsurprising. It was born from the French government's capricious decision-making, which tried and failed to control migration.

Renegotiating Family

As Algerian families relocated permanently to France, the French government sought a stricter protocol for selecting them. Funds for razing bidonvilles, remediating unsuitable housing, and constructing new buildings and apartments made up a considerable portion of the Social Action Fund's budget. In the eyes of French policymakers, these expenditures were a justifiable part of employing migrant workers, but their families fell outside of this contract. As more families arrived through loopholes, evasion, and even successful petitions, French administrators attempted to force Algerian officials to renegotiate the immigration protocol established in the 1964 Nekkache-Grandval agreement and extract better terms for themselves.

A new unilateral circular in 1967 began the process. Signed by the Minister of Social Affairs Jean-Marcel Jeanneney and the Minister of the Interior Roger Frey, the circular modified the existing 1964 agreement to focus on housing conditions and family resettlement. The 1967 circular offered veto powers at virtually every step of the family resettlement process. The prefecture could deny a resettlement application when it first arrived for concerns about public order or members of the family. Demographic or "social" questions were also grounds for a desk rejection of the application. Unacceptable housing continued to provide a convenient justification for the limitation of families. The circular proclaimed that housing had to be "equivalent to those considered normal for French workers," despite the vagueness of this requirement and clear obstacles to this mandate.[70] If a dossier made it to the social services inspector, the circular mandated a rental contract to avoid the earlier inspection loophole. The French had caught on: "Experience has shown that some workers never take possession of a house that they have declared that they occupy."[71] After the social services inspector signed off on the dossier, it could still be rejected once back at the prefecture for any reason. If the family was accepted, the regional office made a follow-up appointment to verify the composition of the family and their occupancy of the home. If anything seemed amiss, the family could be repatriated.[72]

The 1967 circular also set the definition of what constituted the "family" to restrict family resettlement. As historian Muriel Cohen has shown, this definition contracted sharply between 1964 and 1967.[73] The French administration now aligned the Algerian "family" with the Franco-European one. The family included a husband, his wife, and their girl children under the age of twenty-one and boy children under the age of seventeen.[74] The attitude toward potential workers and their gestating wives was always ambivalent. The circular sought to account for—and limit—the population of Algerians whenever possible. Requests to resettle only elder sons without their mother or sisters were rejected. Purely economic considerations, such as "work readiness," could not justify partial family resettlement; rather, the logic of family stability prevailed. The conjugal family hung in the balance, suspended somewhere between its previous appeal and its current undesirability. Five years removed from the end of empire, French administrators raised serious doubts about the future of Franco-Algerian migration.

The circular was effective on another level: it drew the Algerian delegation back to the negotiating table. Since the previous accords were signed, Houari Boumediene, the former minister of war and veteran of the National Liberation Front, had organized a bloodless coup in 1965 that ended with him instating himself as president of Algeria's new Revolutionary Tribunal while placing his predecessor, Ahmed Ben Bella, under house arrest.[75] Boumediene's foreign policy took a much stronger line against Franco-Algerian cooperation agreements that prioritized French interests. Nekkache-Grandval was one such example. The Algerian delegation hoped to renegotiate the 1964 agreement to extract better terms for Algerian workers and especially to insist upon Evian's promise of freedom of circulation. They contested French unilateral agreements, especially the circulars that passed without consulting their Algerian counterparts and that created more roadblocks to Algerian migration across the Mediterranean.[76]

The Algerian delegation was also frustrated by the French failure to create the professionalization and pre-professionalization programs that they had agreed to in 1964. These programs were a key part of incentivizing labor migration but not permanent relocation abroad.[77] The general consul for Algeria in Paris, A. Benghezal, spoke to the unfriendly welcome that Algerian workers received, and stated that they were "less desired" by employers "despite their equal and increasing level of instruction and preparedness for the job."[78] This compounded the discrimination they faced. Another Algerian leader, Bacouche Salah, attested to the "systematic discrimination" against Algerian workers queuing up in labor offices. They rarely were able to use this national infrastructure to find gainful employment and instead found themselves going door-to-door after being told their papers were not in order. Professional training had failed. In 1962, he pointed out, seven thousand Algerians got extra employment training, but without sustained efforts that number had dropped to around a thousand in 1966.[79] The coordinator for the central administration of the Algerian labor union in Europe argued that emigration in Europe helped develop Algeria *through* this training, which both improved conditions of life and work while abroad and later at home in Algeria. This general and professional training helped form the next generation of Algerian citizens destined to improve Algeria.[80]

The French delegation was equally eager to renegotiate, though for different reasons. The French Ministry of Foreign Affairs argued that "workers [were] no longer a determining element" in migration. Instead the French delegation focused on the problems created by women and children, who composed 44 percent of the net migration between October 1967 and September 1968.[81] The Ministry of Foreign Affairs went on to argue that Algerian emigration was "not just about labor but about establishment. The contingent of workers is becoming a secondary problem."[82]

The resulting December 1968 bilateral agreement continued to privilege worker migration over family migration and dramatically curtailed all Algerians' ability to migrate—even temporarily—to France. It set in writing many of the restrictions initially put forth in French circulars. The new protocol adopted the definition of "family" offered in the 1967 circular and submitted the arrival of families to the successful request for a certificate of residence by the head of household. This decision reinforced women and children's structural dependence on male heads of household not only for their livelihood but for the papers permitting their stay in France. These protocols created a sharp demarcation between those families who "resettled" according to the procedure and those who came clandestinely. Only those with their papers could gain access to French benefits.

In exchange for these concessions, Abdelaziz Bouteflika, Boumediene's minister of foreign affairs, increased Algeria's worker quota to thirty-five thousand workers annually and guaranteed France's commitment to professional and paraprofessional development of the workforce. The French also agreed to simplify the transition to this new agreement by issuing five-year resettlement certificates for all Algerian workers and families who could prove they had been legally admitted to France since 1965. Workers and families who had resided in France for more than three years could have a ten-year certificate of resettlement. While these measures should have eased the transition from the Nekkache-Grandval regime to the new 1968 agreement, these certificates still required proof of identity and employment.[83] The 1968 protocol represented a more concerted effort to prevent "dependent" family migration based on the lessons the French had learned—or believed they had learned—over the past six years. The Algerian delegation accepted French demonization of family migration as a price for guaranteeing continued employment to Algerian workers.

Bottlenecks and Whistleblowers at ONAMO

The family resettlement process separated desirable from undesirable migration on two levels. First, it submitted all families to an additional procedure, which winnowed their migration. Second, this procedure rejected families on the basis of their perceived maladaptation and projected cost to social aid. Administrators denied families who seemed posed to cause sanitary, social, or institutional problems. Of course, in the minds of many French administrators, *all* family migration carried these inherent threats. These narratives helped public perception swing against immigration in the early 1970s as the postwar economy slowed. Algerian families were easy targets after decades of policies and rhetoric describing them as problems.

Consider *sanctioned* migration after the 1968 agreement—this was already a large enough problem for French and Algerian diplomats; the pace of arriving mothers and children from Algeria outstripped ONAMO-sponsored workers. The 1968 agreement as well as ONAMO's own internal protocol bore the blame for slowing the migratory process. As a result Algeria often failed to hit its 35,000-worker quota. In 1969, for example, only 27,000 workers gained sanctioned entry into France through ONAMO, while 32,000 women and children arrived through family resettlement petitions (see figure 3). For the next five years, more women and children arrived than ONAMO workers. New procedures such as mandatory medical visits and certificates of establishment made it onerous for men to come to France through legal channels. To compound ONAMO's difficulty hitting the quota, the office rejected around 10 to 15 percent of the applicants in this period.[84] Requests for family resettlement, however, were still granted around 75 percent of

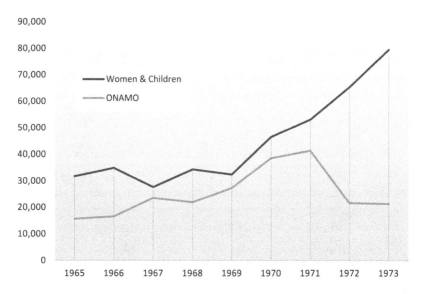

90,000
80,000
70,000 ── Women & Children
60,000 ┈┈ ONAMO
50,000
40,000
30,000
20,000
10,000
0

1965   1966   1967   1968   1969   1970   1971   1972   1973

3. Algerian women and children vs. ONAMO workers. Data compiled from Tapinos, "Chronique de l'immigration," *Population* 23, no. 6 (1968): 1107–14; Tapinos, "Chronique de l'Immigration," *Population* 24, no. 6 (1969): 1169–86; Auboiron, "Comparaison des mouvements migratoires en 1968–1973,"Tableaux A–C, 8 February 1974, Archives nationales de France, 19960134 art. 11.

the time.[85] Algerian workers could come to France without ONAMO permission, skewing French administrators' careful tables balancing arriving and departing workers and families. The "official numbers" were troubling enough to French administrators: Algerians' arrivals were mostly women and children.[86]

The medical procedures included in the 1968 accord provided fertile ground for fear and xenophobia by suggesting tendentious links between infectious diseases such as tuberculosis and venereal disease and the arrival of Algerian families.[87] French public health officials baselessly asserted that Algerians arrived without going through proper medical procedures, despite the fact that families as well as workers were required to have medical exams before or immediately following their arrival in France. Since 1964, two years after ONAMO was established, the French medical missions had sent staff to medical centers in Algeria to help with the migration protocol. The French medical missions were part of Franco-Algerian cooperation agreements fostering technical development in Algeria.[88] France provided technical support and temporary personnel until Algerian doctors could be trained to take over the process. The medical missions were ripe for controversy. The Algerian delegation complained that the language of "cooperation" and "technical training" was only neocolonial window dressing, and that the French benefited more from the medical missions that policed potential worker migration than the Algerians.[89]

One whistleblower, a French doctor assigned to the Constantine ONAMO offices, lent credence to French fears in a report asserting that his office had none of the necessary equipment and was in disrepair. The missions were severely understaffed, he complained, and each ONAMO doctor was supposed to complete thirty exams a day, five days a week, forty-four weeks a year. With only six or seven licensed practitioners at work, they could scarcely meet their quotas, given a 25 percent rejection rate. This crunch led the Constantine office to order the missions' doctors to allow Algerians suffering from syphilis to receive a quick treatment that would mask their symptoms until they could enter France, according to the whistleblower.[90] Syphilis was on the list of diseases posing a public health threat to France, as were tuberculosis, plague, cholera, and yellow fever.[91] This report created a scandal at Michel Massenet's Bureau of Population and Migrations, which had long asserted the fruitlessness of the medical missions. In their view the medical missions were understaffed, unprepared to examine enough workers to hit Franco-Algerian labor quotas, and unable to prevent the migration of unfit workers.[92]

More fact-finding missions into ONAMO exposed the gendered basis of medical clearances. The French government learned that Algerian authorities were "refusing to give the ONAMO card to women, only male candidates are authorized to present their candidacy to go work in France."[93] Ablebodied women were denied entry as workers into France to preserve spots for men. Though Algerian women became part of the official Algerian labor market in the 1960s, they were important parts of the under-thetable colonial economy and central to cottage industries.[94] Yet in 1966 only 1.86 percent of Algerian women were employed outside their own homes.[95] The ability to work—especially abroad—was tied to gendered constructions of migrant labor and the male worker. Since women could enter France under the terms of family resettlement, Algerians hoped to conserve ONAMO cards for men who would receive training to help develop the country's infrastructure.

Even with hard-won increased quotas for Algerian workers, ONAMO's bureaucracy failed to send more migrant workers to France. Crises about public health drummed up by the Bureau of Population and Migrations created further rhetorical grounds for the exclusion of Algerian families. ONAMO's own procedures also hampered Algerian migration, and particularly Algerian women's official channel to migration. With only legal or extralegal family resettlement open to women, labor remained gendered in French and Algerian officials' eyes, enhancing French administrators' view of Algerian families as "unproductive" dependents.

The Portuguese Case in the 1970s

In the early 1970s Algerian migrants outnumbered other national communities in France for the first time. In 1972 the migrant population in France grew to over 2 million people, including nearly 750,500 Algerians, 703,000 people from the European Economic Community, and 694,000 Portuguese migrants (formerly the largest population). The Bureau of Population and Migrations asserted that nearly 95 percent of migrating families did not come through the "normal" means (with medical examinations through the National Immigration Office or ONAMO). Migration was not in itself a problem, Director Michel Massenet's office was quick to note. Instead, it was the growing numbers of women and children, and especially women from North Africa, who, Massenet believed, "rarely worked." He concluded that the "active population" could not keep pace with the growing inactive population represented by wives and children. To wit: "The strictly economic interests of foreign immigration diminishes to the extent that the rate of activity of foreign populations is reaching that of the national population as a result of deliberately favorable politics of family resettlement." Family resettlement weighed on the French economy in Massenet's mind. His office noted that foreigners were responsible for 40 to 50 percent of the annual population growth in the early 1970s. In their view not only were women inactive in the French labor market, but they were also responsible for producing even *more* inactive members of the population through their reproduction.[96]

Since its creation in 1966, which I describe in chapter 3, the Bureau of Population and Migrations had argued for limiting the number of Algerian families on French soil, a position that held constant in the 1970s. Early in his tenure, Massenet commented that Algerian family migration was creating "qualitative and quantitative" problems. In a meeting with French and Algerian diplomatic authorities, he quoted an SSFNA report that argued that "too large a number of Algerian families are not adapting to French life, and these disorderly arrivals are destroying adaptations that have already been accomplished."[97] Resolving family migration was crucial because of its ramifications for social aid. He echoed interwar xenophobic arguments made by Georges Mauco, when he suggested that "Muslim" families from North Africa and Turkey—which constituted the majority of family resettlement requests in 1972—were less assimilable than those who arrived in the past from the European Economic Community or Spain or Portugal.[98] Massenet proposed a slew of new legislation and protocols, from limiting family resettlement to workers who had been in France for an established period, offering bonuses to workers whose families remained in their home countries, and asking employers to pay for some of the costs of social work for workers from whose labor they benefited. Immigration was encouraged only in the context of the needs of the job market.[99] Families need not apply.

Franco-Portuguese immigration accords juxtapose the Algerian case in revealing ways. Portugal negotiated a labor quota agreement with the French government whose terms far outrivaled other bilateral agreements. Since the postwar period, the French National Immigration Office organized Portuguese migration through its general immigration protocol. It established an outpost in Lisbon to recruit workers to France with such success that Portuguese migrants made up the majority of foreign migrants in France for much of the 1960s. As in the Algerian case, the French government had agreed to pay family benefits at a lower rate to the families of Portuguese workers who remained in Portugal, accidentally incentivizing family migration.[100]

Yet French and Portuguese officials tacitly allowed Portuguese clandestine immigration. Portuguese families migrating to France outstripped the number of Portuguese workers by the end of the 1960s.[101] Responding to

Portuguese concerns about family migration and French concerns about employment, the two parties agreed on a quota system much more favorable to Portuguese workers than the analogous 1968 Franco-Algerian quota system. The two delegations settled on a sixty-five-thousand-person quota per year (compared to the Franco-Algerian thirty-five-thousand-worker quota per year) with guaranteed higher social benefits for families remaining in Portugal.[102] This renegotiation afforded Portuguese workers and their families beneficial terms for arriving in France through the National Immigration Office in the same years that the labor market was contracting and tolerance for Algerian workers and families withered. Historian Vincent Viet points out that the administration's "cultural preference" for Portuguese migration over Algerian migration was clear in these agreements.[103]

The transnational politics of Europeanness, or perhaps Europeanness as whiteness, led French authorities to promote the Franco-Portuguese accords and the benefits Portuguese workers brought to the French labor market. This fact did not go unnoticed. The president of the Algerian workers' union abroad, the Amicale des Algériens en Europe, Abdelkrim Gheraieb, spoke out against the hiring practices faced by Algerian workers in France and tied these concerns to Algerian migration as a whole. Gheraieb pointed to the Franco-Portuguese quota as a sign of France's promotion of "white" immigrants over North Africans. Gheraieb argued that because Portuguese families contributed to the "right" kind of demographic growth, they were favored over Algerians: "Algerians are just as 'acceptable' as other so-called white immigrations, which would be so, but for historical, linguistic, and cultural reasons."[104] The alignment of whiteness with desirability was not new, though the French understanding of Portuguese desirability emerged in contrast with growing Algerian migration.

Public policy also shaped French public perception against North African immigration. Sociologist Alain Girard conducted a well-known study for the Institute of Demographic Studies that led him to conclude that in any given society there existed a "threshold of tolerance." This threshold, measured through public opinion, was the point at which "the proportion of foreigners in a region or sector above which accommodation is done with difficulty and provokes risks of tension."[105] This shared *perception* grew from the assumption that the arrival of immigrants led *inevitably* to social clashes, that the very fact of immigration was the cause of xenophobia.[106]

Girard's study found that French people believed that Algerians were least suited to life in France.[107] His study legitimatized the layman's sense—and built upon administrators' arguments—that immigration was always a social problem.[108] The threshold of tolerance provided a framework that helped administrators select for migrants in racialized and gendered terms. Family migration and its perceived permanence made integration, belonging, and whiteness more central to the selection.

The economy also showed signs of slowing in the late 1960s and early 1970s, before the oil shock, which led France to reduce labor migration. The 1972 Marcellin-Fontanet circular limited worker migration to those with full-time job offers. It aimed to address the already high French and existing migrant population unemployment rates by preventing further labor migration. It reserved available jobs to workers already in the market, and especially to those from the European Economic Community, who were still guaranteed free circulation. The agreement especially affected Tunisians and Moroccans, who came to France through the National Immigration Office's general immigration protocol, which had now stopped accepting new workers.[109] At the same time, the French also halved the Algerian admission quota from thirty-five thousand to seventeen thousand workers a year. The National Immigration Office had previously offered medical exams to Algerian women and children in France after migration to relieve strain on the French medical missions in Algeria, but no longer. They reversed course: all exams had to occur before arrival in France through ONAMO. Taken together, these agreements amounted to a sharp curtailment of Algerian and North African worker and family migration over the course of 1972.

The renegotiation of labor migration also prompted the Bureau of Population and Migrations to push the government to reconsider Algerians' special status. The office hoped to reorganize all migration through the National Immigration Office, eliminating ONAMO's control over Algerian migration. Massenet argued that France could use the changing economic context to discuss "the future of our politics of immigration. The moment has without a doubt come to reel our immigration agreements with Algeria into the general immigration protocol [*droit commun*]."[110] Massenet saw Algerian migration as a problem in part because of its exceptionality. The legacies of Evian guaranteed Algerians unique—albeit now severely curtailed—access to France through ONAMO. Renegotiating would bring

Algerians into the general immigration protocol. In Massenet's words, this would "limit the accelerating development of Algerian immigration in France" while also "allowing a better sanitary and professional selection of immigrants."[111] By eliminating ONAMO's sovereignty and the special family resettlement procedures reserved for Algerians, Massenet could achieve the French administration's primary goal since the 1962 Evian Accords were signed: unilateral control over Algerian migration.

Diplomatic Collapse

The early 1970s were diplomatically contentious years in Franco-Algerian relations. Colonel Houari Boumediene, the head of the Revolutionary Tribunal and de facto leader in Algeria, nationalized the oil and gas industries that were previously codirected (or even owned) by French firms. This nationalization directly challenged the terms of the Evian Accords and the cooperation agreements between France and Algeria. These agreements all protected French oil wealth in the Sahara, which was one of France's chief preoccupations at the time of Algerian independence.[112] Long a critic of cooperation and French neocolonialism, Boumediene undermined French interests through his nationalization, pushing the Franco-Algerian relationship to the breaking point.

Soon after, Boumediene, who only rarely commented on Algerian migration, condemned France's immigration politics and the unfriendly welcome Algerian migrants received. At the National Conference on Emigration in Algeria, Boumediene referred to the "heavy heritage of colonialism" that freighted Algeria's economic development. He conceded that his actions in the energy sector had "created problems for emigrant nationals who . . . had to deal with provocations and insults . . . reaching sometimes the assassination of innocent Algerians."[113] To his nationals, he added: "You cannot dissolve yourselves into European societies. It is your right to ask the state to pay particular attention to your fate."[114] In an implicit rebuke of the politics of immigration restriction, integration, and xenophobia, Boumediene reframed Algerian migration much as earlier Algerian diplomats had, around the history of French colonial exploitation of workers and extraction of resources.

Events spiraled in the summer of 1973. Between June and July 1973, the French Ministry of the Interior noted at least six attacks on Algerian workers. The responsible parties were not found in any of these cases.[115] *El Moudjahid*, the Algerian newspaper, printed several articles on violence against Algerian workers in France, which had increased after the nationalization of gas. Then, in August, a mentally ill Algerian man boarded a bus in Marseille and stabbed and injured seven passengers while killing the bus driver. The political and rhetorical backlash was immediate. Papers reported breathlessly on the event and its aftermath, which led, in turn, to an even greater number of attacks against Algerian workers.[116]

The situation boiled over in September when Boumediene halted all further Algerian worker migration. On 19 September 1973, Boumediene announced: "If there are now around 700,000 Algerians currently living in France, the responsibility falls to French colonialism in the first place. . . . This is why we have finally made a decision in which we have decided that as far as conditions of security and dignity are not met in France for our workers, *not one single Algerian will go to work in France.*"[117] This pronouncement shocked the French government, which had been preparing for future immigration talks with the Algerians only days before Boumediene's speech. The suspension had immediate effects: only eighteen ONAMO workers entered France in October 1973, fourteen in November, and none after that.[118]

The "immigration crisis," as it came to be known, developed over the decade following Algerian independence in the context of growing family migration and the perceived failure of French immigration protocols. Especially in the late 1960s and early 1970s, Algerian families were the targets of restrictive policies to prevent resettlement and, therefore, permanent costs to the French social welfare network. Health, housing, and geopolitical decision-making all coalesced around families until Boumediene's worker immigration halt in September 1973. Still, families were central. By preventing *worker* migration, Boumediene's ban reaffirmed the binary of the productive worker versus the unproductive family member. French immigration officials believed they only benefited from worker migration. When Boumediene halted worker—but not family—migration, he again proved the centrality of the family to immigration and social welfare policy.

New answers to old questions arose in the 1970s as diplomatic conceptions of the family changed. After the Algerian War and the establishment of independent Algeria, French and Algerian administrators turned their focus to the supposed problems of welcoming migrant families from Algeria in France. Both France and Algeria seemed to agree in principle on the importance of limiting family migration because family migration represented permanence. Permanent family migration threatened independent Algeria's reconstruction, but France especially demonized this migration pattern. Families from Algeria were purely dependent: on the male head of household and the French midcentury welfare state. French administrators architected ad hoc policies that distinguished freedom of establishment from circulation, regulated housing suitability, and narrowed the definition of the family. Women and children's migration were contingent upon the head of household's successful quest for housing and employment, which only heightened impressions of their dependency.

The thread of family migration raises questions that haunted administrators in the decade following independence. Franco-Algerian relations remained tense, and tussles over everyday families bore the imprint of this deteriorating relationship. What protections were owed migrating families from Algeria? Was migration itself a social right? What rights accompanied labor, and what did France owe workers' families? As the oil shock reverberated across Europe in the 1970s, it became clear that social welfare was the determining factor in restricting family immigration. Yet this was not a story that began with the economic downturn. The framework had already been set. Algerians were marginalized over the long period of decolonization as diplomats in France and Algeria regulated the place of Algerian families. Algerian families' supposed permanence and inability to integrate drove a clash-of-civilizations narrative. I consider this dilemma in the next chapter, in which I turn from the "immigrant problem" to the integration of "problem immigrants" that freighted the midcentury welfare state.

5

Disorderly Families

In the spring of 1971, Madame Ourdia A. received disappointing news: she would not be awarded the Medal of the French Family.[1] The medal, created as a pronatalist initiative in the wake of the First World War, rewarded mothers of multiple children for service to the *patrie*.[2] Gold medals were reserved for only the most fecund mothers of eight of more children, while silver and bronze went to progenitors of six and four, respectively. As a mother of nine, Madame A. ought to have been a candidate for gold, but the president of the regional committee rejected her application.[3] Madame A., he wrote, did not fulfill the necessary criteria.[4]

Though the president provided no justification, Madame A.'s social worker, Madame Glorieux, was suspicious of her refusal, suggesting it was because Madame A. and her family had migrated from Algeria.[5] Glorieux explained that Madame A. and her family had fled Algeria in the wake of independence following Monsieur A.'s years of service as a *harki*—indigenous—soldier in the French army. Glorieux complimented Madame A.'s well-appointed household and her attention to her children's education and health.[6] The family had adopted French citizenship in 1963, Glorieux reminded the committee, and she attested to Madame A.'s "morality," another requirement for the prize.[7] She requested that the committee review their decision but never received a reply.

Madame A. was certainly not the only woman to be refused the Medal of the French Family, but her experience underscores the cold reception of migrant families from Algeria in French society in no small part because of their families' imagined multitude.[8] The midcentury welfare state preserved care for Algerians within its institutional structure in the early Fifth

Republic, serving families from Algeria who continued to migrate after independence. In this chapter, I focus on a third thread, social work relationships themselves, which I analyze here as the care practices that evolved through the dynamic interactions between social workers, their clients, and the dictates they received from their employers and the midcentury welfare state. In the 1960s this thread frayed over the question of integration, a predetermined goal for migrants from Algeria that now seemed impossible to attain. As Madame A.'s experience suggests, racist legal and social practices persisted within the midcentury welfare state and particularly targeted women from Algeria who bore disproportionate responsibility for the integration (or disintegration) of their family in France.[9]

While historians of France have focused on immigration trends after empire as well as funding and welfare provisioning, I follow the ties between social workers and their Algerian clients.[10] I demonstrate that social workers attempted to transform the directives of integration to better address their clients' needs and respond to their feedback. Though integration had originally been part of a geopolitical framing of France's multiethnic empire, social workers now considered it as a social problem, borrowing a colonial framework and repurposing it. Over the decade after independence, however, social workers began conceding that integrating men—whose migration was seen as temporary—was beyond their mandate. They placed even greater onus on women's and children's belonging instead. Through these efforts, social workers positioned themselves as moral neocolonialists, attempting to help but ultimately doing harm.[11] Migrating families' imagined permanence translated into concerns about their ability to integrate. The family—and not the single male worker—embodied a troubling barrier to integration and, therefore, to the French social fabric. By the early 1970s the script about families from Algeria was written: men could be accommodated by focusing on their role as employees. Women and children, however, represented a potential future that threatened white France's vision of itself.

This chapter proceeds by examining a series of family stories.[12] In the decade after Algerian independence, social workers from the North African Family Social Service (SSFNA) documented their growing case load of Algerian families in a scarcely explored archive of more than two thousand dossiers. These stories represented years of interventions with families, friends, and entire neighborhoods through word of mouth and drop-in visits. To be sure, historians only encounter them as incomplete translations of conversations between social workers and clients, recorded from the social workers' perspective. Yet these stories also provide an opening for analysis of Algerians families' precarious place in the midcentury welfare state as much as a case study of how and why these stories came to be unheard.[13] I argue that social aid associations built upon the family stories to shape French perceptions about the Algerian family. While social workers may not have intended this outcome, the stories represented in these dossiers outlasted the Algerian War and came to define the "problem" of Algerian family migration.

Resettling the Harkis

For many Algerians in France, 5 July 1962 represented an important moment of political rupture and joy. Some repatriated to Algeria to take part in reconstructing their newly independent nation. For families like Madame A.'s, whose husband fought for the French army as a so-called harki soldier, there was little choice but to resettle after independence. The French government classified European settlers as repatriates returning to France despite—in some cases—having never been to the former metropole. They made few allowances for harkis, however, who were forced to flee Algeria or face retribution. Once in France, these "French Muslims" faced procedural as well as social barriers.[14]

In the months leading up to Algerian independence, French lawmakers struggled to make clear that harki migration should be discouraged or prevented altogether. One official threatened that harkis who arrived in France would be "sent back."[15] Authorities in the French army nonetheless arranged housing for harki families in makeshift camps marginalized from metropolitan French society with few plans for their gradual integration.[16] Upon their arrival in France, Madame A.'s family first found shelter among hundreds of other harki families at Rivesaltes, a former internment camp for Jews during World War II and political prisoners during the Algerian War. There, the family welcomed their sixth child in September 1963. By March 1965 at the birth of the seventh family member, Madame A.'s family had relocated to another former internment camp, St. Maurice l'Ardoise in the Gard.[17]

As more harki families arrived, it became clear that the French administration had no plan or funding in place to help them. The Ministry of Health quickly recruited volunteer social workers to a two-week intensive training session at a school for social work auxiliaries, L'École de Nantes, an army-run training facility during the Algerian War that provided an overview of basic social work without offering an official social work degree, a normally three-year course of study. As had been the case during the war, these volunteers lacked sufficient expertise and training in social services to aid the displaced harki population.[18]

Once in France, harkis reported difficulty declaring citizenship.[19] Between 5 July 1962, the date of formal independence, and 31 December of the same year, the new arrivals could request French citizenship *only* from French soil by making a declaration with a judge who rendered a verdict to the Ministry of Public Health and Population. The ministry could reject this application for a period of three years for unspecified reasons of "unworthiness."[20] From 1963 until 1965, the period in which the A. family adopted French citizenship, migrants from Algeria could declare citizenship outside the official naturalization process. This exception was precisely tailored to exclude the harkis, who French administrators worried would come to France and declare citizenship to "avoid consequences" in Algeria.[21] The Ministry of Public Health and Population required that the A. family provide their family civil registry booklet, the birth certificates of their children, and other official evidence of their crossing and Monsieur A.'s service to complete the dossier. But many petitioners found themselves caught in the crosshairs of politics and paperwork. According to one police report, only a small percentage of former harkis opted for citizenship, as many were still awaiting the arrival of their families from Algeria. The A. family resettled together, but for those who arrived in stages, adopting French citizenship might make families targets of reprisal in the interim in Algeria.[22]

Even if harkis gained citizenship like Madame A., social aid associations did not necessarily treat them differently than the general population of men, women, and families arriving from Algeria with Algerian citizenship, the majority of migrants from Algeria. The ssfna maintained that the difficulties posed by harkis' arrival were no different than any other family from North Africa, a problematic assertion that overlooked harkis' history as well as the conflicts that arose between these two communities during and after the war. Even the terminology French administrators used contributed to this confusion. Under empire, French law delimited "French Muslims from Algeria" or, later, "French with North African roots" from European settlers ("French with European roots"). After independence administrators and social service provisioners continued to use this term (though it was no longer legally applicable) to refer to harkis such as Madame A.'s family who petitioned for French rather than Algerian citizenship.[23] Although they were theoretically part of the French body politic, the status still set the A. family apart. Madame A.'s declined application for the Medal of the French Family is only one example. She—and other women like her—were marked by their imagined religious, ethnic, and racial difference.

Official and unofficial terminology served to obfuscate the recipients of social aid, though social aid associations also had practical objections to creating too stark a divide between the French Muslim and Algerian communities. The Lille office of the ssfna initially neglected to provide specialized harki social aid altogether and reported that it had welcomed over two hundred families to its offices in 1963 alone, eighty-seven of whom were "Muslim families." "The problem of the repatriates and harkis has significantly increased our task," wrote the Nord headquarters of the ssfna that year.[24] Yet the central administration resisted separating their services. Chief social worker Renée Bley insisted that she was "not convinced by the necessity [of the separation]" of Algerians and French Muslims on principle and instead argued that it created more difficulties for social aid services, since they relied on the same staff and same offices (but different funding) for the French Muslim and Algerian populations.[25] This perspective did not take into account the political backlash against harkis among some Algerians and particularly among members of the fln. Instead Bley promoted a totalizing approach that grouped Algerian migrants and naturalized French Muslims together. This direction implicitly linked the problems faced by populations migrating from Algeria as a whole and added legitimacy to conceptions of a hegemonic "Muslim" or "Algerian" culture that distinguished these new arrivals from other European migrants and French citizens.

The harki community certainly did not view itself as part of the same immigrant body as other families from Algeria. The National Committee for French Muslims (cnmf), the national pro-harki association directed by former colonial officials, fought for dedicated aid. Created in 1963, the committee received earmarked funding from the Social Action Fund for harki-specific initiatives, such as rehousing the community into new low-income housing units and social action specifically tailored to them. By 1966 the CNMF claimed to work on behalf of sixty thousand men, women, and children like the A. family who chose French nationality following their migration to France. The association was responsible for the salaries of fourteen social workers, forty family home aides, and ten advisers stationed in various national social aid associations, such as the SSFNA and the Aid Commission for North Africans in the Metropole (CANAM).[26] Partial funding divided employees' tasks according to their underwriting: some jobs were split in half, requiring 50 percent time addressing Algerian migrants and 50 percent time working on behalf of French Muslims. As was the case for most specialized associations funded by the Social Action Fund, the hazy public/private distinction muddied the waters of the social work provided. The result was confusion—bureaucratic as much as ideological—about the goals and methods of social aid for various populations from Algeria.

For social aid associations, grouping the disparate populations from Algeria served a strategic goal: demand for their services increased as did their funding. Rather than disappear alongside French empire in Algeria, specialized social aid associations expanded in the post-independence era. Even as the French bureaucracy adjusted to reflect the fact that Algeria was no longer a part of France, social aid associations insisted upon the importance of continuing to treat migrants from Algeria as a particular, if homogeneous, population with needs apart from the rest of the migrant body. Private associations cited the increased number of naturalized French and Algerian nationals to make the argument for more funding, more staff, and more visibility.

Creating a Dossier for Madame Yamina M.

Consider another family story that provides insight into the relationship between Algerian clients, social workers, and the midcentury welfare state after empire. The M. family first encountered the SSFNA in April 1954, before the start of the Algerian War, when Madame Yamina M. began taking homemaking classes at the new Roubaix office in northern France.

According to a social worker's record of their first meeting, Madame M. arrived accompanied by her sister-in-law at the suggestion of another "Muslim friend."[27] At that meeting the social worker on duty created a dossier for the family, then composed of Madame M., her husband Ali, and their two children.[28] The dossier noted that they were a "regular"— legitimate—"Muslim family" from Tizi Ouzou, a city not far from Algiers that was home to a large population of Kabyle families.[29] Monsieur M. worked at a smelting plant, and the family rented a studio in a small house shared with Monsieur M.'s brother. As part of her usual rounds, the social worker went to visit Madame M. a few days later. She found Madame M. and her two children in good health. She also met Madame M.'s mother, who had traveled with the family from Algeria.[30] Yet, within the month, the dossier noted that Madame M. no longer attended class, and her husband had a heart condition that kept him home from work. By the beginning of June, the family disappeared from the social worker's notes for thirteen years.

This dossier originated in the Roubaix office of the SSFNA, a suburb of Lille in the Nord, the mining region of France. Many families from Algeria chose the Nord over Marseille, Lyon, or Paris because of the density of work opportunities, especially in mines and automobile factories. Just one of over 2,700 individual family dossiers created between 1952 and 1972, the M. family's file holds an unusual level of detail. Many dossiers only include the last name of a family and their French address, though some make mention of the names of family members and their previous home addresses in Algeria. Diligent social workers added the place and date of birth of the members of the family—important for understanding families that spanned many generations and the Mediterranean—as well as their health, occupation, and ability to speak, read, and write French. Fewer dossiers still include a memorandum sheet on the visits family home aides made to a family's home, relaying the matters discussed while there. Madame M.'s visit sheet comprises only a couple of lines, though others were much longer.

Madame M.'s dossier is especially telling of social workers' continued efforts after independence when we consider the handwritten follow-up report from November 1967. That month, thirteen and a half years after her first meeting with the SSFNA, Madame M. returned to the association's sewing classes and requested that the home economics instructor come to her house to teach her daughter Djamila, now eighteen, how to sew. The instructor of the course demurred, saying that the classes allowed many students to learn together. When a family home aide followed up with Madame M. at her home, offering to drive Djamila to the sewing classes so she would not have to go alone, Madame M. refused while showing her the door.[31]

As a young mother, only twenty-two when she first arrived at the SSFNA office, Madame M. had not come alone. Social workers were quick to note when Algerian clients arrived in the company of a brother, husband, or female relative because it denoted—to them—a more rigid adherence to Islam, which thus required more "emancipatory" work. Though many women from Algeria, and indeed Muslim women, circulated without chaperones, social workers persistently feared the "autocratic Muslim father" who sequestered his wife, sisters, and daughters in the family home. Madame M.'s request for in-home tutoring for her unmarried adult daughter seemed to similarly reflect the conservative religious or societal practices that social workers sought to break down in their work with Algerian women. The social worker suggested that Madame M. seemed "unhappy" at the idea that her daughter would go out alone, an interpretation that aligned with the social worker's explanatory framework if not Madame M.'s emotions. Women-only sewing and home economics classes were meant to create a space for female sociability that would assuage the fears of fathers while providing empowerment. Yet this was unsuitable to Madame M., who refused the social worker's offer to accompany Djamila. The subtext of these case notes is clear: even after thirteen years in France, Madame M. had "yet" to accommodate to French dictates about sexual equality.[32] For the social worker, Madame M.'s refusal was proof of the continued demand for this kind of coursework.

Relationships between social workers, family home aides, and families developed over the long term and within the context of family drama, a crucible of its own. But Madame M.'s dossier also reveals how these relationships did not always play out in the ways that the SSFNA intended. After meeting with the social workers of the SSFNA in the early 1950s, Madame M. turned to them in times of need. Moments of conflict appear in her file as her life and the lives of her husband and children hit unexpected bumps. The SSFNA aimed to bring stability to families, particularly through the idiom of the emancipated homemaker and the modernized home. The association does not appear to have achieved its own goals, however, despite the long-standing relationship established with the M. family. After years in France, Madame M. prohibited her daughter from taking part in activities that the SSFNA believed would help integrate her into French society, attesting to the continued importance that social workers assigned to coursework, family intervention, and the specialized associations for North African families more generally.

Madame M. and her family are one example of how social workers made arguments for expanded funding as they emphasized the structural problems that Algerian families—newly arrived or long established—faced in France. There was overwhelming continuity of services and business in the Nord offices and other SSFNA offices throughout France. The Lille office saw their number of new cases grow steadily from 139 in 1961 to 244 in 1964 to over 500 by 1968.[33] Even with the departure of families to Algeria after independence, the office noted that the number of new arrivals "counterbalanced" the departures.[34] When families left for Algeria, social workers often noted when they returned, disappointed, citing the lack of employment possibilities in Algeria for those without professional degrees.[35] This increasing workload left the Lille office feeling exhausted, and social workers often complained about scarce resources and long hours.[36]

Bundles of dossiers from the post-independence period document an expanding capacity for interventions. They also represent an accumulation of trust between social workers and clients and a paucity of options for families facing hurdles. Some families took advantage of their contacts' expertise to work through administrative red tape together. The average length of the relationship established between social worker and client contained in these dossiers was nearly five years, but this number is misleading.[37] Half of the families who entered the SSFNA offices had relationships that lasted two or fewer years, while most families had relationships that lasted less than a year or, sometimes, only a visit. The SSFNA was one of the few options for families from Algeria arriving in the Nord, and if the office failed to provide answers, families had little recourse.

Families who failed to return did not leave records of their decision. They may have come seeking new answers but found only old methods.

The SSFNA's work remained remarkably consistent over the colonial to early postcolonial period. Its structure did not change because of Algerian independence. Indeed, as the national offices of the SSFNA proudly stated in their 1965 funding proposal, "The independence of Algeria transformed Algerians into foreigners; but on a juridical plane, their situation remains idiosyncratic, and on a human and social plane, we cannot hide that they will still pose difficult problems for a long time."[38] The association mined its expertise from the colonial period to reach out to families from Algeria: family home aides and social workers worked directly with women and families as in the colonial period, and home economics and family course instructors planned and directed classes with similar content.

The SSFNA continued to offer courses such as homemaking, sewing, stitching, and darning to its predominantly female clientele. Courses geared toward Algerian women had, in fact, known greater success in the decade following Algerian independence than during the Algerian War as the SSFNA's reputation (and budget) grew. And women continued to attend. In 1964 the Lille office offered five separate sewing and knitting classes for over forty students each, as well as a French language class exclusively for women.[39] As in Madame M.'s case, the continuity of the coursework provided support to a population in flux. Home help—the sort that visited Madame M's foyer in the early years—continued to make rounds to families in need. They brought wives to grocery stores and helped them find ingredients to cook meals for their families, taught daughters to sew, and tried to gain the trust of neighborhood families. For those who bristled against colonial tropes, the SSFNA could offer few options in the early post-independence period.

Families such as Madame M.'s contacted the SSFNA at moments of crisis or change, moments that had the potential to become "family stories" that historians of the midcentury welfare state only encounter through administrative documents. These are intimate moments that become visible to us through casework files, when "private life allowed itself to be seen, visited, rifled through," melting the distinction between public and private as family matters became matters of state.[40] Yet the dossiers of families represent a moment of dramatic uncertainty about the future: individual, collective, social, and geopolitical. Their sheer number overwhelms; privacy laws guard the names of those involved. These factors and required anonymity could easily transform family stories into stories about *those* families. This was precisely the operation that occurred as social workers tallied their annual successes and failures in yearly reports. Social work relationships were contingent and individual, yet funding schemes demanded neat categorizations to justify annual subsidies. Associational leadership translated individual meetings, conversations, and administrative paperwork into aggregates and outcomes. Faced with an abundance of human need, social aid associations such as the ssfna demanded more resources, more personnel, and greater attention for their clients, even after the end of empire.

Family (Dis)integration

Integrationist social work formed the backbone of associations' demands for funding. It was also a moving goalpost according to which migrants from Algeria fell short. The continued rhetorical and practical importance of integration set the framework for measuring social work after independence. In their public-facing materials, including brochures, annual reports, and quarterly subsidy proposals submitted to the Social Action Fund, the ssfna and other specialized associations balanced positioning their work as important and as yet unachieved, requiring further support. They had another intractable problem: their primary goal, integration, was difficult to achieve because it was based on a negative vision. Its tenets reflected French officials' perceptions about Algerians' failure to adhere to visions of the modern nuclear family. French immigration officials repeatedly worried about the extended nature of Algerian families: grandparents, aunts, uncles, nieces, and nephews, echoing interwar-era concerns about Portuguese, Spanish and Italian migrants.[41] To mitigate this fear, French immigration protocols limited this definition of the "family" to immediate blood relatives and focused integrationist actions and rhetoric on shaping the Algerian family into a nuclear one.

From its inception, integration was an imperiled project based on analyses of the aggregate. Thousands of ssfna clients fell short of the goal. Colonial-era integration had recognized supposedly inherent Algerian difference, especially as it imagined Islam and secular French society as incompatible. These policies' insistence on Algerian *difference* made all subsequent integration impossible; Algerians could approach, but never meet, the objective.[42] When families failed to integrate, French administrators placed the blame at the wife's or mother's feet. Work with husbands and fathers, in contrast, stressed situational and short-term solutions, such as professional or paraprofessional training or French language instruction. Increasingly in the 1960s, social workers steered Algerian male children toward Arabic language classes as part of the persistent belief that, for men and boys, life in France was temporary.[43]

Classes offered by social aid associations fostered relationships between new and more established Algerian migrants as well as with French social workers. Islam was the primary marker of difference in the classroom regardless of individual students' religious beliefs. Being Catholic or Protestant did not pose a problem for the social workers who modeled "modern" behaviors, but being Muslim was seen as a threat to emancipation. Social workers pointed to the dangers of uneven integration—when wives and daughters became more at ease in French society than their husbands and fathers, especially if wives compared themselves to European women. What good could they do, they asked, in a case in which an Algerian woman became aware of "the injustices of which she is the victim" at the hands of a "husband she did not choose?"[44] Social workers recycled tropes about Islam's supposed subjugation of women as they dissected marital relationships, which further fueled their concern about the migrant family unit. Most courses relied on these assumptions, even if they remained unspoken. Classes included skills that many women already had—cooking and sewing, for example—but were then reintroduced and tailored toward cultural integration. For example, women were provided with patterns for pants and modern blouses, an implicit critique of the dresses and haïks that Algerian women often wore.[45] The classes were one arrow in a quiver of strategies aimed at assuring integration through French cultural citizenship.[46]

Cultural citizenship seemed much less central to classes offered to Algerian men and boys. In 1965 the SSFNA in the Nord hired Marcel Viane, a credentialed social worker, as the "specialized educator" responsible for helping Algerian boys and teenagers adjust to life in France. Social workers and home help noted that many of the family crises of the early 1960s related to disequilibrium within the home. Resolving these disputes proved difficult when confronted by a disapproving patriarch, female social workers contended as they again rehearsed tropes about the dictatorial Muslim man. Only an equally strong masculine figure could counterbalance the authority of the head of household and allow the family to make progress. Viane served Lille, Roubaix, and Tourcoing in the Nord and divided his time between the sons of Algerian migrants and young French Muslims in the region.[47]

Viane was one of the few men certified as a social worker, and his role at the SSFNA was specific: he was the chief educator and classroom leader for young men from Algeria.[48] The adolescent boy from Algeria, he wrote, was "raised with the privileges of his future role as head of household . . . raised in an atmosphere of total freedom, adored by his mother, spoiled by her," which led to a rude awakening when confronted with life in France. Without proper preparation and psychosocial support, Viane argued, these boys found themselves adrift.[49] He placed the blame for young men's maladaptation at their mother's feet. His analysis suggests acceptance of a popular perception that the troubled Muslim boy was a product of maternal overindulgence as well as the paternalist dictates of Islam.

Viane did not simply focus on the social. He was also interested in the often-overlooked interior lives of the young men he instructed in small group classes on social belonging and pre-professional training. He argued that the growing feeling of resentment toward life in France among young French Muslims consigned them to marginalization rather than the other way around.[50] He also favored adapting social aid and revising the definition of integration to better reflect French administrators' belief that young men might return to Algeria. "If the behavior of a North African man seems to be poorly adapted to French social habits," he reasoned, the "worst possible technique" would be to try to correct him.[51] Instead, Viane claimed French social workers sought to integrate Algerians to ease their own (French) problems, rather than considering the goals of the Algerian population. Viane insisted that a boy should be himself so long as he did not "[disrupt] the host environment."[52] This boys-will-be-boys approach included the pursuit of "universal" values, such as job satisfaction and self-improvement. Not by accident, these "values" overlapped with men's roles as laborers, impressing upon them the importance of work to the creation of self.[53] This emphasis stood in stark contrast to women's roles as potential members of French society and mothers to French children.

As if to reaffirm Viane's analysis, the Liaison Committee for Literacy and Promotion (CLAP), a left-leaning cooperative, organized reading and writing courses with a secondary goal of training migrant populations to return home.[54] Specialized social aid associations outsourced literacy programming to associations such as CLAP, which in turn focused on the relationship between literacy and hiring opportunities for men in their language classes. Their course packets titled "Learn to Read and Write" intended to teach migrants vocational vocabulary. The illustrations depict discouraged men of North African and Southern European descent looking for work (see figure 4) as well as images featuring men in hard hats and overalls, holding painting and blacksmithing tools.[55] At home, women are pictured serving a young family dinner and supporting their husbands (see figure 5).[56] In one image a tired-looking mother who we understand is illiterate sits at a kitchen table with her young daughter as the daughter writes a letter (see figure 6).[57] These portrayals reinforced stereotypes about migrant laborers and family life while implicitly distinguishing between "normal" and "abnormal" conditions of living. The illustrations depicted a small but clean home that relied upon maternal labor. They portrayed nuclear families of four or five that did not extend to in-laws or other relatives. Wives and mothers were illustrated as disenfranchised, especially in contrast with their literate—"liberated"— daughters. CLAP instruction materials envisioned migrant men as goal-oriented and in steady pursuit of employment opportunities.

These popular depictions of the Algerian family insisted upon cultural difference. Each member of the family could just as easily be disciplined as fall prey to the seemingly inevitable stereotypes corresponding to their familial role: the subservient mother, the authoritarian father, and the maladjusted (delinquent or sexually deviant) children. These perceptions were generalizations and hardly new. But now that Algerians were migrants and primarily prized for their labor, social workers embraced gendered market logic in the home. They, too, contributed to the idea that the families implied permanent relocation (bad) while male migrant workers were only temporary guests in France (good). By the early 1970s, social workers had made clear that men's integration was less important because they assumed men's presence in France to be temporary whereas women and children *needed* to integrate or they risked upending French society.

Discussion of *race* is mostly absent in social work literature and reports, but mention of cultural incommensurability is everywhere. The challenges of integrating Algerians into life in France stood as proof that Algerian

4. Migrant men from Algeria, Mauritius, Yugoslavia, and Senegal with flags. Comité de Liaison pour l'Alphabétisation et Promotion Class Materials, *Apprendre à lire et à écrire: Introduction à la relation parole/écriture: Matériel collectif*, Dossier 6, Bibliothèque nationale de France.

family migration frayed France's social fabric. The father fulfilled his role as head of the family if he held a job and provided for his family, but his wife bore the responsibility for adapting to life in France. Though the 1968 Franco-Algerian agreements urged social aid associations to provide job training services to Algerian men and boys, their work with women remained remarkably similar even in the face of marked reticence. The continuation of these family policies even as social aid associations adjusted their work with Algerian men meant that women were set up for failure as they continued to fall short of—or even actively resisted—integration.

5. Migrant woman serving family dinner in a small, shared room.
Comité de Liaison pour l'Alphabétisation et Promotion Class Materials,
Apprendre à lire et à écrire: Introduction à la relation parole/écriture:
Matériel collectif, Dossier 3, Bibliothèque nationale de France.

The ssfna acknowledged these difficulties, stating that, despite its efforts, it was unsuccessful in its attempts to integrate Algerian women. Yearly course reports written by home help and language instructors for use in internal and external communications document continued difficulties achieving course goals. "After making good progress with women," one 1970 report stated, "for a couple of years, we have had the impression of a 'blockage,' of a return to traditions, a withdrawal into themselves—a defensive attitude."[58] In reaction to attention paid to integration, women from Algeria seemed to dig in their heels and—at least from the perspective of ssfna social workers—resist their overtures. Social workers argued that this recalcitrance led to more problems with individual members of the families, as well as an increased number of suicide attempts by teens and mothers, more runaways, more mental illnesses, and more difficulties between spouses.[59] Social aid organizations' efforts during this period reveal that welfare policies contributed to the perceived migration crisis. The focus on training and repatriating workers was at odds with the families' experiences, including difficulties in their new homes, administrative roadblocks,

6. Migrant woman with daughter, discouraged by illiteracy. Comité
de Liaison pour l'Alphabétisation et Promotion Class Materials,
*Apprendre à lire et à écrire: Introduction à la relation parole/écriture:
Matériel collectif,* Dossier I, Bibliothèque nationale de France.

and the stutter steps of starting a new life. The cumulative costs—economic,
demographic, and social—of hosting families from Algeria and sustaining
the project of integration proved untenable.

In annual reports filed with the Social Action Fund, the SSFNA consistently positioned itself as a crucial but precarious entity. The board of
the fund met quarterly to debate the subsidies provided to the SSFNA and
other semi-private social aid organizations. The supporting documentation
the SSFNA sent attested to the increasing difficulties they faced: "Can
the SSFNA be accused of pessimism in the face of the problems posed in
France by Maghrebi family migration, and let's be clear, mainly Algerian
family migration?" The report went on to underline the prejudice Algerian
families faced in France and the SSFNA's hardships attaining the necessary
funding and support to help their charges. When tasked with helping
the "most difficult cases," they reasoned, they naturally faced failure.[60]
And yet the tone and content of these amassed reports acted as a yearly
reminder of the insufficiencies of specialized social aid and the impossibility
of integration.

Social workers filled an important intermediary role between Algerian migrants and the French state, which attempted to limit families' presence after empire. They interpreted state and departmental policies to the benefit of their clients while also explaining the work they failed to accomplish to state funders and immigration officials. Integration was at the heart of this triangular relationship: if and when families from Algeria failed to cohere with French definitions of belonging, then, in social workers' minds, they had a ready-made explanatory framework for this failure that blamed family migration. Not only did families' resettlement symbolize permanence, but it could also mean instability and the degradation of the French social fabric.

Social Work in Flux

The crises of immigration and integration led specialized social workers of the midcentury welfare state to reevaluate their goals at the same moment that the social work profession more generally interrogated its mission and its structure. This self-study would allow social workers to provide better support to their clients, yet it also exposed their clients' vulnerabilities. Private social aid associations were susceptible to unreflective practices, but few historians have questioned the line of analysis set down by Jacques Donzelot, following Foucault, that the social worker (replacing the education system) sought to civilize the social body. Using the provocative language of empire, Donzelot argued that families were "colonized" by the "double network of social guardians and technicians."[61] This view of social work is derived in part from the roots of professionalization at the apex of empire, yet it misses the shifting nature of the practice. Social work transformed alongside and within French institutions after Algerian independence.

Twenty years after the start of their mission, specialized social workers confronted distinct roadblocks in the form of funding, their clients, and the very mandate of integration they strove to fulfill. They also faced growing public disinterest in the Algerian population and an uphill battle toward recruiting new personnel and retaining those who had grown weary of or disillusioned by repeated interventions. In 1971 the ssfna was relieved to rethink social work in the Nord according to a new organizational framework called "sectorization." This ostensible rationalization of social work delineated the division of labor between social workers, home aides, and course instructors. It also streamlined services for North Africans by making them answer to the departmental social welfare system.

In 1964 the central administration created regional governmental offices for social work, the Departmental Office for Social and Sanitary Action (known as DDASS), which took control of departmental budgets and supervision of social workers.[62] DDASS wanted to equalize tasks among social workers to better equip each team. Yet the reform struggled to promote versatility [*polyvalence*] among social workers, not least for administrative reasons. Who paid social workers' salaries? What tasks would they therefore prioritize?[63] Semipublic social aid associations were especially difficult to regulate and organize. These associations guarded their "freedom" from the DDASS, which they feared would implement national protocols that did not respond to the unique needs of their clients.[64] Private social aid associations' differing organizational designs allowed them to escape attempts at reform in the 1960s, but this changed with sectorization.

Beginning in April 1971 towns in the Nord were divided into districts, each of which had its own "polyvalent" social worker in charge of newly formed teams. The social workers in charge of each team were generalists, those trained to work in a variety of settings (factories, help desks, departmental administration), and they managed several other social workers and team members with more distinct specialties. SSFNA social workers might be placed in these teams but would not lead one. This meant that the generalist leader of the team might only ask an SSFNA social worker to step in in extraordinary cases requiring specific language or cultural expertise. This reorganization relieved the SSFNA and other specialized social aid offices from working with clients with run-of-the-mill requests such as paperwork procedure or job-seeking aid. Since, in the new administration's thinking, these clients could just as easily work with departmental agencies, then the SSFNA was less important as an intermediary.[65]

This cooperative vision again raised existential questions about the SSFNA's necessity, though social workers documenting these changes did not always reflect on them. Echoing the Algerian War–era debates on the double bind of specificity discussed in chapter 3, some reports contested sectorization from its start. What was the specialized role of the SSFNA if "polyvalent" social workers increasingly replaced it?[66] What was the future of an organization whose goal was to render itself obsolete through the integration of the population it was created to serve? Others embraced this finite future for the SSFNA, viewing sectorization as a step forward, even if a bit premature. The SSFNA's Vienne office in the Nord argued that specialized services were only useful to the extent that they were public services and part of the rationalization and reorganization of social work: "Specialized social services should not be private associations but public services since, on the one hand, such services are a foreigner's right . . . and, on the other hand, it's in France's interest to understand welcome, in the broadest sense of the word, for *all* foreign workers to avoid racism and social maladaptation."[67] Sectorization became another means through which social workers could debate the place of their services within the tapestry of the midcentury welfare state.

Whatever the philosophical orientation of sectorization, it was part of a broader reorganization that was beginning to take shape in the national social services. That year, 1971, social workers convened in the capital for a meeting at the Ministry of Population to discuss the costs and benefits of individualized social work. According to the report given by chief SSFNA social worker Renée Bley, two economists had asked the assembled social workers to calculate the precise costs of classes and work with a North African family to economize their time. Bley reported that the current administration wanted to move from subsidies provided by the Social Action Fund to contract work with different geographic sectors. Bley assured SSFNA social workers that she had argued against this kind of devaluation of the profession. She reminded the economists at the Ministry of Population that it would be impossible to evaluate the cost of a family, since that would also require evaluating the cost of families who did *not* seek the SSFNA's help and needed it. Further, she argued that interventions with an individual family had a cascading effect on those around them: each family served might influence two or three others, allowing the SSFNA's teaching to spread.[68]

If the 1970s was the apex of social work, as Donzelot suggested, this fact certainly escaped the notice of specialized social workers struggling to justify their roles to a recalcitrant French administration.[69] Though generalist social workers benefited from sectorization, administrators and funders nickeled-and-dimed specialized social workers. The SSFNA struggled to define the roles of each member of its team: the social worker, the family home aide, the family instructor, and the home economics instructor all worked with individual families to different ends. Social workers, who held the most advanced degrees, were meant to be the liaisons between the SSFNA and state services, such as the DDASS and housing offices. They led a team at their town or region's SSFNA office, including at least one family home aide and one course instructor. Family home aides, who made visits to individual families, and home economics and family instructors, who taught group classes, received less training but were no less important. For practical and economic reasons, they were frequently called upon to fill roles for which they were unprepared.

Moreover, in the decade after Algerian independence, it became more difficult to recruit social workers to specialized services. Social work, family home aide, and course instructor programs also failed to recruit from the North African population. While the SSFNA occasionally made mention of "North African" or "Muslim" instructors, these cases were rare. Some pedagogical materials referred to "translators" who rendered course materials in Arabic or Kabyle, but the SSFNA does not seem to have used these translators as teachers in the classroom setting.[70] The chief social worker in the Nord, Madame Detrez, noted declining job applications for SSFNA positions, which were seen as arduous and underpaid. Even with "language bonuses"—social workers received a 5 percent salary bonus for speaking Kabyle or Arabic—social work was under-remunerated in the face of a growing caseload and an apathetic public.[71]

For its part the SSFNA attempted to reduce redundancy and better define the roles of their various employees. Social workers designed uniform education and degree work for course instructors, who often lacked clear job descriptions or even basic training before entering the classroom. Home aides doubled as course instructors in the face of budget cuts. Individual visits at home could create enough trust to lead a woman to enroll in group classes. Classes were also more expedient for training women in French language and home economics, especially as around one hundred new families arrived each year through family resettlement in places such as Roubaix.[72] A family home aide (who was also a family course instructor) at the SSFNA of Roubaix spoke confidently of the need for increased services to the Algerian population in her town. Adopting the language of her administrative underwriters, she argued, "We think that a family instructor, introduced from a family's first weeks [in France] will accomplish a huge form of preventative work (and profitable work, economically speaking). . . . The three family instructors of Roubaix currently work with 120 families."[73] The more cost-effective courses became the SSFNA's focus.

Since their inception in the colonial era, women's courses remained little changed despite disappointing results. Social workers, family home aides, and instructors all worked together in the classroom, so the downturn in interest toward women's courses affected all three positions. In the late 1960s the SSFNA had difficulty attracting new clients to the courses, especially since the courses tended to attract women who had already taken them. In 1967 about half of the women who signed up had already attended the courses for at least two or three years.[74] As a result, Nelly Forget, a SSFNA employee and a veteran social worker of the Algerian War, proposed integrating home economics coursework with language skills to help women make better progress. "Home economics courses offer opportunities to practice the French language," she noted, which would have the secondary result of revamping these classes that had remained much the same since the 1950s.[75] Forget sought to renew interest in the classes by making them more applicable to women's lives. In an era when men's courses focused more on skills, so too should courses for women.

Forget argued that home economics courses were outmoded. Though social workers at the SSFNA did not directly comment upon the events of 1968 in their discussions of Algerian women, changes to the home economics courses and social work generally reflected shifting perspectives on the role of women in the workforce and the household. Since early 1969, social workers at the national level had proposed changes to the home economics class, even its unique focus on women, "a pretty arbitrary limitation," they conceded.[76] Although they did not fundamentally reconceive traditional femininity in their coursework for Algerian women, social workers questioned the use value of home economics. In the next year national training programs for course instructors pivoted away from "homemaking" toward "social and family economics" (ESF), which emphasized the overlap between language coursework and "practical life" work, including grocery shopping, bill paying, laundry, and bank errands.

Course structure was not always so quick to change, however. It still tended to create a negative feedback loop: coursework set out goals that participants could not or did not choose to meet. Instructors then reported on their students' shortcomings. A 1972 CLAP survey postulated the reasons that migrant women from all national backgrounds might fail to attend classes. More than two-thirds of the 963 women surveyed regularly left their homes unaccompanied and enjoyed a relatively autonomous life in France, while 254 women reported never leaving their homes alone. The majority of those who remained at home were Algerian.[77] These findings reaffirmed social workers' existing assumptions. The survey generated data on the reasons migrant women attended courses: to understand and speak French, to learn to sign their names, and to enjoy the company of other women. The collective aspect of the course was key to its success. In social workers' interpretation, women wanted to "leave their isolation" and become more self-sufficient.[78] Yet according to the survey's findings, associations fell short of helping Algerian women achieve these goals by their own measure. The survey concluded that "written language is useless for women" because basic exchanges and conversing with friends were the course goals. This logic further distanced women from the professionalizing aims of courses for men.[79] At this transitional point for social work, there was little certainty about courses' effectiveness or, more fundamentally, their goals.

In these same years, the SSFNA raised doubts about the possibility of integrating Algerian families into French life and, indeed, families' abilities to ease the troubles of single migrant men. Between 1962 and 1972, the number of families with which the SSFNA worked grew from thirty-five thousand to sixty-five thousand (representing an 85 percent increase over ten years).[80] As the number of families petitioning for resettlement and arriving through tourist visas increased, so too did the magnitude of problems the SSFNA faced. In an annual report for funders, the association noticed "an increase in conflicts" within families that it "linked to maladaptation."[81] The SSFNA blamed the uneven integration of family members for these conflicts. Social workers in Paris categorized three potential outcomes of social work with Algerian families: family members could reject "civilization," embrace integration, or assume a "surface level adaptation" to French norms.[82] Although social workers had previously insisted that families fostered mutual integration, the SSFNA in Paris now questioned that assumption. Social workers classified the adaptation of women in this region on a scale from very good to completely inadaptable. They ranked 21 percent of women as having achieved "very good" integration, but they also ranked 35 percent between somewhat and completely inadaptable. Further, they suggested that about 45 percent of women would only make progress toward adaptation with difficulty.[83]

Because of the limitations inherent in this mission, the SSFNA pursued two seemingly mutually exclusive aims: integration in keeping with French social policy that dated to the colonial years and insistence on the difficulty of integration. Measuring integration was notoriously complicated—how did one quantify success over years of contact with some families? Social work was individual and interpersonal. The vicissitudes of life in France, the quarterly course schedule, and cycles of expanding and contracting employment for course workers and their supervisors often led the SSFNA to proclaim in its yearly reports that it had fallen short of integrating Algerian families. The SSFNA regularly blamed itself as well as Algerian women and families for "failing" to integrate, though this perception ignored the ways integrationist policies impeded success.

Private social aid associations such as the SSFNA faced internal challenges while external reform limited their reach and impact. As social workers engaged in self-study, they questioned the validity and utility of "specialized" social work. Cooperation between public and private services could only go so far in this political and socioeconomic context. Restricted access and constrained resources undermined all social work operations but hit private associations especially hard. These cracks in the infrastructure of the midcentury welfare state became newly apparent, contributing to the bureaucratic rationale for specialized social work's slow elimination.

Ending Integration

Two metaphorical headlines emerged about specialized social work in the decade following independence: first, that integration work for Algerian families was difficult and often failed; second, even in cases when families "succeeded" in their integration, the very definition of integration prevented acknowledging their success as such. As the primary mouthpiece for integrationist work, social aid associations unwittingly helped French administrators make the case that Algerian migration posed the greatest challenge to the midcentury welfare state because of supposedly inherent and unresolvable differences, including worse public health, a tendency to live in overpopulated housing, and an unequal balance between the conjugal couple.[84] Reading social aid associations' yearly reports also allowed officials to continually describe Algerian families as social problems and drains on the welfare state.[85] State officials' conclusions followed: Algerian families could not belong, integrationist efforts over the previous two decades had proven this fact, and social workers' continued failures (well documented in funding requests and internal correspondence alike) were evidence. The burden of integration fell to women and children, which further shored up the reigning impulse to prevent family resettlement altogether.

It was not surprising, then, that crises of funding and confidence hit social aid associations especially hard at the dawn of the new decade. The board of directors of the Social Action Fund debated how to rectify budget shortfalls and the decreasing priority of social aid and social action. In the early 1960s social action had a hearty budget, which reflected the arrival of families, while by the early 1970s the fund allocated the majority of its budget to housing for single workers, including as much as 75 percent of the 1971 budget. The demographics of migration had changed in the intervening decade—by the early 1970s Algerians had become the largest foreign population on French soil. At the same time, funding shifted away from integrating migrants and toward incentivizing the arrival of single male workers by limiting family housing and constructing single bedroom units.[86]

These budgetary difficulties were part and parcel of the French ambivalence toward Algerian migration. Since 1964, representatives from the Ministry of Finance on the board of the Social Action Fund could veto any spending that went to vote, regardless of the support voiced by the majority. This veto power became increasingly important in the years before the oil shock, as Sylvain Laurens has shown, when the representatives from Finance vetoed an average of five subsidies per monthly meeting.[87] Social aid associations understood these new restrictions. For example, in 1971 the SSFNA forecasted an annual budget of 2.9 million francs but requested a subvention of 1.9 million francs (200,000 more than in 1970). While the Social Action Fund had previously covered the entirety of the SSFNA's operating budget, the association now looked elsewhere for fiscal support, including public-private associations such as the National Committee for French Muslims (cnmf).

Funding mandates came from the top. The Ministry of Finance's hesitations drew support from administrative consensus about the importance of "mastering the flow" of immigration to prevent societal anarchy. The collapse of diplomatic discussions between France and Algeria in the early 1970s also restricted aid for Algerians. All North Africans in France, and especially Algerians, faced heightened xenophobia. Boumediene's decision to halt worker immigration allowed family resettlement to continue. The halt thus paradoxically served to justify further cuts to social aid for Algerian families under the guise of the temporary end to worker migration.

How, then, did families from Algeria in France experience the freeze? I offer one more family story. Despite a decade of policy and social work, integration was not an assurance of belonging. Even integrated Algerian families faced hostility in their communities during this period of heightened tensions between France and Algeria. Madame Tassadit A. arrived in Roubaix from Kabylia in 1961 and moved into an apartment in an HLM with her husband and ten children. By Madame A.'s account, they had lived peacefully in Roubaix for over a decade. Yet in the 1970s, her (white) French neighbors began targeting her family. When she left her children to bring one of her sons to the hospital, she reported to the police that her neighbor's sons had thrown a bottle of gasoline into her home to disturb her children. When her children brought it outside, the neighbor's sons beat them. After reporting this incident, Madame A.'s neighbor's sons assaulted her, which caused her to miscarry. She complained of the slurs hurled at her children and the tragedy of her loss. In the weeks that followed, her reports had not yet led to a single charge.[88]

The ssfna in the Nord made it clear that Madame A.'s experience, while traumatic, was not unique. Like our first Madame A., rejected applicant for the Medal of the French Family, the victim was the mother of many children. Racist demographic concerns about Algerians' supposed fecundity underwrote the mixed messages about reproduction that Algerian women received. Although coursework and social work interventions focused primarily on women's roles as mothers, in practice the growing Algerian population had been the subject of French concern since the colonial era.[89] As mothers of large families, both women were targets of a eugenicist inheritance that prized white French births.

This attitude no doubt shaped the prejudice Algerians faced. In letters to the National Institute of Demographic Study, ssfna social workers noted increased racism in communes across the country. They explained that "autochthonous"—or white French—teachers in predominantly North African neighborhoods were leaving for other areas and that the population no longer frequented swimming pools or supermarkets in areas where North Africans were the majority population, characteristics of the "white flight" taking place in towns and cities across the integrating globe.[90]

Over the course of the decade following Algerian independence, French administrators and social workers alike consistently positioned family migration from Algeria as a "problem" to resolve. Rather than acknowledging the long history of migration as a social phenomenon wrought by over a century of colonialism, public policy and public discourse assumed that immigration created societal dissolution. Social welfare offered to migrants made the source of the problem clear: supposedly recalcitrant and inadaptable women and children. Madame A.'s integration made no difference because integration was a rigged game. Regardless of the efforts of social workers to educate their clientele and reform their profession, the result was the same. Dissolving Franco-Algerian relations only heightened the stakes of this purported failure.

In the aggregate, family stories served as evidence of the failures of integration. In individual cases, however, we see the perils of success. There was no winning for families from Algeria. French social work interventions repeatedly demonstrated how integration delimited belonging through its very definition. Even when they acquiesced to French definitions of belonging, Algerians still faced obstacles to inclusion. When viewed from this angle, racism and xenophobia are less grassroots phenomena than state-cultivated ones, promoted through public policy and the welfare apparatus.

French sociologist and family planning activist Catherine Valabrègue expressed the central paradox of family migration: "The closed world of the family is at once a source of security that gives migrants the ability to overcome the inherent difficulties of *déracinement* [uprooting] and a brake on adaptation to a new world."[91] As we have seen, the family embodied these multiple possibilities. Although during the Algerian War French administration saw the family as an important helpmate in the "normal" adaptation of the family to metropolitan life, the family came under fire as the reason for slow or inadequate adaptation in the 1960s. The family stories reflected in archives of social aid associations show how these associations promoted the integration of families while insisting on their inability to do so. As the 1970s dawned, Algerians faced an ever more uncertain welcome in France despite the guarantees offered to them by their independence. The intimate lives of families were refracted through the geopolitics of decolonization.

The relationships created between social work teams, their clients, and the French administration served as one tenuous thread connecting social work to empire. As social workers redefined the meaning of integration, so too did the French state redefine Algerians' ability to migrate and belong. By 1973 French administrators and the French public called into question social aid associations' ability to help Algerian families negotiate life in France. Their services had evolved over the ten years since Algerian independence—they had more experience, more knowledge, and better teams to help with family integration—but they could not achieve the tenets of integration by design. Social workers and the specialized social aid associations that employed them were increasingly adept at pointing out the flaws in integration contributing to diminishing faith in their efforts. Yet while specialized services were far from perfect, the holes in the midcentury welfare state that necessitated them in the first place had hardly been mended. By following this thread from the moment of independence to 1973, I have shown in this chapter how social work practice and the relationships social workers formed evolved without ever losing their colonial framework. In the final chapter I weave this thread back into the others, braiding a narrative about how immigration policy, specialized services, and the midcentury welfare state entered a new crisis in light of the oil shock.

6

A New Politics of Immigration

In October 1977 the new secretary of state for immigrant workers, Lionel Stoléru, appeared on the French public television program *Mosaïque*, a weekend morning show "celebrating" immigrant culture.[1] The short spot began with a besuited Stoléru confidently sipping an espresso in a sunny café in the traditionally immigrant and working-class neighborhood of the Goutte d'Or in Paris. As he and the interviewer walked through the neighborhood, migrants from North and Sub-Saharan Africa looked on while Stoléru plugged an initiative developed by his office called the "Week of Dialogue."[2] The event aimed to establish connections between French citizens and migrants in hopes that the two populations would "get to know each other to understand each other better." Stoléru looked past his interlocutor directly at the camera as he invited migrants from "all" national communities—he listed Algeria, Sub-Saharan Africa, and Morocco—to engage with fellow migrants and Frenchmen.[3]

The Week of Dialogue was the newest social outreach attempt advanced by Stoléru's office to reconcile foreign labor and the French population. In the late 1970s Stoléru and other administrators tasked with managing migration reallocated funding for Algerians' social aid toward the broader migrant community and cost-effective initiatives for workers in place of substantive social services for migrant families. In this chapter, I bring together all three of the book's threads—midcentury welfare, family migration, and the relationships social workers and clients formed—to make sense of the French policy and political decisions that ended support for Algerian-specific social services in the shadow of the global oil shock.

After the election of centrist president Valéry Giscard d'Estaing in May 1974, the government closed the country's borders to foreign laborers and families. As the country slowly reopened to migrant workers in subsequent years, it did so gradually, only welcoming migrants arriving from member states of the European Economic Community or from those countries with bilateral treaties with the National Immigration Office, including Portugal, Spain, Tunisia, and Morocco.[4] However, the ban remained the law of the land for workers and families from Algeria and Sub-Saharan Africa, whose presence in France administrators claimed threatened the "threshold of tolerance."[5] These migrants from decolonizing countries, and especially Algerians, as the largest foreign national population on French soil, bore the brunt of the xenophobia involved in migration management. The administration argued that the previous decades' focus on services for Algerians had the perverse effect of marginalizing Algerians from the immigration system rather than integrating them. This alleged failure of social services to create belonging was both a product of the midcentury welfare state's structure (which administrators sought to reform) and immigration policy targeting Algerians (whom administrators sought to exclude).

I argue that the "new politics of immigration" explored in the 1970s echoed earlier restrictive policies that targeted families from Algeria. In doing so France expanded its ability to manage migration, while excluding migration from Algeria. The French administration ended specialized services for Algerians, a thread precariously tethering the midcentury welfare state to the colonial era, arguing that social services were a benefit for those who worked, men and women. Because the state argued that women from Algeria did *not* work, while European women did, women from Algeria faced more obstacles to receiving their previously guaranteed benefits. France became more adept at streamlining legislation to prioritize European migrants and only those who worked, eroding the last of the country's special protections negotiated at the Evian Accords in 1962.

Immigration after the Thirty Glorious Years

From the beginning of his administration, Giscard d'Estaing sought to tie immigration to labor policy rather than family resettlement. Even before the migration ban went into effect, he resurrected the secretary of state for immigrant workers position as part of a campaign promise to resolve

France's immigration question.[6] His first appointee, André Postel-Vinay, worked alongside the Bureau of Population and Migrations, which had moved to the Ministry of Labor in 1970.[7] Together they consolidated control of migrant social aid, labor, and housing. They operated according to the fiction (and helped create the bureaucratic rationale) that all migrants were laborers and their families remained at home. If the organizational structure represented a wish for the future of immigration as economic and temporary, this wish diverged sharply from the administration's current reality.

André Postel-Vinay quickly confronted the limitations of his position and lasted only two months in the job. Ironically, it was Postel-Vinay who initially suggested that France institute a migration freeze to address the problems facing France's existing migrant population. In his mind this proposal followed the approach of left-wing parties to managing migration, drawing attention to the needs of the existing migrant body without accepting the conservative demand to slow migration.[8] The administration, concerned with limiting expenditures, did not support the social and educational goals for the existing migrant body that Postel-Vinay's policy would have demanded.[9] Disappointed, he stepped down after discovering, in his words, "the truly stunning tendency [of the government] to underestimate the human and social problems of our country."[10]

Despite Postel-Vinay's departure, the President's Council of Ministers nonetheless took up his suggestion to suspend worker migration, though they extended this suspension to include workers and their families.[11] They put out two circulars that dramatically curtailed migration. The first in early July 1974 halted all worker migration, and the second, signed a few days later, ended family resettlement for foreign families.[12] The Council of Ministers consulted major businesses and labor union leaders, who largely approved of the measure.[13] France's ban reflected—and surpassed—those in place in other European countries. Although Britain, a European Economic Community member, had closed its borders, other member states of the EEC had restricted or suspended only their guest worker recruitment programs in the wake of the oil shock.[14] Family resettlement was still permitted. Even in France the rhetoric of the total ban did not hold up in practice. The freedom of circulation guaranteed by the Treaty of Rome exempted families and workers from the EEC from the ban.

The ban affected everyone else: any workers and families entering France from outside the EEC through the National Immigration Office as well as Algerians, subject to a different administrative regime. Since signing the Evian Accords, France had tried and failed to subsume Algerian migration into the National Immigration Office. As written, the ban therefore restricted the movement of migrants from southern and southeastern Europe, ex-colonial territories such as Tunisia and Morocco, and former territories of the French Union such as Laos and Vietnam, who all entered France through the National Immigration Office. It also halted the less regulated but no less contentious migration from Mali, Mauritania, and Senegal.[15] Nonetheless, memos and letters fluttering through the Ministry of the Interior in the months following France's suspension made it clear that Algerians were the especial subjects of this freeze because of their alternative immigration path.[16]

Only five months later, in November 1974, the ban's limitations had already begun to erode. The French Ministry of the Interior argued that Portuguese and Spanish families *should* be permitted to cross the border and apply for resettlement. Though Portugal and Spain were not part of the European Economic Community and ought to have petitioned the closed National Immigration Office for renewed resettlement access, administrators made an exception. Much as they had been in decades past, the lines of migrant desirability were reiterated by circular according to perceptions of whiteness, ethnicity, and soft measures of "social integration." Families from Algeria, regulated by ONAMO, and North Africa and Sub-Saharan Africa, regulated only loosely by National Immigration Office, remained excluded.[17]

Confusion wrought by the many policy loopholes compelled Postel-Vinay's replacement, the comparatively junior Paul Dijoud, to develop a new plan, which he called a "comprehensive politics" of immigration.[18] Following Postel-Vinay, Dijoud argued that the migration ban allowed France to maintain the delicate balance between France's economic imperatives and its ability to provide homes and jobs to migrant workers, though Dijoud placed much less emphasis on supporting France's existing migrant communities. In a presentation to the President's Council of Ministers, he outlined a plan for immigration, which he suggested was fundamentally new. Instead, it was reminiscent of Franco-Algerian agreements over the past decade. He suggested strengthening France's borders, ending "illegal" immigrant and false tourist visas, as well as the "humane" repatriation of those who came to France without papers. He drew attention to the living conditions of migrants already in France and proposed new professional training to incentivize migrants' return home. These initiatives conceded the presence of families, but Dijoud also seemed to envision all future migration as a masculine affair. He supported a continued family resettlement ban. Pleased with this balance of immigration restrictions and social benefits initiatives, the Council of Ministers approved of the plan.[19]

Migrant rights' groups challenged the government's family resettlement ban in court and pressured France to reopen its borders to family reunification.[20] While the freeze was in place, nine of every ten families entering in this period did so through "irregular" means, such as the tourist visa. Suspending family resettlement was unethical and un-republican, the Group for Information and Support for Immigrant Workers (GISTI) argued, and against the United Nations' Universal Declaration of Human Rights. As one of the largest and most vocal pro-immigrant groups, GISTI claimed ending family resettlement upended the family system: separating the father, the wage earner, from the family would create anarchy and ran counter France's political system and values.[21]

These groups successfully petitioned the government and the Conseil d'État (High Court) to end the ban, which was ruled unconstitutional. Cowed, Dijoud announced in December 1974 that family resettlement would restart in the new year. Nonetheless, during its implementation as after its repeal, the ban succeeded in marginalizing men and families from former colonies. Over the next few years, successive administrations nonetheless pursued alternative means of selecting families for resettlement, especially prioritizing European families. In the longer term the xenophobic assumptions underwriting the ban prevailed. Further, the government failed to improve the situation of the current migrant population. Although the administration promised to study the question of "family immigration," the resolution to the legal and ethical quandaries created over the past decade remained elusive.

Creating Family Reunification

After the Conseil d'État overturned the family resettlement ban, Dijoud sought advice on how best to manage this migration, which the administration now called "family reunification." In January 1975 he ordered the creation of two commissions to study the place of migrant families in France. Jacques Doublet, the president of the National Immigration Office and former director of the Social Action Fund, led a commission investigating family immigration, while Germaine Tillion, former director of the Algerian social centers, convened a study on migrant women's place in France. The commissions' published reports received administrative praise, and the policy proposals they made eventually shaped practices. These reports together advocated a politics of universal family reunification and integration, which called into question the decades of specialized work on behalf of Algerians. Their recommendations nonetheless reflected careful knowledge of the protocols for Algerians following independence because they precisely outlined those procedures for general use with migrants from the European Economic Community and moving through the National Immigration Office.

The reports also had another important rhetorical effect: both leaned on earlier configurations of the migrant family that conflated culture and cultural difference with migrant women. Therefore, family migration was posited as the specific source of social disintegration. According to this view, as long as migrant women arrived in France, migration would continue to be a problem. Families with the most difficult time integrating—with the most different "culture"—remained the crux of the issue.[22] While the commissions worked independently, they reinforced each other's findings. Both reports singled out families from Algeria—and mothers specifically—as deficient. Obstacles to Algerian family resettlement only grew as the government actively promoted these controls.

The Doublet Commission confirmed migrants' right to family reunification in theory while submitting that right to burdensome petitions and procedures. Like so many immigration regimes of the twentieth century, the commission argued that not all families were created alike, asserting that it might be easier for an Italian than a Turk to "understand and learn French." Further, the report maintained that "the status of women in Maghrebi countries is an obstacle to the adaptation of families." It made use of colonialist measures of women's emancipation to argue that North African cultures were too different to be integrated. Giving voice to bad faith cultural relativism, the authors wrote, "we cannot underestimate the influence of civilization, culture, religion" on migrant integration. For those migrants unhabituated to France, "the shock is brutal."[23] In the past decade social work had substantiated these assertions as specialized social aid associations had failed to enact meaningful integration according to their own proclaimed goals.

In its deliberations about family reunification policies, the Doublet Commission drew parallels to—and inspiration from—Algerian family migration protocols.[24] Composed of members of government administrations such as the Social Action Fund and state-subsidized housing associations such as SONACOTRA, as well as members of social aid associations (including the SSFNA), the commission was familiar with the existing welcome structures. In a meeting of the working group, the committee members reviewed the current controls regulating Algerians' "right" to family resettlement: proof of employment and suitable housing whose monthly rent could not make up more than 15 percent of a worker's salary. They also appreciated the local and regional checks on Algerian families' applications. They pointed out that Algerian families submitted their dossiers for resettlement to the local mayor's office, which could accept or reject the application based not only on the formal requirements, but also on regional or departmental national quotas.[25]

When the group finished reviewing existing statutes and scholarly literature, they concluded that foreign workers should fulfill three conditions to request family resettlement: they must have a home, have a job, and have been in France for a year.[26] These recommendations reflected earlier protocols for Algerian family resettlement but were extended to the National Immigration Office's immigration apparatus, which excluded Algerians. The committee suggested that families entering through the National Immigration Office and EEC protocols be eligible for a family resettlement bonus and help getting established once in France. As in years past, the committee also suggested offering round-trip tickets to workers to encourage them to return home rather than resettle their families.[27] But these provisions were destined only for "desirable" migrants, with the goal of limiting, rather than promoting, family reunification.

In the same year, 1975, the Tillion Commission took up the question of migrant families from the perspective of the wife and mother, and it was the Algerian mother whom they found deficient. While it was clear from the work of the Doublet Commission that European migrant women and women entering through the National Immigration Office would be the beneficiaries of the new policies, Algerian women—in their negative example—again gave these policies shape and context. The perception of the Algerian family migration "problem" provided the vocabulary for intervention. Dijoud's invitation to Tillion to chair the commission asserted that migrant women faced difficulties that were "even more trying than those faced by workers themselves."[28] He asked the commission to issue a report that proposed reforms for migrant women and girls.

There was a clear paradox facing the Tillion Commission: they feared that previous administrations' inability to help Algerian families integrate with specialized aid created the problem of "ghettoization" that integration was meant to solve.[29] For her part Germaine Tillion had worked to dispel many French myths about North African or "Muslim" women. In her most recent book, *The Republic of Cousins*, she argued that the subordination of women in the Maghreb was not a result of Islam, but rather of historical and cultural traditions stemming from Mediterranean tribal marriage between cousins and siblings—endogamy.[30] Tillion did not question the second-class status of women in North African society—that was evident enough to her—but she contested the common interpretation of Islam as the root cause. Tillion rejected the equation of Islam with oppression, and therefore of secularism with emancipation, a striking reinterpretation of the terms through which French officials were accustomed to viewing the Muslim family.[31]

Perhaps as a result, the Tillion Commission's report seemed to disavow cultural differences altogether. Women's issues were migrant issues, the report argued, and moreover, "certain difficulties known by immigrant women are not only their own, but also affect French women."[32] Migrant women were simply an aspect of the general migration problem, and the issues migrant women faced were no different than those faced by French women. Tillion's commission explicitly recentered the problem of education and emancipation around a shared sex, rather than nationality, religion, or ethnicity. The commission wrote, "All politics which aim to improve the fate of immigrant women must then be included in the broader politics of the promotion of women."[33] If migrant women were alienated, it was because all women felt alienated, or migration on the whole created alienation.

Like the Doublet Commission, the Tillion Commission proposed an easily achievable solution: a national welcome network, which already existed. Nationalized and rationalized "social work antennae" in various migrant neighborhoods across France would make it easier to reach the migrant population and develop contacts between different ethnic and national communities across the territory.[34] Endorsing the Giscard d'Estaing administration's approach, the report emphasized flexibility rather than specialization with certain migrant populations (which they called "segregation").[35] Tillion's report also served the prevailing logic that Algerian women had self-segregated as a result of (or as protest against) their inability to integrate. The network Tillion proposed was not for specialized social aid, but for camaraderie among all women.

Finally, the report emphasized possibilities for work, explicitly suggesting that French social services were predicated on women's wage labor as well. Training programs with an emphasis on French language and remedial education for women were well and good, but the commission also sought opportunities for pre-professional and professional training to engage migrant women in the workplace. While migrant women's welcome in France was usually linked to their husbands' jobs, Tillion's report emphasized the importance of facilitating immigrant women's access to work visas and job training, which were currently out of their reach based on family resettlement procedures. Beyond the benefits of a two-income household, the report argued, "work outside the home for many immigrant women represents the possibility to leave an often very closed social milieu to have access, at least psychologically, to a form of independence."[36] Training migrant women to become active participants in the workforce served the prevailing market logic of decreasing the cost of dependents' benefits by pairing the possibility of migration with a work contract. Finally, it supported the imagined link between labor and emancipation. As Joan Wallach Scott has argued, insertion in the job market demanded this internal "emancipation" as a precondition of belonging in the modern state.[37]

The previous decade of Algerian family resettlement gave context and meaning to the debates held in the Doublet and Tillion Commissions. When read together, these reports formed the perception that families from Algeria had become trapped by specialized and individualized immigration policies and services. Families' supposed inability to adhere to French definitions of belonging, especially in cases including a reluctant wife or mother, led the commissions to question previous approaches, which had always separated services for Algerians from the larger migrant body. The future could be different, the commissions agreed, if Algerians were no longer considered as separate from the migrant body or as the primary recipients of specialized services. The Doublet Commission's suggestions could result in new regulations for family migration, and the Tillion report changed the focus from Algerian women to migrant women writ large. By reconceiving of family resettlement as a right for those in the EEC and those working with the National Immigration Office, social services could reorient care. Dijoud's office thus orchestrated a new politics of immigration that was both explicitly and implicitly focused on families from Algeria. There was little that was truly "new" in terms of policies or practices in either commission's report; the plan instead re-created the existing system built for Algerians while excluding them from it.

France formally enshrined "family reunification" as the law of the land in April 1976. Its protocol applied to family members of EEC migrants and those arriving through the National Immigration Office. Under the new law nationals from the EEC and those with bilateral treaties with the National Immigration Office could petition the French government to resettle their minor children and their spouse.[38] Even while avoiding mention of Algerians, the law conspicuously mirrored the Franco-Algerian family resettlement procedures established in the previous decade. Dijoud proudly proclaimed that family reunification "constituted an essential social and human right," a French commitment that families should remain together.[39] However, the very existence of such a procedure suggested it was less a right than a *possibility*. Equally revelatory, family reunification did not extend work visas to resettled family members, nor was it available to everyone. Families from Algeria and from Sub-Saharan Africa were still barred.[40]

Under this new law, a worker who applied for family reunification after having "fulfilled certain conditions with the goal of ensuring the stability of his stay and the existence of resources" received special benefits, thus linking immigration to integrationist incentives and labor to social rights.[41] Following the Doublet Commission's recommendations, families who came to France through the family reunification procedure received priority access to welfare services, guaranteed support from family home help, and financial inducements of up to three months' rent to defray the costs of the application. But these conditions were difficult to meet. Workers needed to hold a job for a year and secure a large enough place to live.[42] While borrowing from the structures created for Algerian family resettlement in the 1960s, the 1976 family immigration law denied Algerians access to the French territory on the same terms as other migrant family members.

"Guardians of Tradition" or Women Who Work?

Family reunification was the law of the land in 1976, and once again French policymakers sought to craft social welfare procedures that would promote belonging for migrant families. Since integrationist policies were widely believed to have failed in the 1960s, what would they be replaced with? In the wake of the economic downturn and with increasing distance from the colonial era, government officials and social workers alike began to argue that families from all nationalities and backgrounds could be beneficiaries of the same generalized social aid. In their eyes, depending on the culture, cultural difference no longer posed the same threat.

This shifting appreciation for the place of migrant culture was not just a reflection of a changing attitude toward migration, but also an evolving idea of who migrants were and where they came from. These changes mapped neatly onto a growing number of European migrant women entering the French labor force. Simply put, European women's wage labor mitigated the threats supposedly created by cultural difference. This understanding of migration as primarily European and focused on labor replaced the idea of the Algerian family as migrants. It especially excluded Algerian women from consideration because of the popular belief that they did not work. Without recognized work, the French administration questioned women's right to social services.

With the wife as a potential worker, the migrant family was no longer purely a helpmate to or brake on a male migrant's integration. Instead the family became a haven from culture shock, one that preserved traditions from their home country and yet nonetheless contributed, as a unit, to the French labor market. The introduction of migrant women into the workplace made integration a fait accompli, at least insofar as the family's interactions with French society were concerned. A woman in the workforce could be educated by the same assimilatory forces as a woman in classes with other migrant women or a child in a French classroom. Her presence in the market and in the public square presumed her engagement in the French social sphere. Of course, migrant women had long been engaged in the French labor market, whether officially or under the table. But this fact was of little interest to commentators and researchers who celebrated this "new" phenomenon. Unemployed women or women employed off the books because of industry standards or immigration status were outliers, excluded from French society.

Yet women's labor was always a double-edged sword. If social aid associations saw it as a potential resolution to the "cultural" problems of family migration, French immigration officials still considered the country's demographic bottom line. The number of migrant women entering the country was rapidly increasing, which effectively grew the migrant labor pool. The government anxiously studied this "feminization of labor" and found that the number of women entering France through the National Immigration Office and as members of the EEC grew from 18 percent in the late 1960s to 28 percent after the immigration suspension.[43] In those same years the government granted only about 25 percent of all migrants' requests for family resettlement.[44]

While market forces and the oil shock helped explain these dynamics, researchers and government officials still noted that the number of women in the workforce could be greater than they realized. Migrant men received priority access to factory jobs, but government officials noted that the number of women employed as so-called skilled workers rose to nearly 40 percent (up about ten points since 1968), while the number of women working in domestic services fell to 27 percent (down from 36 percent).[45] Without the ability to account for those working under the table or as undocumented migrants, the report noted that these numbers could be much higher, which left them without a doubt that the migrant workforce included a high share of women.

Understanding women's and family migration as economic migration also shifted administrators' thinking about benefits. If husbands and wives provided their labor to French industry and both partners' wages covered the cost of their benefits alongside their employers' contributions, then family migration as worker migration was less of a problem for the mid-century welfare state. This template assumed that work made migration less expensive because benefits were part of the labor exchange rather than a question of French largesse on behalf of dependent female and minor populations. Nonetheless, this line of thinking was also out of step with more than fifty years of welfare legislation designed along a male breadwinner/female homemaker model.[46] Further, according to this logic, nonworking dependents were the problem and *not* family migration as such. This rethinking conveniently comported with the logic of the recent "family reunification" legislation.

This shift in thinking also mirrored the national and international labor market as more women entered the workforce in this decade. Between 1954 and 1975, married French women in the workforce increased from 28 percent to 41 percent.[47] The shift also provided a new metric by which to measure migrant women in France. In a special issue of the social work journal *Migrant Training* on migrant women's professional preparation, the editorial asserted that the public powers now thought of migrant women as potential workers, though worker migration had previously been gendered male. Echoing the Tillion report, these social workers argued that pre-professional training and French language immersion for migrant women were important in new ways: for integration and to be productive members of the workforce.[48]

The government's secretary general of the Committee on Women's Work reported that migrant women, like French women, had changed. Migrant women in France did not arrive solely through family reunification but also on their own work visas. According to the secretary general, 47 percent of migrant women were not married when they entered France in 1975. Statistics from the Ministry of the Interior broke employment down by nationality: 43 percent of Portuguese women and 31.5 percent of Spanish migrant women in France were employed (this was an increase from 1968, when only 15 percent of Portuguese women were part of the "active" work population in France).[49]

Table 1. Migrant women workers in France

NATIONALITY	TOTAL	WOMEN ACTIVE IN THE WORKFORCE	% WOMEN ACTIVE
"Latin Countries"			
Portugal	220,000	95,000	43%
Spain	190,000	60,000	31.5%
Italy	185,000	45,000	24%
EEC (except Italy)	60,000	20,000	33%
"Other European Countries"			
Poland	35,000	10,000	28.6%
Yugoslavia	35,000	20,000	57%
"Maghreb"			
Algeria	95,000	15,000	10.5%
Morocco	40,000	15,000	37.5%
Tunisia	35,000	10,000	28.6%

Source: Ministry of the Interior statistics, 1974; *Hommes et Migrations* in "Des chiffres et des hommes," 1974, reprinted in "Quelques chiffres sur la presence féminine étrangère en France," *Migrants Formation*, no. 14–15 (March 1976): 67.

Public discussions compared working European women to their "unemployed" North African counterparts. These same statistics showed that just over 10 percent of the population of Algerian women in France were active members of the workforce.[50] This low number stood in contrast with European women. Equally revealing, Moroccan and Tunisian women were much more likely to be involved in the French workforce than their Algerian counterparts. These analyses missed many important caveats, most notably Algerian women's under-the-table work in France and their exclusion from ONAMO-sanctioned work permits. However, the narrative was set: Algerian women fell squarely outside this new normative of the gainfully employed, industrious, two-income migrant family. Critics instead portrayed them as women who did not work. Work became another means by which to measure (and inculcate) belonging in French society, another category in which Algerian women came up short.

The SSFNA defended Algerian women's place in France by rejecting the logic of labor-as-integration. Instead they returned to their old argument about the gendered division of labor. North African women were "guardians of tradition," they argued, and none more so than Algerians.[51] Taking part in the workforce, they reiterated, was out of step with their cultural and religious values, though some women may "evolve." While the social workers in the SSFNA noted that they had welcomed more "open" women in their classes over the past three or four years, these women were mostly Tunisian or Moroccan. They attributed this fact to an increase in schooling in independent Tunisia and Morocco.[52] This education, however, did not lead to a simple acceptance of the French feminine model, but rather allowed women to accept certain aspects of "modern life" while "maintain[ing] familial traditions to which they are legitimately attached."[53] In this view Tunisian and Moroccan women were educated, and so their choice to retain certain unnamed aspects of their lives at home was valid. For these women cultural pluralism was possible, but only in limited circumstances, and not in the case of Algerian women, supposedly the most reticent.

SSFNA social workers put pressure on the Tillion Commission's conclusion that all "migrant women" faced analogous problems because of their femininity, preserving their specific courses for Algerian women. One course instructor in the Nord wrote of a home economics class that it was "difficult to integrate various requests" from women of diverse nationalities. She argued only a "homogeneous" population in her class would "assure progress" with migrant women.[54] Advocates tried to make clear that the "failure" of integration was actually a result of French definitions of what constituted a modern, French household. Through these justifications, social workers pointed out—in contrast with their North African and European peers—Algerian women had failed to conform to French models of femininity, which increasingly included work outside the home. When course instructors advocated for the continued importance of targeted interventions—such as the SSFNA's courses for North African women—their intention was to protect specialized services and expertise built over decades to aid Algerian women. However, their arguments paradoxically highlighted the "remedial" work needed for Algerian women when compared with other migrants.[55]

By conceding the shortcomings of integration and advocating for certain women's embrace of cultural pluralism, social workers inadvertently opened the door to the renegotiation of specialized social services. As conversations about women's labor evolved, so too did the belief that work was part of the exchange for social support. Algerian women were doubly excluded: from the workforce and from benefits. This new attitude about labor substituted work for social services, insisting that the workplace could help create belonging. It also decisively linked labor to social services provisioning, now that women were no longer necessarily dependents (to the extent they ever were). Both developments hastened the end of specialized services for Algerians.

Insertion: The New Melting Pot?

Work had become a major factor in finding a sense of belonging in France. Work, which for French officials and social workers alike was by definition *outside* the home, was an incubator for French values. In the 1970s, as the Tillion report had suggested, social services belatedly reoriented care toward shaping women into workers. This metamorphosis could potentially alleviate pressure on social services as well as provide an avenue for improving the reputations of migrant families. To speak of migrant women's labor was to introduce their use value to the French job market and to shift responsibility for their social rights onto themselves and their employers. It also moved the conversation away from integration. The marketplace could provide the forum for some integrationist techniques, but social workers and employers alike began to speak of *insertion*, or the idea that the public square could include all kinds of people with different backgrounds, as long as they sequestered this "culture" in the home. In other words, proof of labor was proof of insertion, taking the focus off what happened in "private." Social workers and researchers began to call this mode of life "bicultural," where families could straddle the divide between France and their countries of origin.

What did this new "bicultural" attachment mean for migrant women? For specialized associations previously tasked with integrating specific populations? One study advanced the argument that migrant women were not, by nature, inassimilable; rather, they were actively resisting assimilation. The authors argued that in their examination of training programs for migrant women, they found women rejected the approach to education pursued in many courses. Coursework for women was "strongly marked by the ideology of modernity," they held, which repelled migrant women.[56] It was not that women were incapable of education because of their "cultural specificity," but rather that migrant women rejected the cultural specificity of the training programs.[57] This study's hypotheses overlapped with the popularity of insertion as a mode of migrant belonging. The authors questioned the dominant approach to migrant social aid of the previous twenty-five years and asked social workers to become more aware of their own presuppositions. Insertion compelled social work to rethink its goals for migrants. It also made the case for a mindful consideration of the prevailing trend to systematize social aid. Understanding France's cultural specificity could have generated a similar understanding of migrants' own cultural specificities and, therefore, the divisions among migrant groups.

However, insertion *did* prioritize certain types of behaviors and belonging. Researchers still scrutinized migrants' exteriors—their homes, habits, dress, and performance—to measure the degree to which different nationalities functioned within the French environment. One generally optimistic study appealed to clichés to celebrate the possibility of French modernity at the heart of migrant homes. It testified that "Iberian women are cutting their hair, Maghrebi women abandon the veil and adopt pants, but keep the head scarf on their hair." They trained their vision on the household and found that "cooking is less strictly national and certainly some urban practices are adopted (frozen food, prepared foods)."[58] The cultural expectations that migrant women balanced included all aspects of their lives, but social workers' measurements included little in the way of introspection or discussion of choices. The observable—the dynamics of the home—instead represented a supposedly transparent translation of women's interior lives to their external surroundings. These choices, which weighed home against home country, also made potential return possible.

The myth of return had assuaged French administrators' paralyzed with concern about continued migration: temporary workers would return home. Others were less convinced of this idea and instead emphasized the persistent ways that France's capitalist and colonialist history of resource and labor extraction labeled Algerians as outsiders. Abdelmalek Sayad, born in Kabylia, trained first under Pierre Bourdieu in Algiers during the Algerian War and later completed his doctorate in France. His first and most famous essay, "The Three Ages of Algerian Emigration," appeared in 1977. In it he argued that considering only immigration created an "ethnocentric" view of migrants' trajectory that only focused on the "host society." His work, in sum, drew sociological attention to the experience of both emigration and immigration. While this article focused on the subsequent waves of Algerian workers (from adult men to permanent family resettlement), he also gave weight to the economic factors that conditioned Algerians' political and social exclusion.[59] In doing so Sayad emphasized the capitalist rationality that all actors, migrants and hosts alike, shared—the illusion that conditioned the entire operation.[60] To be a migrant, he argued, was to position oneself as a laborer, and this labor-centered definition of migration created the conditions for the host society's constant tallying of "immigration's social balance sheet."[61] For Sayad, the persistent "myth of return" paralyzed social analysis of immigration and burdened entire families with the mandate to labor and produce. He did not comment on Algerian women's work outside the home; instead he presumed that Algerian women and children were dependents beholden to masculine labor.

Models of insertion and cultural difference also had ramifications for continued specialized social aid, which paradoxically further damaged administrators' perception of Algerians. The new politics of immigration had rested on broadening the specialization of social work experts. Social workers pushed back. Considering the challenges migrant families faced without attention to their nationality meant offering a poorly conceived one-size-fits-all solution. Yet government family resettlement procedures had provided a crucible to test the mettle of migrant families against each other: Who could achieve "insertion" and how? To what effect? Though social scientists and local experts drew from the reserves of information they had accumulated about Algerian families over the previous decade, they also used this knowledge (and these practices) against them. Since the oil shock, Algerian labor—and the arrival of supposedly nonlaboring family members—was presented as too burdensome for the already overwhelmed social welfare state. But if the woman was a worker, she paid her own way, undermining the assumption that work was a masculine sphere. Paradoxically, the family from Algeria, which conformed to the welfare model of the male breadwinner and female homemaker, no longer kept up with the emerging female workforce or new models of migrant belonging in France.

The End of the Specialized Social Welfare Network

The French immigration suspension and resulting reforms failed to limit migration, whether by law, loophole, or family reunification. However, these changes were much more successful in heralding a period of cuts to social welfare. As Minayo Nasiali has explained, the immigration freeze included attempts to prevent future immigration (which failed), encouragement for migrants to leave (often unsuccessful), and the further development of migrant welfare services.[62] Yet any development of migrant welfare services that took place responded to directives from Secretary of State for Immigrant Workers Paul Dijoud, which restricted aid to only migrants entering through the National Immigration Office. This period reflected the government's desire to support only working migrants and to abandon specialized social aid associations created to integrate families from Algeria.

After the 1974 suspension the National Immigration Office became the focus of funding and resources for migrant welcome.[63] Social workers greeted people entering through regional National Immigration Office offices in train stations and airports to process their entries. Rather than subcontract social workers from private associations with specialized knowledge of migrating populations, the National Immigration Office awarded the contract to the Social Service for Aid to Emigrants (SSAE), the largest national organization for migrant acculturation.[64] The SSAE was created in 1926 and had longstanding administrative support. However, it was not a part of the network of specialized social aid associations. The decision had two effects: first, it made a statement that the administration was pursuing migrant workers of all nationalities; second, it prioritized social aid for migrants entering France through the EEC and the National Immigration Office.[65]

Prioritizing the general immigration protocol prompted a rethinking of social services at the structural level, which led the Social Action Fund to cut funding to associations that specialized in work with North Africans and favor associations that approached migration irrespective of nationality.

The Bureau of Population and Migrations argued that distance from the colonial era justified this shift: times had changed. The bureau criticized the "irrational division of activities and expertise across our territory" created by the network of specialized social aid associations.[66] It described these services as vestigial organs, extant but ill-suited to present-day concerns. It would be better to reorganize these services, the bureau director wrote to the director of the Social Action Fund, and to reconceive social aid as a universal tool. This bureaucratic reshuffling, if pursued, could strip specialized social aid associations of their autonomy and original purpose as helpmates to integration.[67]

The Social Action Fund streamlined associational funding procedures, reduced redundancies, and cut back extraneous services to refocus the network according to the Bureau of Population and Migrations' proposal. For example, in 1974 the board of the Social Action Fund complained that the Commission for Aid to North Africans in the Metropole (CANAM) had not been properly integrated into the National Immigration Office's national welcome network.[68] In turn the Social Action Fund reduced CANAM's budget for welcoming families, which overlapped with the goal of the national network, forcing the association to take part in the general immigration protocol. President of CANAM Maurice Sabatier defended his association's approach, which relied on welcoming North African men and families into their offices and then sponsoring social aid and education for them.[69] In CANAM's view a tailored "welcome" was the condition by which social aid took place. Slashing funds for this aspect of their mission affected the mission in its entirety.

These arguments ultimately fell on deaf ears, leading to the most dramatic shift yet. In 1978 the SSFNA underwent a major reorganization that brought the age of specialized social services for Algerians to a symbolic close. At the request of the Bureau of Population and Migrations, the SSFNA redefined the scope of its work. The SSFNA extended its educational and cultural action to families of *all* nationalities.[70] A few months later the SSFNA changed its name from the North African Family Social Service to the Migrant Family Social Service Association (ASSFAM).[71] This "broadening" of its services exposed the underlying shift nearly accomplished by the Giscard d'Estaing administration: the end of the era of specialized social services for Algerians.

The name change also signified a closer union between the immigration administration and social aid associations. In its yearly report ASSFAM attested to its continued role as the "hinge between the [migrant population] and the environment." Yet the report conceded, "The world evolves, French society evolves, techniques evolve, the migrant public evolves. . . . It is certain that on the whole we observe and feel the need for the enlarging and deepening of responses to the migrant public."[72] ASSFAM's role negotiating between migrants and the French state remained the same; its importance as a translator between French cultural norms and uprooted migrants held weight. But its expertise was no longer required. The politics of immigration prioritized EEC and other migrants from the National Immigration Office as the memory of colonialism faded. While ASSFAM still believed in its importance as an intermediary body between newly arrived immigrant populations, the French public, and French bureaucracy, the era of robust specialized social service funding had come to an end.

The debate around social services for the migrant family had two potential outcomes, but it was the government's that prevailed. Specialized social aid associations argued—as they had over the past twenty-five years—that their services helped integrate a marginalized population through targeted outreach. This outreach, in turn, would ameliorate the "social issues" supposedly caused by these families. The government had another interpretation: that special focus on Algerians was the cause of their marginalization, and that Algerians should be treated the same as other migrant populations. Moreover, because Algerian women did not work outside the home to the same extent as other migrant women, these services were undeserved. With sapped support for specialized services, the administration hollowed out some of the essential services that had scaffolded the midcentury welfare state, removing protections for Algerians and providing a powerful example for future cuts.

Aide au Retour or Forced Deportation?

As specialized services for Algerian migrants reoriented, French diplomats and bureaucrats from the Bureau of Population and Migrations were hard at work rolling back Franco-Algerian immigration accords. According to the 1968 Franco-Algerian accords still in effect, Algerian workers with three years' work experience in France before 1968 could apply for ten-year residency permits, while Algerians with less experience could apply for five-year renewable permits. In 1978 both five- and ten-year residency permits were on the brink of expiration, affecting over half a million Algerians in the country. The 1968 accords stipulated that the French government would renew those permits. After the oil shock and immigration freeze, the French government was reticent to extend Algerians a helping hand, however. In France Giscard d'Estaing's center-right party had received poor results in the spring 1977 elections, and in 1978 he lost his parliamentary majority.[73] Facing a choice between acquiescing to the growing number of Socialists and Communists urging freer migration and doubling down on a politics of immigration restriction, Giscard d'Estaing chose the latter.

In June 1977 the administration piloted a repatriation policy known as a "return stipend" (*aide au retour*) that offered 10,000 francs to unemployed migrant workers upon return to their home country.[74] The stipends drew from the Social Action Fund's budget usually reserved for housing and subsidies for associations. It guaranteed 10,000 francs to any unemployed migrant, as well as 10,000 francs to his unemployed wife and 5,000 francs for each dependent child, to return to their home country. The new secretary of state for immigrant workers, Lionel Stoléru of *Mosaïque* fame, received all applications for *aide au retour* transmitted from departmental directors to the Bureau of Population and Migrations. They vetted each request to ensure that applicants had certificates of residency and unemployment paperwork.[75]

Although the return policy was theoretically open to migrants of all origins, in practice it applied narrowly. Members of the European Economic Community were not eligible, nor were refugees from Laos or Vietnam, nor people from France's overseas departments. Further, migrants with residency cards with over ten years of validity, migrants married to a French or EEC spouse, refugees, and students were also excluded. Thus, the policy specifically targeted out-of-work contract laborers from North Africa and France's other former colonies (apart from those with refugee status). The proposed flight paths in Stoléru's letter introducing the policy testified to this fact, as the cost of flights (covered by the return policy as well) included a list of destinations between France and North and West African cities (Casablanca, Algiers, Tunis, Dakar, Yaoundé), in addition to Madrid and Lisbon.[76]

Return stipends further strengthened the implicit connections between labor, social benefits, and the precarious migrant family; initially only the unemployed were eligible. The official reasoning may have been to alleviate strain on the French labor market, but many who took advantage of the policy were reaching retirement age, so it hardly changed France's economic bottom line.[77] In a follow-up directive Stoléru reaffirmed the policy's intent to repatriate entire families to maintain their integrity.[78] Of utmost importance and underlined for emphasis was that departmental directors could only submit Algerians' dossiers for a return stipend if their certificate of residence stated that they had permission to work in France.[79] In these notes to his departmental appointees, Stoléru's unwritten concerns become legible. His office billed the return stipends as a policy targeting unemployed migrants and their families, but they tailored them to deport Algerians on five- and ten-year residency visas in the months before the renegotiation of their status in France.

Despite these efforts the policy failed to send Algerians to Algeria. In December 1978 the National Immigration Office found that only 1,339 Algerians had received stipends, compared to 13,580 Spaniards and 18,888 Portuguese.[80] Algerians made up only 3 percent of the overall requests.[81] In an attempt to correct this unintended consequence, Stoléru's office issued a mandate for an expanded return stipend program that included currently employed migrants with at least five years of salaried activity in the French workforce. When this measure proved insufficient, the Budget Ministry exposed the true goal of the policy, announcing that Spanish and Portuguese migrants were no longer able to take advantage of the stipends.[82] They reserved the majority of the budget (468 million francs of a total 670 million francs) for Algerians.[83]

Not content to incentivize returns or to limit social aid for the remaining migrants, Stoléru also reopened the question of family immigration in the fall of 1977, only a year after his predecessor had declared it a universal right. Mere weeks before Stoléru appeared on *Mosaïque* to publicize the Week of Dialogue, he held a press conference in which he floated the possibility of suspending all family immigration for a period of three years, making reference to a similar policy underway in the Federal Republic of Germany.[84] While the Bureau of Population and Migrations was still in the process of determining the legality of a potential suspension (the Ministry of Foreign Affairs protested that it might be "difficult" to implement), Stoléru's provocation caused panic among migrant communities and outrage from the political left.[85] One deputy from the French Communist Party aired his outrage in the Senate, calling the proposal "illegal and devoid of any economic foundations."[86] To address these concerns Stoléru simply revised his proposal: family migration was suspended for members of a family who sought to enter the French job market in November 1977.

Plenty of social aid associations and parties across the political left spoke out successfully in favor of migrants affected by Stoléru's new policies. As had occurred after the immigration suspension in 1974, the Movement against Racism and Antisemitism and for Peace (MRAP) and the General Confederation of Labor (CGT), one of France's oldest and largest labor unions, challenged Stoléru's circulars for their unilateral and unlawful attempt to coerce the "voluntary" deportation of migrants. They asked the Conseil d'État to review the legality of the government's return stipend policy and succeeded in overturning it.[87] Similarly the cooperative for immigrant rights, the Group for Information and Support for Immigrant Workers (GISTI), protested Stoléru's planned suspension of family migration with the help of organized labor and forced the Conseil d'État to reaffirm the universal right to family resettlement in 1978.[88]

This flurry of activity and legislation around family migration and Algerian migration culminated in Stoléru's attempt to force a renegotiation of the 1968 Franco-Algerian Accord. By 1978 some 530,000 Algerians, including 400,000 people with ten-year residency cards from the 1968 agreement, faced expulsion if the governments could not agree on temporary measures to renew their paperwork.[89] To bring the Algerian delegation to the table, the French administration put forth legislation in the National Assembly that would facilitate the expulsion of Algerian migrants living in France with expired residency permits. The French government threatened to create an apparatus that permitted the forced deportation of migrants by a quota system that automatically excluded EEC members, refugees, and "future Europeans," such as Spanish and Portuguese migrants.[90] This effectively left only North and Sub-Saharan Africans.

Between 1979 and 1980, the French government made good on this threat, forcibly repatriating Algerians whose residency paperwork had expired.[91] The Bureau of Population and Migrations as well as the French

Ministry of Foreign Affairs worked to bring the Algerian delegation to the table to renegotiate the 1968 accords. They brainstormed ways to force the Algerian delegation's hand: Had Algeria violated the Evian Accords? Did the treaty violate the Vienna Convention? Could they convince Algeria that it was *they* who wanted to renegotiate the treaty?[92]

As a result of pressure on multiple fronts, and especially because of the large population of Algerians in legal limbo after their ten-year permits issued in 1968 had expired, the French delegation succeeded in crafting an "exchange of letters"—a short-term diplomatic fix—that permitted Algerians who had lived in France since before Algerian independence to renew their residency cards for ten years. This was an especially dramatic change for the hundreds of thousands of Algerians who had arrived in France between 1962 and 1965, the previous cutoff for ten-year residency cardholders. Now those migrants, as well as any who arrived after, could renew their residency cards for only three years and three months. The policy incentivized the return of Algerian workers and families through pre-professional training in Algeria and "reinsertion" in the Algerian economy. The exchange of letters did not invalidate the quotas and protections of the 1968 agreement as the French government had hoped, but it did change the tenor of the debate between France and Algeria. It made France's persistent efforts to end their "special relationship" with Algeria clear.

Return stipends and other policies with the goal of repatriating Algerians were not simply a function of the economic conditions. In the six years since the oil shock, attempts to limit, halt, or reverse migration had led the Ministry of Labor—and the French public more generally—to confront the place of foreigners in French labor markets and on French soil. No foreigners were more marginalized or maligned than Algerians, who had long been portrayed as symbols of the "human problems" of migration, the problems that Lionel Stoléru sought most urgently to politicize. In a speech to the Council of Europe in 1980, Stoléru staged the issue as such: "The problem of immigration is posed in terms of civilization. What kind of coexistence do we want to create between different groups in our civilization?"[93] Far from a philosophy of immigration that concerned itself with the suffering of migrants, Stoléru focused on undermining what he called the "dream" of open borders in favor of a realpolitik of border control.

Stoléru and members of the Giscard d'Estaing administration more generally had capitalized on depictions of Algerians and families from Algeria especially as the source of the migration problem, and the saturation of the French labor market made them into convenient scapegoats. Fears of the permanent relocation of Algerian workers along with their families had motivated anti-immigration policies since the end of the Algerian War. In the 1970s these fears provided the government with momentum to finally renegotiate the 1968 Franco-Algerian accords and to limit family resettlement to worker migration. These policies were not long for the world, however. Giscard d'Estaing was voted out of office in May 1981, and François Mitterrand was elected the first Socialist president of the Fifth Republic.

Giscard d'Estaing's presidency offered very little that was new in terms of managing migration or social welfare. After the short suspension at the beginning of his term, his solutions to the immigration problem were remarkably uncreative when viewed through the prism of Algerian decolonization. The Giscard d'Estaing administration attempted to rationalize the welcome network, limit family resettlement under the guise of creating it, provide jobs and language training for migrants, and urge return after a short stay in France. The administration saw these threads of decolonization as problems to untangle and unwind as best they could. Nonetheless, immigration remained roughly steady in the seven years of Giscard d'Estaing's presidency, even as the number of Algerians declined.

For all the administrative uncertainty, the Giscard d'Estaing administration managed to drive the Algerian question, a question that had preoccupied immigration officials for the past two decades, to its logical conclusion. They limited family resettlement to the National Immigration Office and the European Economic Community, expanded the category of migrant workers to include women, and reconceived of social assistance. These changes did not solve the economic contraction of the end of the Thirty Glorious Years, but they did manage to bring the era of Algerian specificity to a close. By the end of Giscard d'Estaing's term, the only solution the administration could envision was deportation and diplomatic bullying that reneged on the promises of Evian.

While at the center of the political debate, Algerians were pushed to the margins of social services for migrant populations. The programs and policies created for Algerians in the previous decades lost support even as French officials drew from these templates to craft their new migration protocols. Economic crisis, draconian immigration restriction, and the slow shift toward prioritizing European workers—men and women—restructured the social welfare network. As the Algerian War faded into historical memory, so too did protections for Algerians. Despite bilateral accords and the terms of Evian, Algerians found the rights of their families seriously threatened. The end of specialized social aid associations and threats of deportation made it clear that the period of decolonization was drawing to a close. The damage was therefore done.

The close of the 1970s meant the end of many things: the end of specialized social aid associations for Algerians, which hollowed out some of the crucial support systems of the midcentury welfare state, the end of the prioritized Franco-Algerian relationship facilitating migration, the end of Giscard d'Estaing's presidency. But it also ushered in new beginnings, especially the presidency of the first Socialist president of the Fifth Republic and a rejuvenated commitment to the vision of France as a potentially multicultural society. The slow disintegration of empire in France finally came to fruition in the 1970s. But the foreclosures of the 1970s created the exact conditions questioned by second-generation children in the early 1980s: the lack of acknowledgment of France's colonial past, the paltry protections for migrant families, and the racism and xenophobia faced by these marginalized communities.

Coda

The French Melting Pot Revisited

In 1972 social worker Monique Hervo interviewed "Colette," an Algerian woman, about her makeshift home in the cité Gutemberg, a French transitional housing estate outside of Paris.[1] Colette lived in this temporary housing unit as she awaited an apartment vacancy in France's low-income housing complexes, which granted priority access to French citizens. Colette complained that Gutemberg was poorly built, there was water everywhere, and during storms, the whole building shook. French families came and went, but Colette remained. Until the social work team was satisfied that she had learned to keep house—"as if I've never kept a house," she retorted—she could not move to a permanent apartment. Colette went on, "An Algerian is an Algerian. A foreigner is a foreigner. . . . They will never become French. We cannot become French." She and other Algerians were left in Gutemberg to live as "savages," or "that's what [the French] think," Colette complained, while French citizens would never be asked to become Algerians, were the situation reversed.[2] The housing support staff, building managers, and social workers all offered advice that they believed would lay the groundwork for her selection for permanent housing. Yet Colette did not welcome or need this input, for, in her assessment, she would never be French by their metrics nor her own.

In this book I have shown the French failure, both short- and long-term, to create a welfare state that supported Colette and all its clients from Algeria in the years surrounding Algerian independence—the era of decolonization. The midcentury welfare state's failure lay in no small part in its foundation. It was colonial in nature, patchy by design, and explicitly concerned with delimiting access to its reputedly generous benefits for non-white and former colonial populations. Especially in the years of migration following decolonization, people from across the globe moved to France to enjoy the benefits of this state. Yet after the end of empire, French policymakers and administrators tasked with managing migration imperiled these services, hemming them in wherever possible, and especially when the applicants were members of families from Algeria. As I have illustrated, opponents—and even supporters—of welfare from across the political spectrum claimed that services for Algerian families overextended the welfare state. They then marshaled this overextension as evidence of the limits of social services.

Though the 1970s closed in crisis, Socialist François Mitterrand's election to the presidency in the spring of 1981 presented an opportunity to revise the politics of immigration, welfare, and integration that divided the country. Mitterrand wrote in 1981, "If France must be united, she must also be rich in her differences. Her unity has enabled our country; respecting her diversity will prevent her undoing. One and diverse, that is France."[3] Some scholars have read these words as a reflection of Mitterrand's commitment to policies the Socialists called *droit à la différence*—the right to difference.[4] This right disavowed the Gaullist insistence on national unity and the historical strength of French Jacobin republicanism. It instead projected an image of France that was a polyglot of cultures, languages, and traditions.[5] Mitterrand's embrace of France's plurality was not an automatic adoption of the erstwhile American myth of the multicultural melting pot, however; nor was he even necessarily embracing France's postcolonial migration.[6] In the years to come, the Socialists did indeed undertake a decentralization of the Parisian administration to protect the specificity of regional identity across France: Bretons should learn to speak Breton in Brittany, Corsicans could direct regional affairs from Corsica. But did this cultural pluralism extend to North Africans in France?

In 1955, following the outbreak of the Algerian War, Mitterrand had promised that Algerians could be both French and Muslim. While this vision was more a fantasy than reality at the time, can we interpret the droit à la différence as a reinvigoration of this promise? Mitterrand's presidential-era political philosophy of equality-through-difference rhymed with earlier proclamations in favor of Algerian integration. His vision for France at the end of the twentieth century was plural and embracing of France's regional diversity, and yet once again he failed to engage with movements that promised to address the causes of social and economic inequality. Even in the wake of the grassroots political movement, the March for Equality and Against Racism organized by second-generation North Africans in France in 1983, Mitterrand focused his response on the "immigrant question" and paperwork regularization rather than the movement organizers' demands for social rights and economic equality.[7] Indeed his record on these issues was mixed. Mitterrand had famously turned to austerity in 1982, freezing wages and devaluing the currency to battle inflation and French unemployment.[8] While he remained in office through a second term, state spending—and certainly social spending—never rebounded.[9] This austerity failed to extend equality of opportunity or access to the most marginalized.

Though France did not take the neoliberal turn of Margaret Thatcher's Britain or Ronald Reagan's United States, French public opinion still framed the welfare state as in crisis. In 1981 Pierre Rosanvallon argued that the ostensible problems associated with the welfare state were not financial. Instead, it was a crisis of the body politic and civic solidarity: "a crisis of the social contract." While he did not explicitly consider immigration, Rosanvallon asserted that the welfare state had failed to create equality and would never achieve this goal. It had become amorphous and bureaucratic, an external force that people looked to in the *absence* of social solidarity.[10] Rosanvallon advocated for a redefinition of the relationship between state and society: the future welfare state should rely upon more rational management, decentralization, and "autonomization," the transferring of public tasks to private institutions. While Rosanvallon imagined that this autonomization would create a more transparent democracy by creating a "welfare society" with enhanced social solidarity, I have shown that the substitution of public services with private initiatives led in precisely the opposite direction. If Rosanvallon saw this decentralization and privatization of welfare as a path forward to greater social equality, Algerians' own experiences with the specialized social welfare system proved the contrary.

The midcentury welfare state's ideal clientele, imagined as white and European, created the powerful argument that Algerian migrant families were a particular drain on the state's resources. Although this was a historically specific argument made during the late colonial and early post-Algerian independence years, the persuasiveness of this framing endured.

In the 1970s conservatives in power seized the opportunity to undermine specialized services for Algerians, and a broader coalition of French political actors in the 1980s and 1990s further exploited concerns about the welfare state's fragility to justify its underfunding.

This crisis was manufactured and began much earlier for Algerian migrant families. Algerians' payments underwrote the Social Action Fund's financing, yet the office worked on a shoestring budget according to which there was never enough to go around. Specialized social aid for Algerians shuttered in the 1970s, but this was only one of many cuts. By the 1990s President Jacques Chirac proclaimed that financing France's social security system was too expensive with high unemployment, leading him to attempt to cut social protections. The persistent recurrence of this theme across administrations over the past thirty years again makes clear that the midcentury welfare state worked only selectively. .

Many heads of state shared the assumption that social spending was the cause of the state's financial precarity. While it has become difficult to imagine alternative methods of state investment to create social solidarity, the welfare state model, as historian James Chappel has pointed out, is also historically contingent and has proven equally vulnerable to changing political economic tides.[11] Put another way, the transformation of the welfare state through austerity politics and neoliberal reform in the last thirty years has proceeded from a central presumption about welfare's failure, or as Amy Offner has suggested, from "a great deal of storytelling about what the midcentury state had been."[12] As we have seen, the robust welfare state never existed for Algerians.

Abdelmalek Sayad called immigration "the temporary that lasts."[13] In this book I have shown that the entire midcentury welfare state created to manage migration could also be described as such. The organization of semiprivate specialized social welfare associations for Algerians in the 1940s and 1950s at the twilight of empire had been part of the promise of a greater France, one that administered to varied constituents, and that nonetheless sought to offer services to all. These Algerian-specific organizations grew during the Algerian War and—paradoxically—even for a period after Algerian independence. The growing population of migrant families from Algeria relied upon these services even as they became segregated from the broader welfare tapestry of the French state. The French welfare state had already attempted Rosanvallon's imagined decentralization and autonomization for Algerian migrant families, but integration—or, as Rosanvallon puts it, social solidarity—proved elusive.

I have traced three disintegrating threads of empire to illustrate this case. The midcentury welfare state composed of specialized social aid associations propped up traditional welfare to supply remedial aid to Algerian families under empire and even after. Family migration from Algeria, including men, women, and children, grew after independence, contributing to the view that *families* were a specific problem for welfare because of their imagined permanent relocation to France. Finally, I have especially elaborated on the development of social work relationships between clients and social workers over this period, a thread that did not disintegrate but certainly transformed through their dynamic approach to care. This care inadvertently singled out Algerian families' specific vulnerabilities and used their family stories to generalize about Algerians' response to welfare. Taken separately, these threads help explain the longer chronology of decolonization that I follow in this book. Together, they make clear that even as these services unwound, decolonization was never complete (and could never be). These disintegrating threads bound France to Algeria.

Finally, a word about the "integration," which these services sought to inspire. Integration, as Sayad explained in the early 1990s, is not a "predictive discourse."[14] Instead, in his view, integration only ever appealed to those most capable of achieving it. It was, in other words, a rigged game. The very marginality of migrants from Algeria made their integration impossible from the start. As Colette, who was awaiting permanent housing, suggested, "We cannot be French." French government policymakers, social service administrators, and social workers alternately envisioned the integrationist project as remaking the geography of greater France, a political community constituted by all France's subjects and citizens, and as a murkier sociocultural phenomenon that sought to prevent or repair tears to the French social fabric, imagined as an inevitable outcome of increased migration. Yet I have shown that integration was an imperiled policy from the start, precarious by its nature and defined by the difference it sought to erase. The midcentury welfare state imagined a French—or at least European—clientele that excluded Algerians as well as the memory of French Algeria and a multiethnic and multiracial French past.

Family migration from Algeria across the divide of Algerian independence shaped the possibilities of the midcentury welfare state in profound ways. Whereas French administrators had preferred Algerian families during the late colonial years, this thinking shifted with independence, though the institutions of the midcentury welfare state only slowly took note. The image of and the imagined problems associated with the "Algerian family" animated French administrators' immigration and social policy so that the two worked together. Administrators constrained the definition of the family eligible for migration and restricted access to the services promised to those families. All the same, they also doubled down on the importance of integration for those same families, a service that historically only specialized social aid associations could provide. These concerted efforts on behalf of Algerian families succeeded in fulfilling colonial prophesies about Algerian difference.

We have inherited this world. Growing support for far-right policies and political parties are part of the problem, but electoral victories alone will not defeat them. To diagnose the failures of neoliberal reforms to French, European, or Global North social welfare systems, we must reconsider a longer history of what the *golden age* of welfare meant and for whom it was assured. As I have shown, those years were robust precisely because of the politics of austerity and racism waged against migrating communities and, in the French case, especially families from Algeria. To create a more just network of social support, we need to begin by thinking critically and historically about the racial politics of the welfare state, which decades of policy decisions nurtured through the era of decolonization and beyond.

NOTES

A NOTE ON LANGUAGE

1. Dubois, *Avengers of the New World*, 5.

INTRODUCTION

1. Glorieux to Société de Saint Vincent de Paul, 3 June 1969, Dossier 1331, Archives départementales du Nord 2229 W 10.
2. Farge and Foucault, *Disorderly Families*, 48.
3. Scott also employs a "threads" metaphor to signify themes that work together; she analyzes this separately in *Politics of the Veil*, 18. In her case, however, this metaphor serves primarily as a narrative device, rather than an illustration of argument.
4. On rupture and continuity across 1962, consider Shepard, *Invention of Decolonization*, for the French case; Rahal, *Algérie 1962*, for the Algerian case. On chronology and teleology in thinking about decolonization, see Wilder, *Freedom Time*. Considering the terminology of the Algerian War, see the discussion in Vince, *Algerian War*, as well as Shepard, "Making Sovereignty," and Sidi-Moussa, "Devenirs Messalistes." Here I use the Algerian War, foregrounding the implications of the conflict during the decolonization of the French midcentury welfare state.
5. F. Cooper, *Colonialism in Question*, 19.
6. The historiography of the civilizing mission under empire is vast. My work has been especially informed by the literature on gender and the civilizing mission. See especially Stoler, *Carnal Knowledge and Imperial Power*; Burton, *Burdens of History*; Eichner, *Feminism's Empire*. On Algeria and France specifically, see Rogers, *Frenchwoman's Imperial Story*; Surkis, *Sex, Law, and Sovereignty*.
7. Fernando, *Republic Unsettled*.
8. Historians have debated the presence of memory about the Algerian War at a high level and often from the perspective of collective memory and state recognition.

Stora first analyzed the presence and absence of this history; see *La gangrène et l'oubli*. Other historians have focused on legacies of the war in political culture or society. This literature is growing, but see, for example, Ross on the cultural afterlives of decolonization in *Fast Cars, Clean Bodies*; Branche on the publication of memoirs and popular histories in the decade after Algerian independence in *La guerre d'Algérie*; Shepard on the persistence of "sex talk" about Algerians as a symbol of continuity in *Sex, France, and Arab Men*; Choi on pro-French former colonial subjects in *Decolonization and the French*.

9. On racism in the welfare state in the interwar, see especially Camiscioli, *Reproducing the French Race*; Frader, *Breadwinners and Citizens*. After the Second World War, consider Lyons, *Civilizing Mission in the Metropole*; Nasiali, *Native to the Republic*; Byrnes, *Making Space*; Harris, "Centre d'Accueil Nord-Africain"; E. Naylor, "'Une âne dans l'ascenseur'"; Wadowiec, "Afterlives of Empire." In Europe, see Bailkin, *Afterlife of Empire*; Stokes, *Fear of the Family*; Schields, "Science of Reform and Retrenchment."

10. I engage especially with Shepard, *Invention of Decolonization*; Lyons, *Civilizing Mission in the Metropole*. Both suggest that the Fifth Republic bore lasting imprints of the Algerian War, though they end their histories in 1962. I take up this suggestion.

11. Nasiali, *Native to the Republic*; Muriel Cohen, *Des familles invisibles*.

12. This term refers to a public administration and management and social work studies discussion about the role of social workers vis-à-vis the state. See Lipsky, *Street-Level Bureaucracy*; and more recently on this question, Maynard-Moody and Musheno, *Cops, Teachers, Counselors*; Rowe, "Going Back to the Street."

13. For general histories of Algeria, see especially McDougall, *History of Algeria*; Ruedy, *Modern Algeria*. On the invasion, see Sessions, *By Sword and Plow*.

14. On the military intervention, see Brower, *Desert Named Peace*. On territorial assimilation, I take my cue from Surkis's argument that in 1848 Algerian land became French but not Algerian *people*; see *Sex, Law, and Sovereignty*, 5.

15. Prochaska, *Making Algeria French*; Legg, *New White Race*; Andersen, *Regeneration through Empire*.

16. For a discussion of the effects of the Algerian War on France and Algeria, see especially Stora, *La gangrène et l'oubli*.

17. Here I am referring to Spire, "Semblables et Pourtant Différents." Spire's work, however, is indebted to Scott, who coined the term "paradoxical citizenship" in *Only Paradoxes to Offer*. On the specifics of Algerians' citizenship, see Weil, *How to Be French*. On "social rights" as a term, see Marshall, *Citizenship and Social Class*, 106. For challenges to Marshall's analysis in historical context, see Frader, *Breadwinners and Citizens*; Nasiali, *Native to the Republic*.

18. Lyons, "French or Foreign?"
19. On Algeria's circumstantial relationship to the European Economic Community, see Brown, *Seventh Member State.*
20. Shepard, *Invention of Decolonization.*
21. For another "long decolonization," see Lewis, "Legacies of French Slave-Ownership."
22. Nord, *France's New Deal*; Chapman, *France's Long Reconstruction.*
23. See literature on welfare in the interwar and Vichy period: Camiscioli, *Reproducing the French Race*; Barton, *Reproductive Citizens*; Frader, *Breadwinners and Citizens*; Pollard, *Reign of Virtue*; Childers, *Fathers, Families, and the State.*
24. Nord, *France's New Deal*, 170.
25. Offner, *Sorting Out the Mixed Economy*, chap. 1. While scholars understand decolonization as a postwar phenomenon, the welfare state was not. As I read the history of the welfare state through the prism of decolonization, I characterize the welfare state as "midcentury" to underscore the chronological disjuncture between traditional narratives of decolonization and the welfare state.
26. My analysis is especially indebted to Robcis, *Law of Kinship.*
27. Davis has convincingly characterized this phenomenon as a "racial regime of religion" in *Markets of Civilization.*
28. On the distinction between pronatalism and familialism, I follow Andersen, *Regeneration through Empire*; Dutton, *Origins of the French Welfare State.* Both argue that pronatalism was generally concerned with population numbers, while familialists were concerned with quantity *and* perceived (moral) quality. Pronatalists also held racist views, as Andersen and Camiscioli have shown. In addition to Dutton, on the origins of the European welfare state, see Pedersen, *Family, Dependence, and the Origins*; Ambler, *French Welfare State*; J. R. Horne, *Social Laboratory for Modern France*; Nord, "Welfare State in France."
29. I quote Barton, "'French or Foreign, So Long as They Be Mothers.'" For her argument about pronatalism overriding xenophobia in some cases, see Barton, *Reproductive Citizens.* On whiteness in French history, see especially Peabody and Stovall, *Color of Liberty*; Beaman, "Are French People White?"
30. Lyons, *Civilizing Mission in the Metropole.*
31. The French state—and later independent Algeria—framed workers as men and families as women and children according to the gendered dynamics of the welfare state and labor migration. If this trend holds true demographically in this period, it by no means exhaustively describes the conditions of Algerians in France. Algerian women worked both inside and outside the home in unpaid, under-the-table, or waged labor. Further, while my research revealed exclusively heterosexual couples, this is not proof of the absence of same-sex partnerships.

32. Lyons, *Civilizing Mission in the Metropole*, chap. 5; MacMaster, *Burning the Veil*; Seferdjeli, "'Fight with Us Women.'" In metropolitan France, consider Beaujon, "Policing Colonial Migrants"; Byrnes, *Making Space*; Prakash, *Empire on the Seine*.

33. This was especially acute in humanitarian work during the Algerian War. Consider Johnson, *Battle for Algeria*; Fontaine, *Decolonizing Christianity*.

34. On social services across 1962, see Franklin, "Defining Family, Delimiting Belonging"; Nasiali, *Native to the Republic*; Harris, "Centre d'Accueil Nord-Africain"; Lyons, "French or Foreign?"; E. Naylor, "'Une âne dans l'ascensceur.'"

35. Some migrants from Algeria claimed French citizenship in the years following independence, though French internal record keeping notes them as "French Muslims." See especially Choi, *Decolonization and the French*.

36. On workfare in the United States, see Mittelstadt, *From Welfare to Workfare*. In the European context, workfare is framed as well as the "right to work" in, for example, Rosanvallon, *New Social Question*.

37. Stokes argues this point about guest workers in her study of family migration in West Germany; see *Fear of the Family*.

38. Handler, *Social Citizenship and Workfare*, 2.

39. There is a growing literature on neoliberalism; see especially Harvey, *Brief History of Neoliberalism*; more recently, Slobodian, *Globalists*. On neoliberalism and the welfare state, see especially Mittelstadt, *From Welfare to Workfare*; M. Cooper, *Family Values*; Offner, *Sorting Out the Mixed Economy*.

40. Roediger, *Wages of Whiteness*.

41. For commentary on the crisis of the French welfare state, consider especially liberal (rather than socialist) reformers' arguments, especially Rosanvallon, *La crise de l'État-providence*; Ewald, *L'État providence*.

42. Sayad, "Three Ages of Algerian Emigration." The literature on Algerian migration is vast. Consider MacMaster, *Colonial Migrants and Racism*; Blanchard, *Histoire de l'immigration algérienne*.

43. Lyons, *Civilizing Mission in the Metropole*; Muriel Cohen, *Des familles invisibles*.

44. When I refer to family migration from Algeria rather than "Algerian family migration" I indicate that, after independence, some migrating families opted for French citizenship after arriving in France, a nuance I develop further in chapters 4 and 5.

45. On linking immigration to social problems, which Chin euphemistically calls, following the concerns of contemporary policy analysts, "managing migration," see *Crisis of Multicultural Europe*, chap. 2.

46. Italy received these benefits prior to the Treaty of Rome in 1957 (21 March 1947 decision), while Spanish and Portuguese workers received them through binational treaties outside of the EEC (as non-EEC members).

47. Article 7 of the "Déclaration des principes relative à la coopération écononique et financière," in the Evian Accords, published in the *Journal officiel de la République française*, 20 March 1962.
48. This integrationist policy was related to but distinct from other French postwar integrationist efforts, notably European integration and failed Françafrique policies. On the convergence between the two, see Brown, *Seventh Member State*; Marker, *Black France, White Europe*.
49. Sayad, "Weight of Words," 221–23. Sayad's understanding of integration was tied to the 1990s-era revival of the term to describe second-generation children's contingent belonging in France rather than the earlier colonial iteration.
50. Shepard, *Invention of Decolonization*. On Soustelle's integrationism, see Tyre, "From *Algérie Française* to *France Musulmane*."
51. As Hall writes in "Race—The Sliding Signifier": "What matters about science or religion is not that either one contains the actual truth about difference, but that each functions *foundationally* in the discourse of race to fix and secure what cannot be finally fixed and secured" (56–57).
52. Surkis, *Sex, Law, and Sovereignty*, chap. 3.
53. Cohen suggests that administrative visions of integration risked papering over the "invisible integration" of the many Algerian families who did *not* follow the dominant stereotypes. I emphasize here that integration itself created an archetype that Algerians could not emulate by design. See Muriel Cohen, *Des familles invisibles*, 22–23.
54. The debate on assimilation has petered out, but the term itself referred to republican universalist mission of imposing of cultural sameness through France's civilizing mission. On assimilation versus other relationships to colonial subjects in empire, see Betts, *Assimilation and Association*. On the debate over assimilation, see Belmessous, *Assimilation and Empire*; Conklin, *Mission to Civilize*; Wilder, *French Imperial Nation-State*. On territorial assimilation and dispossession, see Surkis, *Sex, Law, and Sovereignty*.
55. Stora draws a connection between second-generation Beurs movements and empire in *La gangrène et l'oubli*, 297–300. On the Beur movement more generally, see Hajjat, *La Marche pour l'égalité*, recently translated as *The Wretched of France*. On the resurgence of neo-republicanism, see Chabal, *Divided Republic*.
56. On the idea of the "intermediary" in French political culture, see Rosanvallon, *Demands of Liberty*.
57. On the policy and political dynamics of immigration, see especially Viet, *La France immigrée*; Weil, *La France et ses étrangers*; Spire, *Étrangers à la carte*. New studies include Barton, *Reproductive Citizens*, for the interwar; Nasiali, *Native to the Republic*, in the postwar period.

58. On the relationship between policing and social work, consider first Donzelot, *Policing of Families*. More recently, see Blanchard, *La police parisienne et les Algériens*; Prakash, *Empire on the Seine*; Beaujon, "Policing Colonial Migrants."

59. Muehlebach, *Moral Neoliberal*, 9.

60. On the historical configuration of whiteness through immigration, see Allen, *Invention of the White Race*. On the exclusion of Algeria from European integration, see Brown, *Seventh Member State*.

61. Fontaine, *Decolonizing Christianity*. Social Catholicism underwrote humanitarian work in France and was equally important to the foundation of specialized social aid associations for Algerian families. The largest public-private associations for Algerians were founded by Père Blanc Catholic missionary Jacques Ghys. His organizations published a journal, the *Cahiers Nord Africains*, dedicated to sharing knowledge about Algerian ethnicities, languages, and cultures, though in a colonialist vein. On Ghys, see Escafré-Dublet, "Aid, Activism, and the State."

62. My interpretation is guided by Hartman's claim, drawing from Foucault, that we "stumble upon" stories in the archives that reflect "exorbitant circumstances that yield no picture of the everyday life," and yet we are compelled to explain these stories as either "exemplary or typical" to make broader claims about the past. See Hartman, "Venus in Two Acts," 2. I sampled one in five case files for each archive where I accessed them (the North African Family Social Service archives at the Archives départementales du Nord and Cimade's [Inter-Movement Committee for Evacuees'] archives at La Contemporaine, then the BDIC [Bibliothèque de Documentation Internationale Contemporaine]).

63. Fourastié, *Les Trente Glorieuses*. On the periodization of the Thirty Glorious Years for migrants, consider Blanc-Chaléard, *En finir avec les bidonvilles*; Kozakowski, "From the Mediterranean to Europe."

1. A GREATER FRENCH FAMILY

1. On "Muslim" as a legal and political signifier, see Shepard, *Invention of Decolonization*; on the social construction of Islam, see Davidson, *Only Muslim*. On the "origins-" and "religion-based" language of identity, see Shepard, "Algerian Nationalism, Zionism, and French Laïcité," 445–67.

2. Table 2, "Principaux problèmes posés par les familles et pour lesquels le SSFNA a été sollicité," in "Rapport d'activité du SSFNA dans le Département du Nord," 1953, Archives départementales du Nord (hereafter Nord) 2585 W 1.

3. On the history of non-state care work, consider first Smith's classic *Ladies of the Leisure Class*. This phenomenon is not limited to France. On the charity and the foundations of social work in the United States, see Kunzel, *Fallen Women, Problem Girls*. For works about feminism in the empire, which often undergirded these

projects, see Eichner, *Feminism's Empire*; Burton, *Burdens of History*; Wildenthal, *German Women for Empire*.

4. On these specialized social aid associations under empire in France, consider Lyons, *Civilizing Mission in the Metropole*.

5. On familialism in French legal regimes, see Robcis, *Law of Kinship*, chap. 1.

6. The literature on the family in French political culture is vast. In addition to Robcis, see, for example, Desan, *Family on Trial*; Heuer, *Family and the Nation*; Surkis, *Sexing the Citizen*; Fuchs, *Contested Paternity*.

7. On the relationship between pronatalism and familialism, see Andersen, *Regeneration through Empire*, 14–18; Dutton, *Origins of the French Welfare State*.

8. Fenet and Ewald, *Naissance du Code Civil*, 68, as cited in Robcis, *Law of Kinship*, 21.

9. For two interpretations of European integration and Françafrique, see Brown, *Seventh Member State*; Marker, *Black France, White Europe*.

10. The rights guaranteed by French citizenship mattered a great deal to the foreign migrants and colonial subjects promised them. On claims for citizenship rights—and especially social citizenship—in the metropole, see Barton, *Reproductive Citizens*; Nasiali, *Native to the Republic*.

11. For a comprehensive history of Algeria, see McDougall, *History of Algeria*.

12. On the history of the French Union, see F. Cooper, *Citizenship between Empire and Nation*. Other historians have positioned barriers created by racism more centrally to the history, including Wilder, *Freedom Time*; Semley, *To Be Free and French*; Childers, *Seeking Imperialism's Embrace*; Marker, *Black France, White Europe*.

13. For this discussion, see Brown, *Seventh Member State*, 59–60.

14. See the preamble of the Constitution of the Fourth Republic: "In the morrow of the victory achieved by the free peoples over the regimes that had sought to enslave and degrade humanity, the people of France proclaim anew that each human being, without distinction of race, religion, or creed, possesses sacred and inalienable rights." See the preamble to the Constitution of 27 October 1946 (Constitution of the Fourth Republic) as translated and published at https://www.elysee.fr/en/french-presidency/the-constitution-of-27-october-1946 (accessed 25 May 2023).

15. On these articles, see F. Cooper, *Citizenship between Empire and Nation*, 121–31.

16. Colonial subjects acquired the "quality of the citizen" but not citizenship, full stop, as F. Cooper explains in *Citizenship between Empire and Nation*, 126.

17. Davis, *Markets of Civilization*, 3–9.

18. Davidson, *Only Muslim*. On the exception of Jews from the Mzab, see Stein, *Saharan Jews*.

19. See Title VIII, "De l'Union française," of the Constitution of the Fourth Republic. On personal status as the justification for unequal legal protection, see Shepard, *Invention of Decolonization*, 20–43. On the roots of this distinction, which was

born from French attempts to make Algerian land—but not the families that lived upon it—French, see Surkis, *Sex, Law, and Sovereignty*, chap. 3.

20. See article 74 of the Constitution of the Fourth Republic: "The Overseas Territories shall be granted a special status which takes into account their particular interests with relation to the general interests of the Republic."

21. Shepard, *Invention of Decolonization*, 41.

22. In Algeria the European settler-dominated Algerian Assembly declined to extend the rights of citizenship to Algerian women or enforce benefits.

23. Vergès makes this argument regarding French overseas departments in *Wombs of Women*, chaps. 2 and 3.

24. Shepard notes that the term "French Muslim of Algeria" emerged unevenly after 1944 and became codified in usage in 1956; see *Invention of Decolonization*, 49.

25. Lyons, *Civilizing Mission in the Metropole*, 66–73.

26. On this tension, see Spire, *Étrangers à la carte*, 115–18.

27. Ordinance no. 45-2568 of 2 November 1945, *Journal officiel de la République française*, 4 November 1945.

28. Chapman, *France's Long Reconstruction*, 64. The SGI allowed French businesses to work together to recruit foreign laborers without the oversight of the state. See Barton, *Reproductive Citizens*, 23–30.

29. Viet, *La France immigrée*; Spire, *Étrangers à la carte*; and Chapman, *France's Long Reconstruction*, have all noted the continued emphasis on selection even as postwar migration specialists disavowed earlier xenophobia.

30. On interwar antecedents, see Camiscioli, *Reproducing the French Race*, chap. 1.

31. Chapman, *France's Long Reconstruction*, 63–70.

32. Viet, *La France immigrée*, 280–81.

33. Spire, *Étrangers à la carte*, 119.

34. Spire, *Étrangers à la carte*, 116.

35. Weil, *La France et ses étrangers*, 84.

36. Chapman, *France's Long Reconstruction*, 119.

37. De Gaulle as cited in Weil, *La France et ses étrangers*, 69.

38. See especially Camiscioli, *Reproducing the French Race*.

39. For debates on Mauco's postwar influence, see Weil, "Racisme et discrimination"; Burgess, "Demographers' Moment"; Nord, *France's New Deal*, 173–78.

40. Camiscioli, *Reproducing the French Race*, 63–73.

41. On the "demographic intelligence" that shaped INED and the French state's populationism in the postwar, see Rosental, *L'intelligence démographique*.

42. Lyons notes how INED reshaped its Vichy roots in the post–World War II period in *Civilizing Mission in the Metropole*, 33–35.

43. Alain Girard and Jean Stoetzel, "Nouveaux documents sur l'immigration en France," *Population* 9, no. 1 (1954): 44.

44. Lyons, *Civilizing Mission in the Metropole*, 33–35.
45. Weil, *La France et ses étrangers*, 83–84. On the tension between Mauco and others in the committee who wanted a more open immigration for populationist reasons, like Alfred Sauvy (quoted), see Spire, *Étrangers à la carte*, chap. 4.
46. Chapman, *Long Reconstruction*, 69.
47. Girard and Stoetzel, "Nouveaux documents sur l'immigration," 48.
48. Girard and Stoetzel, "Nouveaux documents sur l'immigration," 48.
49. On embodiment as a framework, see Camiscioli, *Reproducing the French Race*; for the way the French imagined Islam as specifically embodied, see Davidson, *Only Muslim*.
50. My analysis of the "Algerian family" as it relates to colonial politics is indebted to Stoler's conceptualization of the intimate and its relationship to state power in *Carnal Knowledge and Imperial Power*.
51. On LePlay and familialism, see especially Robcis, *Law of Kinship*, chap. 1.
52. This discourse on women's (de)stabilizing role in the home was not specific to Algerian or even colonial women but also included European women and their important roles in shaping the household. Fascist regimes often positioned the family and women as central to the regime and national culture as in de Grazia, *How Fascism Ruled Women*; Koonz, *Mothers in the Fatherland*; Pollard, *Reign of Virtue*; Childers, *Fathers, Families, and the State*.
53. Chapman, *France's Long Reconstruction*, 117–31.
54. "La politique de sécurité sociale en Algérie," *Population* 7, no. 1 (1952): 25.
55. "La politique de sécurité sociale en Algérie," 18.
56. The number of Algerian women may have been greater, as administrators included a stable number of women over the course of the five-year period between 1948 and 1953. On the difficulty of accounting for Algerian demographics and on her calculation of these numbers, see Lyons, *Civilizing Mission in the Metropole*, 73.
57. "La politique de sécurité sociale en Algérie," 20.
58. "La politique de sécurité sociale en Algérie," 17.
59. This was not a new concern. Mauco had published on fecundity and colonial population growth since the interwar. See Camiscioli, *Reproducing the French Race*, 41–47.
60. Jacques Breil, "Étude de démographie quantitative," in "La Population en Algérie," Tome II, Report by the High Consultative Committee on Population and the Family, 1957, Archives nationales d'outre-mer (hereafter ANOM) 81F 1667.
61. Breil, "La Population en Algérie," ANOM 81F 1667.
62. For discussions about pronatalism, familialism, immigration, and empire under the Third Republic, in addition to Camiscioli, *Reproducing the French Race*, see Andersen, *Regeneration through Empire*. On pronatalism in France generally, consult Roberts, *Civilization without Sexes*; Cole, *Power of Large Numbers*.

63. On the National Alliance in the interwar and French populationism and eugenicist thinking, see Camiscioli, *Reproducing the French Race*, chap. 1. On the positioning of the interwar National Alliance within familialism, see Robcis, *Law of Kinship*, 29–38; within familialism and empire, see Andersen, *Regeneration through Empire*, 200–236.

64. Math, "Les allocations familiales et l'Algérie coloniale," 38.

65. See Andersen, "Office de la Famille Française."

66. Lyons, *Civilizing Mission in the Metropole*, 39.

67. FASS was created in 1952 by the Caisse National de Sécurité social (CNSS). See Math, "Les allocations familiales et l'Algérie coloniale," 39.

68. Lyons, *Civilizing Mission in the Metropole*, 42.

69. On the network state, see Rosanvallon, *Demands of Liberty*, chap. 13.

70. Hegel, *Hegel's Philosophy of Right*, par. 255.

71. Lyons, *Civilizing Mission in the Metropole*.

72. On relative assimilation of the Italian population in Paris during the post–World War II period, see Blanc-Chaléard and Milza, "Les Italiens à Paris depuis 1945," 33–53. On the difficulties of assimilation for Poles, see Ponty, "Une intégration difficile," 51–58.

73. Italy received these benefits prior to the 1957 Treaty of Rome in a 21 March 1947 decision, while Spanish and Portuguese workers received them through binational treaties established outside of the European Economic Community (as non-EEC members).

74. On the SSAE's involvement in promoting family resettlement policies for Europeans, see Chibrac, *Les pionnières du travail social*.

75. See chapter 3 on Guy de Serres-Justiniac's role in the Social Action Fund.

76. On the foundation of CANAM, see Sloan, "Welfare and Warfare," 60.

77. Georges Mauco, "Le problème de l'assimilation des étrangers en France," 1949, Archives Georges Mauco, Archives nationales de France—Pierrefitte-sur-Seine (hereafter AN) 577AP 5 (emphasis added).

78. Mauco, "Le problème de l'assimilation des étrangers."

79. AMANA Report, 2 July 1959, AN 19770391 art. 2. Ghys first petitioned the French government for financial backing in 1948.

80. On the creation of the SSFNA, see Lyons, *Civilizing Mission in the Metropole*, 38–47.

81. As cited in Sloan, "Welfare and Warfare," 48.

82. "Au 'service social' des Nord Africains," *Cahiers Nord Africains*, no. 3 (1950): 7.

83. Le Play argued that the family would act against the social instability wrought by capitalism and industrialization, which also led his followers, familialists and pronatalists alike, to idealize tradition. See Robcis, *Law of Kinship*, 25–38. On

modernization theory and its relationship to industrialization and urban in life in different case, see Weber, *Peasants into Frenchmen*.

84. P. Caltez, "La famille patriarcale en Afrique Berbère," *Cahiers Nord Africains*, no. 7–8 (1950): 19.

85. On gender and the welfare state in the postwar period, see Pulju, *Women and Mass Consumer Society*; Duchen, *Women's Rights and Women's Lives*; Prost, "L'évolution de la politique familiale"; Rudolph, *At Home in Postwar France*.

86. *Venues d'ailleurs, L'accueil et l'intégration des familles en France. Cinquante années d'histoire de l'ASSFAM, 1951–2001,* 5 (internal publication housed in Nord 2585 W 254).

87. For the interwar period, see especially Barton, *Reproductive Citizens*.

88. Chapman, *France's Long Reconstruction*, 149–50. See Jobs, *Riding the New Wave*, chap. 2 as well.

89. "Rapport Moral," Nord 2585 W 14. The only major city in which the SSFNA did not implant was Marseille, where a local organization, the Association for Aid to Overseas Workers (ATOM), had established services for Algerians and other North Africans. On ATOM, see Nasiali, *Native to the Republic*, 79–81; Harris, "Maghrebis in Marseille," chap. 1.

90. On the Nord's interwar investment in welfare, see Pedersen, *Family, Dependence, and the Origins*, 228. As the "primordial land of paternalism," see Donzelot, *Policing of Families*, 152.

91. Table 2 in "Rapport d'activité du SSFNA, bureau de Lille," 25 June 1953, Nord 2585 W 1.

92. "Rapport d'activité du SSFNA du Nord," 1954, Nord 2585 W 1.

93. On some of the paperwork lapses concerning the *livret de famille* and *état civil* experienced during the Algerian War, see MacMaster, *Burning the Veil*, 300–303.

94. "Rapport d'activité du SSFNA, Bureau de Lille," 1953, Nord 2585 W 1.

95. "Action éducative menée par le SSFNA en faveur des femmes musulmanes," n.d., Nord 2585 W 1.

96. "Action éducative menée par le SSFNA."

97. A family home aide describes her work in these years in "Rôle des travailleuses familiales au SSFNA," *Cahiers Nord Africains*, no. 51 (1951): 28–33.

98. "Le Rôle des Assistantes Sociales du SSFNA," 15 March 1954, Nord 2585 W 254.

99. "Le Rôle des Assistantes Sociales du SSFNA."

100. "Rapport d'activité du SSFNA dans le département du Nord," 1953, Nord 2585 W 1.

101. "Rapport d'activité du SSFNA, Bureau de Lille," 1953, Nord 2585 W 1.

102. "Rapport d'activité du SSFNA du Bureau du Nord," 1954, Nord 2585 W 1.

103. "Classifications des 'Cas' Enregistrés," Table 3, in "Rapport d'activité, Bureau de Lille," 1953, Nord 2585 W 1.

104. "Rapport d'activité du SSFNA du Bureau du Nord."

105. "Rapport d'activité du SSFNA du Bureau du Nord."
106. "Rapport d'activité du SSFNA du Bureau du Nord."
107. This logic changed in the 1970s and 1980s, when administrators became concerned about the second generation's position straddling the Mediterranean. They were convinced this generation was neither sufficiently culturally French but were also not Algerian. This problem was coupled with the fact that many second-generation immigrants were legally French, by virtue of the fact that they were born on French soil. For more on double *jus soli*, see Weil, *How to Be French*, chap. 7.
108. On war-era integration, see Shepard, *Invention of Decolonization*, 45–53. For contemporary reporting on Mitterrand's speech, see Pierre-Albin Martel, "Les réformes proposées par M. Mitterrand tendent d'abord à l'application plus complète du statut de l'Algérie," *Le Monde*, 10 January 1955.

2. THE WAR OVER SOCIAL WORK

1. On the terminology of the Algerian War versus the Algerian Revolution as well as the historiographical trends that have shaped these interpretations, see Vince, *Algerian War*.
2. Tillion to Kergomard, 16 January 1969, Centres Sociaux, Box 1, Collection Germaine Tillion, Bibliothèque nationale de France—site Richelieu (hereafter BNF). I consulted these archives with special permission while they were still being processed. The box numbers reflect the temporary organizing system.
3. On Tillion's work with the social centers, see especially LeSueur, *Uncivil War*; Sacriste, *Germaine Tillion*; Durham, "Une aventure sociale et humaine." On social work during the Algerian War, see Doré-Audibert, *Des Françaises d'Algérie*.
4. On the war and the international community, see Connelly, *Diplomatic Revolution*.
5. On the politicization of social work or social work as a means of social control, start with Donzelot, *Policing of Families*. Consider as well Rosenberg, *Policing Paris*; during and after the Algerian War, see especially Lyons, *Civilizing Mission in the Metropole*; Blanchard, *La police parisienne et les Algériens*; Prakash, *Empire on the Seine*; Byrnes, *Making Space*.
6. I paraphrase Muehlebach, *Moral Neoliberal*.
7. Consider postrevolutionary religious engagement in colonial politics described by Curtis, *Civilizing Habits*; or Third Republican efforts at schooling as recounted by Rogers, *Frenchwoman's Imperial Story*.
8. Kunzel, *Fallen Women, Problem Girls*, 12. There is a robust debate on the role of French reforms to attract Algerian women during the Algerian War as part of the French integrationist strategy. See especially MacMaster, *Burning the Veil*; Seferdjeli, "French 'Reforms' and Muslim Women's Emancipation"; Wadowiec, "Muslim Algerian Women"; Franklin, "Bridge across the Mediterranean." Diane Sambron accepts French reforms' stated goals in *Femmes musulmanes*. On

conversations within the FLN, consider Amrane, *Les femmes algérienne*; Vince, "Transgressing Boundaries."

9. See Burton, *Burdens of History*; Wildenthal, *German Women for Empire*; most recently, Eichner, *Feminism's Empire*.

10. Diebolt, *Les femmes dans l'action sanitaire*, 50.

11. Decree of 12 January 1932, "institution d'un brevet de capacité professionnelle permettant de porter la titre d'assistant ou d'assistante de service social diplômé de l'État français," *Journal officiel de la République française* (hereafter *JO*), 3 February 1932. Loi 46-330 of 8 April 1946 "relative à l'exercice des professions d'assistantes ou d'auxiliaires de service social et d'infirmières ou d'infirmiers" declared only social workers who had obtained the diplôme de l'État required by the 12 January 1932 decree could use the title in public or private (except certain exceptions). Written in Code of the Family and Social Aid—article 218. On the branches of social work, see Blum, "Regards sur les mutations du travail social."

12. See especially Auclert, *Les femmes arabes en Algérie*. On Auclert and other women like her in the Third Republic, see Eichner, "*La Citoyenne* in the World." See also Rogers, *French Woman's Imperial Story*; Bowlan, "Civilizing Gender Relations in Algeria."

13. On the codification of social work in the interwar period, in addition to Blum, see Guerrand and Rupp, *Brève histoire du service social*; Rater-Garcette, *La professionnalisation du travail social*. On the various forms of aid in the interwar period in the metropole, see Barton, *Reproductive Citizens*.

14. "Conseil d'État section du contentieux: Mémoire ampliatif," n.d., Archives nationales de France—Pierrefitte-sur-Seine (hereafter AN) 19870527 art. 3.

15. "Note sur l'évolution du service social dans le départment de la Seine," 1948–50, AN 19870527 art. 7.

16. "Note sur le rôle d'un ministère de la population en matière de service social," n.d., AN 19870527 art. 7.

17. Code of ethics articles 3 and 4, reprinted in *Feuillets de l'Association Nationale des Assistantes Sociales et des Assistants Sociaux*, no. 32 (July 1956), supplement.

18. "En marge de la commission de morale et technique professionnelle: Le code de déontologie des assistantes sociales," *Feuillets de l'ANAS*, no. 32 (July 1956): 7.

19. Doré-Audibert, *Des Françaises d'Algérie*, 44.

20. Johnson, *Battle for Algeria*.

21. For the creation of medico-social auxiliaries in Algeria, see the decree of 26 June 1946 by the governor general of Algeria, AN 19770393 art. 4. Cécile Braquehais dates the creation of this service to 1943 in her "Rapport sur le Service Social en Algérie," 1960, AN 19870527 art. 1.

22. Social workers later sought to establish programs for promotion for these aides but not to the rank of social worker. As part of a wartime compromise, some were

employed as full-time functionaries, but the majority worked without contracts and were excluded from functionary status. See Ordinance no. 59-244 of 4 February 1959 "relatif au statut général des fonctionnaires," *JO*, 8 February 1959.

23. On Chéné, see her nephew by marriage Pierre Couette's self-published biography, *Marie-Renée Chéné*. Chéné arrived in Algeria in 1951 as a volunteer for the International Civil Service (SCI), a pacifist organization.

24. Chéné, "Rapport social sur le bidonville Bérardi d'Hussein Dey," 8 March 1955, Centres Sociaux, Box 6, Folder 2, Collection Germaine Tillion, BNF.

25. Doré-Audibert, *Des Françaises d'Algérie*, 45; Fontaine, *Decolonizing Christianity*, 46.

26. Fontaine, *Decolonizing Christianity*, 39–55.

27. Chéné, "Rapport social sur le bidonville Bérardi d'Hussein Dey."

28. Chéné, "Rapport social sur le bidonville Bérardi d'Hussein Dey."

29. Doré-Audibert, *Des Françaises d'Algérie*, 56.

30. Serra, "Itinéraires," n.d., Folder Associations féministes, Collection Germaine Tillion, BNF.

31. Doré-Audibert, *Des Françaises d'Algérie*, 43.

32. Excerpt of the resolution "invitant le Gouvernement Général à constituer un 'Centre Algérien d'action et de Documentation Familiale,' presentée par Mme. H. Charles-Vallin, adoptée à l'unanimité par l'Assemblée Algérienne le 13 juin 1950," in "Naissance du CADAF," *CADAF*, no. 1 (1952): 2, conserved at Archives nationales d'outre-mer (hereafter ANOM) FM 81F 1659.

33. Serra, "Itinéraires."

34. Surkis, "Ethics and Violence," 46–47; Beauvoir, *Ethics of Ambiguity*.

35. For another account of this raid as it affected the politics of solidarity in Algeria, see Fontaine, *Decolonizing Christianity*, 81.

36. Fanon, "Algeria Unveiled."

37. On the army's role in unveiling Algerian women in the *bled* (countryside), see MacMaster, *Burning the Veil*, chap. 6.

38. According to a letter written by Chéné to ANAS reprinted in Doré-Audibert, *Des Françaises d'Algérie*, 48. See also, according to Darcie Fontaine, the archives of Nelly Forget at the Mission de France.

39. Chéné in Doré-Audibert, *Des Françaises d'Algérie*, 50.

40. Agnès de Laage, "Editorial," *Feuillets de l'ANAS*, no. 32 (1956): 1.

41. Letter from de Laage to Lacoste as cited in the "Rapport Moral" of the 1956 General Assembly, *Feuillets de l'ANAS*, no. 34 (1957): 14.

42. M. Cloupet, "En marge de la commission de morale et technique professionnelle: Le code de déontologie des assistantes sociales," *Feuillets de l'ANAS*, no. 32 (1956): 8.

43. Doré-Audibert, *Des Françaises d'Algérie*, 54.

44. Wilder, *French Imperial Nation-State*.

45. As Shepard notes, this was not a new strategy but rather was borrowed from other French projects; see Shepard, "Algeria, France, Mexico, UNESCO."

46. Tillion, *Algeria*. On Tillion, Soustelle, and the politics of intellectuals in Algeria, see LeSueur, *Uncivil War*, chap. 3.

47. Shepard, "Algeria, France, Mexico, UNESCO," 293.

48. The social centers were created by the decree of 27 October 1955, "portant création du Service des Centres Sociaux," *Journal officiel de l'Algérie*, 4 November 1955.

49. Information relayed to Darcie Fontaine by Nelly Forget as cited in Fontaine, *Decolonizing Christianity*, 46.

50. "Les Centres Sociaux," Centres Sociaux, Box 6, Folder 7, Collection Germaine Tillion, BNF, 20–21. The social centers started by Serra and Gallice were the first two incorporated by Tillion's social centers. See Durham, "Une aventure sociale et humaine," 64.

51. MacMaster, *Burning the Veil*, 77.

52. Durham, "Une aventure sociale et humane," 63.

53. The brevet is a national exam taken at the end of troisième (around the age of fifteen). On the problem of employing young Algerian women, see "Projet de scolarisation totale de l'Algérie: Les centres sociaux," December 1955, Centres Sociaux, Box 2, Folder 3, Collection Germaine Tillion, BNF. This was in keeping with Soustelle's integrationist mission, informed by an emphasis on achieving political equality through modernization. Tyre, "From *Algérie Française* to *France Musulmane*."

54. "Journées d'études sur l'éducation de base en Algérie," 2–3 July 1955, Centres Sociaux, Box 2, Folder 1, Collection Germaine Tillion, BNF.

55. "Journées d'études sur l'éducation de base en Algérie."

56. "Projet de scolarisation totale de l'Algérie: Les centres sociaux," December 1955, Centres Sociaux, Box 3, Folder 3, Collection Germaine Tillion, BNF.

57. "Bulletin intérieur: Vie de centres, Centre social de Boubsila," no. 2 (May 1957), conserved in Centres Sociaux, Box 2, Collection Germaine Tillion, BNF.

58. Emma Serra as quoted by Doré-Audibert, *Des Françaises d'Algérie*, 79.

59. See Le Sueur, *Uncivil War*, chap. 3; Fontaine, *Decolonizing Christianity*, chap. 2; Johnson-White, "Christian Anti-Torture Movement."

60. The SAS were created by a decree of 26 September 1955 with the goal, according to their pamphlets, of "[ensuring] the retaking of the population in regions where terrorists are active or those at risk of being contaminated," as cited in Johnson, *Battle for Algeria*, 48–49. On the Arab Bureau, see Abi-Mershed, *Apostles of Modernity*.

61. Johnson, *Battle for Algeria*, chap. 2. Peterson has shown that in addition to humanitarian outreach, SAS and SAU officers were also involved in torturing Algerian

populations; see Peterson, "Counterinsurgent Bodies." On torture in the Algerian War more generally, see especially Branche, *La torture et l'armée*; Branche, *La guerre d'Algérie*; Thénault, *Violence ordinaire dans l'Algérie coloniale*; Thénault, *Histoire de la guerre d'indépendance algérienne*.

62. Johnson, *Battle for Algeria*, 51.

63. Anti-nationalist politics were more important than technical skill. The SAS turned down applicants with a history of protesting colonialism or with family members involved in the nationalist movement. See Johnson, *Battle for Algeria*, 51.

64. MacMaster, *Burning the Veil*, 246.

65. On the EMSI, see especially Seferdjeli, "'Fight with Us Women,'" chap. 5; MacMaster, *Burning the Veil*, chap. 7. On the creation of the EMSI, see "Objet: Emancipation de la femme, Kerrata, 12 December 1957," Service Historique de la Défense 1H2461 DI. See also Lazreg, *Torture and the Twilight*; Sambron, *Femmes musulmanes*.

66. Seferdjeli, "'Fight with Us Women,'" 281.

67. "La femme musulmane contre la rébellion: Action psychologique," n.d., ANOM 932 89.

68. Seferdjeli, "'Fight with Us Women,'" 289.

69. "Création d'un corps 'd'auxiliaires sociales' en Algérie," *Feuillets de l'ANAS*, no. 34 (1957): 13.

70. "Création d'un corps 'd'auxiliaires sociales' en Algérie," 13.

71. "Création d'un corps 'd'auxiliaires sociales' en Algérie," 13.

72. "Note d'orientation: Emploi des attachées féminines des affaires algériennes," [1959], ANOM 6 SAS 64.

73. "Note d'orientation: Emploi des attachées féminines des affaires algériennes."

74. Macmaster, *Burning the Veil*; Seferdjeli, "'Fight with Us Women.'"

75. "Habitants des Douars: Que mangerez-vous cet hiver?" n.d., ANOM 932 89.

76. Vince, "Transgressing Boundaries."

77. Johnson, *Battle for Algeria*, chap. 3.

78. FLN-ALN Wilaya IV, Zone II, "Service Social: Définition des taches," 11 October 1957, Centres Sociaux, Box 6, Folder 8, Collection Germaine Tillion, BNF.

79. For earlier efforts, see, for example, the army's internal report "La femme musulmane contre la rébellion," n.d., ANOM 982 99; or the Ministry of the Interior's attempts to reform the personal status law, ANOM FM 8IF 74.

80. See MacMaster's discussion of the May demonstrations in *Burning the Veil*, chap. 3.

81. Speech by Nafissa Sid Cara, 25 May 1959, AN 103AJ 3. On Sid Cara's role during the Algerian War, see Franklin, "Bridge across the Mediterranean"; Asseraf, "Weapons of Mass Representation."

82. Seferdjeli, "'Fight with Us Women,'" 296.

83. Hal Lehrman, "Battle of the Veil," as cited in Seferdjeli, "'Fight with Us Women,'" 296.
84. "Dossier d'information sur les Milieux Féminins en Algérie, Appendix no. 1," n.d., AN 103AJ 3.
85. The MSF was part of the psychological warfare organized by the Fifth Bureau of the Army. In early 1958 the Specialized Administrative Section published a report titled "La femme musulmane contre la rébellion," in which it laid out the importance of earning Algerian women's trust to gain support for the French cause. See ANOM 932 89.
86. "Une campagne électorale en Algérie," *Bulletin trimestriel du CNFF*, January 1959, 8.
87. Gen. Daillier to Capt. Thier, 21 July 1958, ANOM 932 89.
88. Denéchère, "Les 'enfants de Madame Massu,'" 130.
89. Reid, "Worlds of Frantz Fanon's 'l'Algérie se dévoile,'" 472.
90. Nafissa Sid Cara quoted in minutes from the board of the MSF, 9 February 1959, AN 19830229 art. 6.
91. "Compte-rendu de la trésorière," 9 February 1959, AN 19830229 art. 2.
92. Serra, "Itinéraires," Folder Associations féministes, Collection Germaine Tillion, BNF.
93. "Discours Prononcé Par le Général de Gaulle le 3 Octobre 1958 à Constantine," 3 October 1958, AN 5AG 1 1414.
94. For more on the reform of social services in metropolitan France, see chapter 3. On the trans-Mediterranean politics of social aid in the Constantine Plan, see Lyons, *Civilizing Mission in the Metropole*, 151–59.
95. Cécile Braquehais, "Rapport sur le Service Social en Algérie," 4–20 January 1960, AN 198970527 art. 1.
96. Braquehais, "Rapport sur le Service Social," 12.
97. Braquehais, "Rapport sur le Service Social," 32.
98. Braquehais, "Rapport sur le Service Social," 18.
99. Braquehais, "Rapport sur le Service Social," 38–39.
100. Braquehais, "Rapport sur le Service Social," 42.
101. Braquehais, "Rapport sur le Service Social," 56.
102. Braquehais, "Rapport sur le Service Social," 54.
103. Seferdjeli, "'Fight with Us Women,'" 290.
104. Seferdjeli notes the FLN's concern with the ASSRA as well in "'Fight with Us Women,'" 295. On ASSRA concerns, see MacMaster, *Burning the Veil*, 265.
105. Seferdjeli, "'Fight with Us Women,'" 306.
106. SAS de Mac-Mahon (Batna), "Bulletin trimestriel des questions islamiques," 7 October 1960, ANOM 6 SAS 26.

107. SAS de Bou Akal (Batna), "Bulletin trimestriel des questions islamiques," 28 December 1960, ANOM 6 SAS 26.

108. SAS de Timgad (Batna), "Bulletin trimestriel des questions islamiques," 27 March 1961, ANOM 6 SAS 26.

109. Morel to Sid Cara, 16 May 1962, AN 19830229 art. 6.

110. "Situation du MSF au 12 juin 1962," 7 September 1962, AN 19830229 art. 6.

111. See Durham, "Une adventure sociale et humaine"; Aoudia, *L'Assassinat de Château-Royal*.

3. THE DOUBLE BIND OF SPECIFICITY

1. Dossier no. 1407, T— family, Archives départementales du Nord (hereafter Nord) 2229 W 11.

2. In the case of welfare, see Lyons, *Civilizing Mission in the Metropole*, 209–13; on institutions of state in general, see Shepard, *Invention of Decolonization*.

3. On continuities in welfare provisioning across the era of decolonization, see Germain, *Decolonizing the Republic*; Muriel Cohen, *Des familles invisibles*; Nasiali, *Native to the Republic*; E. Naylor, *France's Modernising Mission*; Byrnes, *Making Space*; Harris, "Maghrebis in Marseille."

4. Fourastié, *Les Trente Glorieuses*. On migration from the Mediterranean during these years, see Kozakowski, "From the Mediterranean to Europe."

5. On this insight, see Offner, *Sorting Out the Mixed Economy*.

6. Barton, *Reproductive Citizens*.

7. Sayad argued that the first integration occurred when Algerian workers left home to emigrate to France to take part in the market economy; see Sayad, "Weight of Words," 222. On the "market-conforming" family in West Germany, see Stokes, *Fear of the Family*, chap. 1.

8. Although the Constitution of the Fourth Republic had offered Algerians French Union citizenship and the loi organique gave them access to social rights while in France, Algerians were not treated as full citizens. In 1958 Algerian men and women were promised full access to their rights regardless of whether they lived in metropolitan France. On the Fourth Republic's citizenship promises, see chapter 1.

9. On the ways de Gaulle's administration reshaped welfare and France's political economy, see Hayward, "From Republican Sovereign to Partisan Statesman." Consider as well the special issue of *Modern & Contemporary France*, "The Fifth Republic at Fifty," including Clift, "Fifth Republic at Fifty"; Levy, "From the Dirigiste State"; Palier, "Les transformations du modèle social français."

10. Letter from Ministry of the Interior to IGAMES and prefects, 10 February 1958, Archives nationales de France—Pierrefitte-sur-Seine (hereafter AN) F1a 5010.

See especially Blanchard, *La police parisienne et les Algériens*; Prakash, *Empire on the Seine*.

11. Viet, *France Immigrée*, 186.

12. On the process of navigating citizenship for Algerians in France after independence, see Lyons, "French or Foreign?"

13. Ministerial circular no. 490, 17 September 1963, as cited in "Note sur le Service des Affaires Musulmanes: Mission-Organisation-Moyens," 20 March 1965, AN FIA 5010.

14. Michel Massenet, "La migration algérienne et l'administration française," 1963, AN 19770391 art. 9. In Massenet's mind, the Social Action Fund and not the Service for Muslim Affairs was best suited for this continued work.

15. On the SLPM's mission, see "Service de Liaison et de Promotion des Migrants" included in a 24 December 1965 memo from the SLPM to Service des Préfets. On the transition, see Lyons, *Civilizing Mission in the Metropole*, 216.

16. The FAS was created by Ordinance 58-1381 of 29 October 1958, *Journal officiel de la République française* (hereafter *JO*), 1 January 1959. On the wartime creation of FAS, see Lyons, *Civilizing Mission in the Metropole*, 147–51; Lyons, "Social Welfare, French Muslims, and Decolonization."

17. The two-thirds of the Social Action Fund budget directed to Algeria was part of the administration's "Constantine Plan" for reconstruction and renewal in Algeria. On the coercive function of social aid in the Constantine Plan, see Lyons, *Civilizing Mission in the Metropole*, 151–59. On the Constantine Plan and the creation of neocolonial economic foundations in Algeria, see Davis, *Markets of Civilization*, chap. 3.

18. On the IGAME, see Blanchard, *La police parisienne et les Algériens*; Prakash, *Empire on the Seine*.

19. See the organizational chart in Viet, *La France immigrée*, 205.

20. Doublet, "Réflexions sur dix années de législation," 14. Doublet wrote the family benefit program alongside other noted pronatalists such as Pierre Laroque (see chapter 1) and Alfred Sauvy, the director of INED. Laroque had also led the Social Action Fund's predecessor organization, the Fonds d'action sanitaire et sociale, according to Sloan, "Welfare and Warfare," 119.

21. Jacques Doublet, also director general of Social Security, ensured continued emphasis on familial integration. Guy de Serres-Justiniac had previously served as director of the Administrative Office of the General Government of Algeria, the colonial government in the Fourth Republic. He remained director general until 1966, when Jacques Revol, the original associate director, took over. Revol stayed on as director from 1966 until 1973.

22. Lyons, *Civilizing Mission in the Metropole*, 149–50.

23. Massenet mentions the increase in family arrivals from 1959 forward in "Note concernant les problèmes posés par l'habitat des femmes musulmanes de souches algériennes," 9 September 1960, AN 19770391 art. 6.
24. Massenet, "La migration algérienne et l'administration française."
25. Massenet, "La migration algérienne et l'administration française."
26. Joxe to the Ministry of Labor, 9 November 1962, AN 19770391 art. 9.
27. Joxe to the Ministry of Labor, 9 November 1962.
28. The Social Action Fund completed the projects begun before Algerian independence in July 1962 to avoid negative public relations or the appearance that France had abandoned its Algerian construction sites, as described in a letter from Pompidou to Joxe, 16 February 1963, AN 19770391 art. 9.
29. Decree no. 64-356 of 24 April 1964. See Viet, *La France immigrée*, 223.
30. "Répertoire des mandatements" compiled from AN 19990118 art. 17. Funding stalled in 1968.
31. Funding compiled from documents in AN 19980118 arts. 17 and 19.
32. "Unlocatable institution" attributed to Michel Yahiel, director of the Social Action Fund in Chirac's government, in "Politique d'une institution. Le Fonds d'action sociale pour les travailleurs immigrés: Entretien avec Michel Yahiel," *Politix. Revue des sciences sociales du politique*, no. 12 (1990): 70. On the long-deferred nature of Algerians' French citizenship, see Shepard, *Invention of Decolonization*, chap. 1.
33. "Carrefour sur quelques problèmes sociaux poses par la migration musulmane algérienne en metropole," 28 January 1959, AN 19760133 art. 17. They noted that this was likely an underestimate. On ATOM, see Nasiali, *Native to the Republic*; Harris, "Maghrebis in Marseille."
34. "Carrefour sur quelques problèmes sociaux poses par la migration musulmane algérienne."
35. See chapter 1.
36. On counterinsurgency and strategies of pacification geared at women in Algeria during the war, see MacMaster, *Burning the Veil*; Seferdjeli, "'Fight with Us Women.'"
37. "Carrefour sur quelques problèmes sociaux posés par la migration musulmane algérienne."
38. "Carrefour sur quelques problèmes sociaux posés par la migration musulmane algérienne."
39. "Carrefour sur quelques problèmes sociaux posés par la migration musulmane algérienne."
40. "Rapport d'activité pour l'année 1959, Département du Nord," Nord 2585 W 1.
41. Racine to Revol, Social Action Fund, 18 June 1965, AN 19850021 art. 22.
42. CANAM, "Conseil d'Administration: Procès Verbal," 16 January 1967, AN 19850021 art. 49. On distinctions between "Muslims" and "repatriates," see chapter 4.

43. "Résidant étrangers en France en 1967 par départements et principals nationalités," n.d., AN 19930317 art. 1 (Source: Ministry of the Interior). A 1962 census compiled by INSEE estimated 109,280 total foreigners in the department in 1962, in Louis Chevalier, "Chronique de l'Immigration," *Population* 19, no. 3 (June–July 1964): 571.

44. The number of Algerians who opted for French citizenship was usually much smaller than the number of Algerians living and working (temporarily or permanently) in France. On these numbers, see CANAM's "Rapport Moral," 1967, 20, AN 19850021 art. 84. On citizenship after independence, see chapter 4 or Lyons, "French or Foreign?"

45. CANAM, "Conseil d'Administration: Procès Verbal," 16 January 1967.

46. CANAM, "Extrait du Procès-Verbal de la Séance du Conseil d'Administration," 3 November 1964, AN 19850021 art. 23.

47. CANAM, "Extrait du Procès-Verbal de la Séance du Conseil d'Administration," 3 November 1964.

48. CANAM, "Conseil d'Administration Procès Verbal," 1 February 1965, AN 19850021 art. 23.

49. CANAM, "Extrait du Procès-Verbal du Conseil d'Administration," 18 March 1966, AN 19850021 art. 23.

50. Social Action Fund, "Rapport d'activité année, 1966," AN 19990118 art. 19.

51. "Réunion des assistantes présidés par M. Racine (SSFNA) en présence de Mme. Berthelot, M. Villey, et Mlle Golube au SSFNA," 24 November 1965, Nord 2229 W 164.

52. "Convention de main d'œuvre entre la France et le Maroc," 1 June 1963, published in JO as Decree no. 63-779 (27 July 1963).

53. "Convention de main d'œuvre entre la France et la Tunisie," 9 August 1963, published in JO as Decree no. 63-1055 (15 October 1963).

54. "Répartition des travailleurs étrangers introduits par nationalité," appendix B, n.d., AN 19930317 art. 1.

55. Numbers compiled from the National Immigration Office by the Ministry of the Interior and published in Francine Siety, "Chronique de l'Immigration: L'immigration étrangère en France en 1966," *Population* 22, no. 4 (1967): 736.

56. On housing after empire, consult Nasiali, *Native to the Republic*; Byrnes, *Making Space*; Blanc-Chaléard, *En finir avec les bidonvilles*. On housing for Algerian families especially, see Muriel Cohen, *Des familles invisibles*; Hmed, "Loger les étrangers 'isolés' en France"; on North Africans, see Harris, "'Capital of Hope and Disappointments.'"

57. Social Action Fund, "Rapport d'activité, 1962," AN 19990118 art. 19. On the growth of the National Society for Construction of Housing for Workers (SONACOTRA) despite the end of empire in Algeria, see Nasiali, *Native to the Republic*, 93–99.

58. "Des divers aspects du problème posé par le mouvement migratoire des nord-africains et des africains vers la France," December 1965, AN 19770391 art. 9, circulated by the préfecture de police. On Préfet de Police Maurice Papon's career as a Vichy official and later his part in the October 1961 massacre of Algerians in Paris, see House and MacMaster, *Paris 1961*.

59. Massenet, "L'évolution de la migration algérienne en France," n.d., AN 19770391 art. 9.

60. Massenet, "La migration algérienne et l'administration française," 1963, AN 19770391 art. 9.

61. Social Action Fund, "Rapport d'activité, 1967," April–May 1968, AN 19990118 art. 19.

62. For housing funding from 1969 to 1974, see Social Action Fund, "Rapport d'activité 1973," AN 19990118 art. 19. For social assistance in those years, see "Répertoire des mandatements, Programme 1967–1971," AN 19990118 art. 17. For earlier numbers, see Board of the Social Action Fund, "Extrait du Procès Verbal," 8 December 1966, AN 19770391 art. 1.

63. "Rapport d'activité du SSFNA, Bureau de Lille," 1965, Nord 2585 W 1.

64. "Rapport d'activité du SSFNA, Bureau de Lille."

65. "Rapport d'activité du SSFNA, Bureau de Lille."

66. Nasiali, *Native to the Republic*, 97.

67. Louis Belpeer, "Le passage du migrant et sa famille du bidonville au HLM," *Colloque sur la migration algérienne*, 13–15 October 1966.

68. A. Benghezal, "L'arrivée et la psychologie du migrant," *Colloque sur la migration algérienne*, 13–15 October 1966.

69. Marc Bernardot as cited in Byrnes, *Making Space*, 10.

70. Philippe Serre, "Le problème de l'accueil et l'adaptation des travailleurs étrangers," January 1966, Haut Comité de la Population et de la Famille, AN 577AP 3.

71. Serre, "Le problème de l'accueil et l'adaptation des travailleurs étrangers."

72. Belpeer, "Le passage du migrant et de sa famille du bidonville au HLM."

73. Nasiali, *Native to the Republic*, 93–99.

74. On the negotiation of social rights in Evian, see chapter 4. On debates over citizenship and social rights for Algerians and naturalized French, see Lyons, "French or Foreign?"

75. Although the West and Central African countries concluded treaties between 1960 and 1963 as they gained independence, in practice migration to France remained limited in these early years. Bilateral treaties that generated more robust migration in the early 1960s included especially Portugal, the terms of which I discuss in chapter 4, as well as Spain (1961), Tunisia (1963), and Morocco (1963).

76. Barton, *Reproductive Citizens*.

77. Chapman, *France's Long Reconstruction*, chap. 4.

78. As described in "Groupe d'étude chargé d'examiner le régime juridique applicable aux Algériens en France," 16 September 1963, AN FIa 5045. See also Lyons, *Civilizing Mission in the Metropole*, chap. 1.

79. Article 7 of the "Déclaration des principes relative à la coopération éconionique et financière," in the Evian Accords, *JO*, 20 March 1962.

80. According to Lyons, the fact that the Social Security Code predated the Evian Accords gave the committee, in their view, the ability to deny these services that were destined explicitly for a "national purpose"; see Lyons, *Civilizing Mission in the Metropole*, 216.

81. "Groupe d'étude chargé d'examiner le régime juridique applicable aux Algériens en France," 16 September 1963, AN FIa 5045.

82. Camiscioli, *Reproducing the French Race*.

83. On the decline of polygamy, see Kamel Kateb as cited in Surkis, *Sex, Law, and Sovereignty*, 238. On French demography and population growth in the colonies after the Second World War, see chapter 1.

84. Dossier no. 1407, T— family, Nord 2229 W 11.

85. Surkis, *Sex, Law, and Sovereignty*, 247.

86. Case notes, Dossier no. 1407, T— family, Nord 2229 W 11.

87. "Rapport d'activité du SSFNA," 1970–71, Nord 2585 W 14.

88. Decree no. 66-486, *JO*, 7 July 1966.

89. Led by the former first French ambassador to Algeria Jean-Marcel Jeanneney, this ministry brought together offices working to solve the problems supposedly wrought by demographic growth, family policy, housing inadequacy, immigration, and the shifting labor market.

90. The Bureau of Population and Migrations included three departments: the Movement of Populations, which included professional training, employment, and labor migration; the Office of Social Programming, which oversaw the Social Action Fund's initiatives and worked with associations dedicated to social aid; and the Office of Naturalizations, which worked in conjunction with the Ministry of Social Affairs. See Laurens, *Une politisation feutrée*, 137.

91. Bureau of Population and Migrations, "Note sur les problèmes créés par la politique de l'immigration," 23 November 1972, AN 19950493 art. 6.

92. Social Action Fund, "Rapport d'activité, 1967," April/May 1968, AN 19990118 art. 19. The SSFNA received 1,100,000 francs and CANAM received 250,000 francs in 1967.

93. Social Action Fund, "Rapport d'activité, 1968," April 1969, AN 19990118 art. 19.

94. FASTI, "Qui sont-ils? Pourquoi viennent-ils?" (1971), Fonds Monique Hervo, Institut d'Histoire du Temps Présent (hereafter IHTP), ARC 3019 art. 13.

95. "La cité du pont de Bezons," 1971, Fonds Monique Hervo, IHTP, ARC 3019 art. 11.

96. Michel Massenet in his interview with Anthony Hartley, originally published in the United States and republished in excerpted form in Massenet, *Sauvage Immigration*, 42.

97. The scholarship on racism and republicanism is immense. See especially the early edited volumes by Peabody and Stovall, *Color of Liberty*; Frader and Chapman, *Race in France*. See also Wilder, *French Imperial Nation-State*; Semley, *To Be Free and French*. On "commonsensical" understandings of race, see Nasiali, *Native to the Republic*; Marker, *Black France, White Europe*.

4. FOREIGN RELATIONS

1. Hurston, *Their Eyes Were Watching God*, 27.
2. On these two communities, see Choi, *Decolonization and the French*; Eldridge, *From Empire to Exile*.
3. On the confusion and double-speak wrought by the so-called exodus, see Shepard, *Invention of Decolonization*, chap. 8.
4. Noiriel, *French Melting Pot*; Weil, *La France et ses étrangers*; Viet, *La France immigrée*. On the three ages, see Sayad, "Three Ages of Algerian Emigration." Sayad dates the movement of individual workers to the metropole from the beginning of the First World War through the end of the Algerian War (these comprise the first two stages). The third stage—the movement of families and the creation of Algerian enclaves in France—occurred only after Algerian independence.
5. Lyons, *Civilizing Mission in the Metropole*.
6. Muriel Cohen interprets families as a secondary but shared concern in Franco-Algerian negotiations and argues that housing primarily conditioned Algerians' migration in *Des familles invisibles*, chap. 4.
7. Sayad, "Exemplary Immigration," 80.
8. Other scholars have noted continuity in administration, diplomatic relations, and the social fabric of migration, though they have not focused on gender. See Laurens, *Une politisation feutrée*; Spire, *Étrangers à la carte*; Katz, *Burdens of Brotherhood*.
9. On power in Franco-Algerian bilateral discussions about immigration, see Sayad, "Exemplary Immigration," 81.
10. Chin, *Crisis of Multiculturalism in Europe*, chap. 1.
11. Bennett-Coverley, "Colonisation in Reverse," 16–17.
12. Chin, *Crisis of Multiculturalism in Europe*, 22.
13. Of the five chapters in the Evian Accords, only chapter 2 focused on provisions for citizens of France and Algeria. The other four chapters focused on military and economic agreements between the states.
14. Shepard, *Invention of Decolonization*, 144–55.
15. Shepard, *Invention of Decolonization*, 215.

16. Shepard, *Invention of Decolonization*, 155–62.

17. Outlined in Chapter II.A.2 of the Evian Accords as appeared in the *Journal officiel de la République française* (hereafter *JO*), 20 March 1962.

18. See chapter 5 on for the legal and social trajectory of post-Algerian independence French Muslims in France.

19. On the legal complications of Algerian and French citizenship, see Lyons, "French or Foreign?"

20. Shepard, *Invention of Decolonization*, 51–52. Shepard argues that the French government shifted usage from "French Muslim of Algeria" to "French with North African roots" to insist upon Algerian difference despite integration, creating a "'racialized' ethnicity."

21. "Déclaration des principes relative à la coopération écononique et financière," in the Evian Accords, *JO*, 20 March 1962.

22. "État comparative des formalités d'entrée en France des travailleurs étrangers, en fonction de leur origine," n.d., Archives du Ministère des Affaires Étrangères—La Courneuve (hereafter AMAE) 29 QO 92.

23. Viet, *La France immigrée*, 280.

24. Migrants arriving through the general immigration protocol were traditionally from southern or southeastern Europe. See chapter 1.

25. Viet, *La France immigrée*, 282–83.

26. On citizenship law in the four communes of Senegal, see Semley, *To Be Free and French*, chap. 2.

27. Viet, *La France immigrée*, 285–86.

28. Mann, *From Empires to NGOs*, 129.

29. In addition, consider migration from France's overseas departments. After Algerian independence, France instituted the Bureau pour le développement des migrations dans les départements d'outre-mer (BUMIDOM), which organized migration from the overseas departments and especially the Caribbean. As French citizens from overseas, the terms of their migration and their access to benefits was guaranteed in theory, if often difficult to attain in practice. On BUMIDOM, see, for example, Pattieu, "BUMIDOM 1963–82"; Childers, *Seeking Imperialism's Embrace*, chap. 7.

30. Evian Accords in *JO*, 20 March 1962.

31. See Lyons, "French or Foreign?," 128; Shepard, *Invention of Decolonization*, 237.

32. Frey to Broglié, 12 July 1962, Archives nationales de France—Pierrefitte-sur-Seine (hereafter AN) 19960134 art. 12.

33. Frey to Broglié, 12 July 1962.

34. "Synthèse des rapports trimestriel établis par les Conseillers Techniques pour les Affaires Musulmanes," 3rd Trimester 1962, AN F1a 5014.

35. Louis Chevalier, "Chronique de l'immigration," *Population* 19, no. 3 (1964): 569–78.

36. Francine Siety, "Chronique de l'immigration," *Population* 22, no. 4 (1967): 736, for the first data. See also AN 19950493 art. 5.
37. On complete figures and their accounting, see Muriel Cohen, *Des familles invisibles*, appendix 2 and 2 bis.
38. For figures on single men, see Chevalier, "Chronique de l'immigration."
39. Lyons, *Civilizing Mission in the Metropole*, 72–73. The number of Algerian women may have been even greater than estimated, as administrators assumed a stable number of women over the course of the five-year period between 1948 and 1953.
40. Lorcin, *Imperial Identities*.
41. For this figure, see Sutton, "Population Resettlement." On the experience of regroupment camps, see Cornaton, *Les camps de regroupement de la guerre d'Algérie*; Thénault, *Violence ordinaire dans l'Algérie coloniale*.
42. According to Bennoune, over 723,000 Algerian peasants relocated to urban centers in the years following the end of the war; see Bennoune, *Making of Contemporary Algeria*, 89.
43. The Algerian Labor and Social Affairs Ministry reported that 7 percent of its requests for immigration came from Algiers and 16 percent from Constantine. While the Kabyle still provided the largest percentage of migrants (45 percent), the increase in migrants from cities actually reflected Algerian underemployment in cities after the rural exodus. Statistics from a 1968 report by the Ministère Algérien du Travail et des Affaires Sociales quoted in Salah, *La communauté algérienne*, 61. Consider as well the table circulated by the French Embassy in Algeria to the minister of social affairs about Algerian emigration, 28 June 1966, AMAE 29 QO 92 in which 1964 emigration included an almost equal movement of Algerian migrants from large urban areas (8,689 from Algiers, Oran, Bone, and Constantine) and rural zones (8,935).
44. Viet, *La France immigrée*, 288.
45. Note for the minister relaying the results of a Franco-Algerian meeting on Algerian worker migration, 29 January 1963, AMAE 29 QO 92. See as well the hand-drawn flow charts of the proposed French and Algerian systems for managing migration that follow.
46. Bachir Boumaza, Ministère algérien du Travail et des Affaires Sociales, "Extrait de la déclaration du 23 October 1962," AMAE 29QO 92.
47. ONAMO was created by Decree 62-99 of 29 November 1962.
48. Boumaza, "Extrait de la déclaration du 23 October 1962."
49. In 1966, 45 percent of the Algerian active population (mostly men) were out of work according to data collected by the Ministère du Travail et des Affaires Sociales Algériennes and cited by Bennoune, *Making of Contemporary Algeria*, 112.
50. See the extract of the Algerian ambassador Redha Malek's press conference in "Emigration algérienne en France," *Documents Nord-Africains* (9 December 1964), 1.

51. Lewis, *Boundaries of the Republic*, 123–33. Lewis refers to France's system of "circulars," procedures without the formal weight of law and often unannounced, which nonetheless governed France's immigration system.

52. "Emigration algérienne en France," 4.

53. Hendrickson, *Decolonizing 1968*, 149.

54. Meeting between Broglié and Nekkache, 24 January 1964, AN 19760133 art. 15.

55. "Emigration algérienne en France," 4.

56. "Protocole franco-algérien du 10 avril 1964," AMAE 29 QO 9.

57. Muriel Cohen, "Regroupement familial," 21.

58. See Nasiali, *Native to the Republic*, chap. 4, for a discussion of the everyday racism that guided the allocation of housing.

59. "Rapport Moral du SSFNA," 1963–64, AN 19850021 art. 24.

60. I consulted the housing inspection forms held in the archive of the SSFNA of the Nord, and especially the Archives départementales du Nord (hereafter Nord) 2229 W 135 and 2229 W 136.

61. This anecdote was relayed to me in an interview with Béatrix Dagras, a social worker for the SSFNA, 29 April 2014, Paris.

62. Detrez to Departmental Director for Social and Sanitary Action regarding the A— family, 1 April 1967, Nord 2229 W 136.

63. Monsieur A. to unknown [SSFNA], 16 February 1967, Nord 2229 W 136.

64. Detrez to Departmental Director for Social and Sanitary Action regarding the A— family.

65. Departmental Director for Social and Sanitary Action to Detrez, 7 February 1975, Nord 2229 W 135. In these files the DDASS regional office refers to Detrez interchangeably as Destrez or Detrez, but they were one and the same person, head social worker for the Lille SSFNA.

66. See decisions from 1965 to 1968 in Nord 2229 W 135 6. This statistic is similar to findings in the Bouche de Rhône where around 82 percent of families were approved for resettlement in 1965, according to Lyons, "Invisible Immigrants," 333.

67. "Mouvement migratoire des Algériens entre l'Algérie et la France de 1914 à 1969," "La migration algérienne," *Hommes et Migrations* 116 (1970): 15. The net increase of migrants was 35,568, of which 6,399 were women and children.

68. This claim appears in numerous sources. See the minutes of the Commission mixte franco-algérien, 24–25 March 1965, AN 19960134 art. 12.

69. The Ministry of the Interior demanded these changes based on pressure from Public Health according to "Note pour M. De Laboulaye," 24 January 1966, AMAE 29 QO 92.

70. Circular no. 112, 27 February 1967, Minister of the Interior for "admission en France des travailleurs algériens." See AN 19760135 art. 2.

71. Circular no. 112, 27 February 1967.

72. Circular no. 112, 27 February 1967.

73. Muriel Cohen, *Des familles invisibles*, 186–90.

74. Circular no. 112, 27 February 1967.

75. On the Algerian regime change, see McDougall, *History of Algeria*, chap. 6.

76. "Note au sujet de l'immigration algérienne," 23 February 1968, AMAE 0034 SUP 122.

77. "Problèmes d'ordre social dans les relations franco-algériennes," 27 December 1968, AMAE 0034 SUP 122.

78. A. Benghezal, "L'arrivée et la psychologie du migrant," *Colloque sur la migration algérienne*, 13–15 October 1966, 43–44.

79. "Intervention de M. Bacouche Salah, chef d'équipe algérien travaillant en France," *Colloque sur la migration algérienne*, 13–15 October 1966, 76–77.

80. "Les travaux du premier séminaire algérien consacré a l'émigration, 8–16 August 1966 à Alger," Génériques, AMANA 42.

81. Auboiron to Ministère des affaires sociales, 11 October 1968, AMAE 0034 SUP 123.

82. Auboiron to Ministère des affaires sociales, 11 October 1968. Auboiron based this argument on statistics he cited earlier. Between October 1967 and September 1968, 25,968 approved ONAMO workers entered France. But another metric was cause for alarm. Auboiron also noted that during the same period, 147,458 salaried workers left France for vacation, but only 123,725 returned, representing a net loss of workers. Therefore, the growth of the male Algerian population in France was not due to workers, Auboiron argued, but rather those who came to France under "other" reasons.

83. Accord franco-algérien drafted 26 October 1968, AMAE 0034 SUP 123 (signed 28 December 1968).

84. Auboiron to Bureau of Population and Migrations, 9 March 1971, AN 19930317 art. 18.

85. Statistics compiled from AN 19960134 art. 11.

86. These numbers do not include the workers and families who arrived in France outside legal channels. Some reports indicate between 230,000 and 400,000 arrivals per year during this period (men, women, and children counted together). It is impossible to know the number of arrivals who arrived only for vacation or a temporary stay versus those who overstayed their visas. In fact, this problem contributed to administrative panic about the number of Algerians arriving each year. See Auboiron to Gorse, "Comparaison des mouvements migratoires en 1968–1974, Tableaux A-C," 8 February 1974, AN 19960134 art. 11.

87. Colonial thinking had long linked venereal diseases to empire and Islam. See, for example, Amster, *Medicine and the Saints*.

88. The new agreement also flagged people with physical disabilities as undesirable ONAMO migrants. French administrators in charge of immigration worried that

Algerians would use ONAMO and other sponsored migration to travel to France for medical procedures, and that migrants would take advantage of bilateral agreements to seek covered medical treatment in France to which they could not gain access in Algeria. Algerians with metabolic, heart-related, and neurological disorders particularly raised concerns about chronic diseases.

89. Series of letters between the French Embassy in Algeria and the DPM and AMAE, November 1969, AN 19930317 art. 18.

90. Report by Bourquin about the Centre médical, 1969, AN 19930317 art. 18.

91. Appendix I, Accord franco-algérien, 26 October 1968, AMAE 0034 SUP 123.

92. Massenet and his office were involved in repatriating ONAMO card holders who failed the medical test, rubber stamping even individual decisions. See AN 19930317 18. Massenet also asserted that the ONAMO testing was not thorough enough, leading to the involvement of the French ambassador to Algeria in the French Medical Missions. See "Procès-Verbal de la réunion interministérielle du 25 mars relative aux négociations franco-algériennes en matière de main d'œuvre," 25 March 1968, AMAE 0034 SUP 123.

93. Telegram, Basdevant to the Ministry of the Interior, 20 August 1969, AMAE 0034 SUP 122.

94. On the invisible labor of North African women, see Clancy-Smith, "A Woman without Her Distaff."

95. Anne Lippert, "Algerian Women's Access to Power: 1962–1985," 222, cited in Vince, *Our Fighting Sisters*, 124.

96. Bureau of Population and Migrations, "Note sur les problèmes posés par la politique de l'immigration," 23 November 1972, AN 20010399 art. 1.

97. Massenet, "Note pour le Ministre," 8 April 1965, AMAE 29 QO 92.

98. Bureau of Population and Migrations, "Note sur les problèmes posés par la politique de l'immigration."

99. Bureau of Population and Migrations, "Note sur les problèmes posés par la politique de l'immigration."

100. Accord franco-portugais de main d'œuvre, 31 December 1963, as described in Viet, *La France immigrée*, 270.

101. Viet, *La France immigrée*, 271.

102. "Protocole sur l'immigration et la situation sociale en France des travailleurs portugais et de leurs familles," 29 July 1971, as cited in Viet, *La France immigrée*, 272–73.

103. Viet, *La France immigrée*, 273.

104. Haddad to *El Moudjahid* as reported in a letter from the French ambassador to Algeria to Minister of Foreign Affairs Maurice Schumann, 8 June 1971, AMAE 0034 SUP 122.

105. Alain Girard, "Attitudes des français à l'égard de l'immigration étrangère," *Population* 26, no. 5 (1971): 850. The survey included 1,337 men and 1,356 women of

all different ages. On the threshold of tolerance, see also MacMaster, "'Seuil de Tolérance,'" 14–28.

106. Chin, *Crisis of Multiculturalism in Europe*, chap. 3.

107. Girard, "Attitudes des français à l'égard de l'immigration étrangère," 837.

108. For more on Girard's study and its context, see Nasiali, *Native to the Republic*, 99–106.

109. Marcellin-Fontanet circular no. 1/72, 23 February 1972. Note as well that there was an earlier Marcellin-Fontanet circular signed in January 1972. Workers from Tunisia and Morocco entered France through the National Immigration Office after both countries signed bilateral treaties with France in 1963.

110. Massenet to Fontanet, "Note à l'attention de M. le Ministre du Travail, de l'Emploi, et de la Population," 14 May 1971, AN 19950493 art. 6.

111. Massenet to Fontanet, "Note à l'attention de M. le Ministre du Travail," 14 May 1971.

112. Stora, *Algeria*, 153, See also P. C. Naylor, *France and Algeria*; Grimaud, *La politique extérieure en Algérie*.

113. Houari Boumediene as quoted in telegram from Soutou to Ministry of Foreign Affairs, 13 January 1973, AMAE 0034 SUP 122.

114. Boumediene as quoted in telegram from Soutou to Ministry of Foreign Affairs.

115. Note, Ministry of the Interior, 4 July 1973, AN 19960134 art. 13.

116. For more on the relationship between racism and Algerians in France, see Nasiali, *Native to the Republic*, chap. 4.

117. "L'avenir de nos relations avec la France repose sur le respect du citoyen algérien," *El Moudjahid*, 26 September 1973, 3 (emphasis added).

118. Catherine Gokalp, "Chronique de l'immigration: L'immigration étrangère en France en 1973," *Population* 29, no. 3 (Summer 1974): 903.

5. DISORDERLY FAMILIES

1. Women from Algeria were not always denied the medal. See Lamri, "Algériennes' et mères françaises exemplaires."

2. On the Medal of the French Family, see Stamler, "Decorating Mothers, Defining Maternity"; Roberts, *Civilization without Sexes*, 131–33; during Vichy, Pollard, *Reign of Virtue*, 11.

3. Mothers of families of eight or more grown children were eligible for the gold medal.

4. Tirloy, President of the Service Départemental de la Médaille de la Famille Française, to Ourdia A., 20 April 1971, Dossier no. 2366, Family A—, Archives départementales du Nord (hereafter Nord) 2229 W 22.

5. Dossier no. 2366, Family A—, Nord 2229 W 22.

6. Glorieux to Tirloy, 29 June 1971, Dossier no. 2366, Family A—, Nord 2229 W 22.

7. The application itself included an attestation about the mother's morality, a nebulous category through which foreign-born and working-class mothers could be found deficient.

8. On the state's biopolitics in the colonial and former colonial spheres, consider especially Vergès, *Wombs of Women*; on independent North Africa especially, see Johnson, "Contradictions of Sovereignty"; Johnson, "Origins of Family Planning." On the nexus of gender, Islam, race, and belonging, see Scott, *Politics of the Veil*.

9. On "Muslim" as a colonial legal signifier, see Shepard, *Invention of Decolonization*. On the conflation of Islam, race, and ethnicity, see Davidson, *Only Muslim*; more recently, Davis, *Markets of Civilization*.

10. On French immigration after empire, see especially Spire, *Étrangers à la carte*. On welfare funding and provisioning, see Lyons, "French or Foreign?"; E. Naylor, "'Une âne dans l'ascenseur'"; Harris, "Centre d'Accueil Nord-Africain"; Wadowiec, "Afterlives of Empire." On housing for Algerians in particular, see Muriel Cohen, *Des familles invisibles*.

11. I borrow from Muelhebach's formulation of the "moral neoliberal"; see Muelhebach, *Moral Neoliberal*, chap. 1.

12. Farge and Foucault, *Disorderly Families*, chap. 1.

13. As Hartman reminds historians, the act of excavating the experiences of the dispossessed requires examining the conditions by which they were dispossessed in the first place; see Hartman, "Venus in Two Acts," 12.

14. French Muslim was the category that usually included former harkis and their families as well as other colonial citizens who had offered support for French Algeria and were now claiming French citizenship. One did not have to have served French Algeria to claim French citizenship, but this was often the case.

15. This threat is attributed to Minister for Algerian Affairs Louis Joxe in Eldridge, *From Empire to Exile*, 25.

16. On harki integration, see chapter 4. See also Crapanzano, *The Harkis*; Miller, "Camp for Foreigners and 'Aliens.'" On the reception of harki soldiers and their families following the war, see especially Choi, *Decolonization and the French*, chap. 3; Eldridge, *From Empire to Exile*, chap. 2.

17. Dossier no. 2366, Family A—, Nord 2229 W 22.

18. Cécile Braquehais, "Note pour M. Trillat," 19 July 1964, Archives nationales de France—Pierrefitte-sur-Seine (hereafter AN) 19770393 art. 4.

19. Members of other religious communities migrating to France did *not* have to declare French citizenship. As Shepard has shown, Jews from Algeria became "Europeans" before the end of the Algerian War; see *Invention of Decolonization*, 169–73. On the liminal legal status of Mzab Jews of the south of Algeria, see Stein, *Saharan Jews*.

20. Shepard, *Invention of Decolonization*, 237.

21. "Conclusions du Groupe d'Étude chargé d'examiner la situation juridique des Algériens en France," 12 November 1963, AN 19760135 art. 2.

22. "Des problèmes posés par l'accueil, la prise en charge, et le reclassement des réfugiés musulmans algériens dans le département de la Seine," Préfecture de Police, 25 June 1963, AN 19770391 art. 9. According to the report, only 143 of the 1,834 harkis in the Seine had opted for French citizenship—around 7 percent.

23. For example, Nafissa Sid Cara, the Gaullist minister who served in the Fifth Republic during the war, was a "refugee" to France. She claimed French citizenship, yet she was also still referred to as a "French Muslim." This was another way in which citizenship failed to ensure belonging. On legal and unofficial terminology, see Lyons, "French or Foreign," 136.

24. "Rapport d'activité du SSFNA—Bureau de Lille," 1963, Nord 2585 W 1.

25. "SSFNA-Remarques sur l'action du SSFNA," 17 September 1965, AN 20120054 art. 95.

26. Augustin-Thierry, Report, Comité National pour les Musulmans Français, May 1966, AN 20120054 art. 5.

27. Case notes on Famille M—, Dossier no. 121, Nord 2229 W 2.

28. Madame M. had, at that point, given birth to three children, though her second child died in infancy in 1952.

29. Dossier no. 121, Famille M—.

30. Case notes on Famille M—, Dossier no. 121.

31. Handwritten case note, November 1967, Dossier no. 121, Famille M—.

32. On sexual equality, emancipation, and belonging, see Scott, "Vexed Relationship," 151–56.

33. See Rapports d'activités du SSFNA, Bureau de Lille, 1961, 1964, and 1968, Nord 2585 W 1. These numbers represent *new* cases only. In 1967, for example, the Lille office also managed 476 old cases. They estimated around 3,700 Algerian households in the region, including over 24,000 adult Algerian men, 3,880 women, and nearly 14,000 children. See "Activité du SSFNA dans le département du Nord durant l'année 1968," Nord 2585 W 1.

34. "Rapport d'activité du SSFNA, Bureau de Lille," 1963, Nord 2585 W 1.

35. "Rapport d'activité du SSFNA, Bureau de Lille," 1962, Nord 2585 W 1.

36. This is a nearly constant source of concern in internal memos and letters between the Nord offices and Paris. See especially Nord 2229 W 165.

37. I sampled 1 in 5 of the 2,700 dossiers in the SSFNA's archives in the Archives du Nord, Nord 2229 W 1 to 24. I calculated this data based on the date the dossier was created and last documented contact.

38. Racine to Revol, 18 June 1965, AN 19850021 art. 22.

39. "Rapport d'activité, Bureau de Lille," 1964, Nord 2585 W 1.

40. Farge and Foucault, *Disorderly Families*, 41.

41. Consider two perspectives on family migration and welfare in the interwar: Camiscioli, *Reproducing the French Race*; Barton, *Reproductive Citizens*. Both emphasize the centrality of the migrant family, at that point conceived of as southern or eastern European, to social benefits.

42. My analysis is indebted to Scott, *Only Paradoxes to Offer*; Scott, *Politics of the Veil*.

43. Arabic language training was part of the Franco-Algerian 1964 and 1968 accords, though only after Boumediene took lead of the government did the Algerian delegation press the French into offering more Arabic language courses.

44. "Rapport d'activité, Bureau de Lille," 1965, Nord 2585 W 1.

45. I viewed course materials, including lesson plans with patterns included in the private archives of Nelly Forget, viewed with her permission at her home.

46. On "cultural citizenship" as a term and a boundary to belonging, see Beaman, *Citizen Outsider*; Beaman, "Citizenship as Cultural." I use this term advisedly, however, because Beaman's analysis includes children of North African immigrants who *were* citizens of France, while I use cultural citizenship to imply the unwritten soft qualities of belonging that were part of integration regardless of the citizenship status of the client.

47. "Rapport Moral du SSFNA," 1968–69, appendix VI, Nord 2585 W 14.

48. According to a representative survey conducted in the National Institute for Health and Medical Research (INSERM) in 1970, less than half a percent of social workers were men. See "Enquête sur la profession d'assistant de service social," 1970, AN 19870527 art. 4.

49. Viane, "Réflexions et Conclusions après trois ans du Travail au SSFNA," 18 March 1969, Nord 2585 W 1.

50. SSFNA, "Rapport Moral," 1968–69, appendix VI, Nord 2585 W 14.

51. Viane, "Réflexions et Conclusions après trois ans du Travail au SSFNA."

52. Viane, "Réflexions et Conclusions après trois ans du Travail au SSFNA."

53. On the secular self and market logic as a strategy for ostracizing Muslims, see Scott, "Vexed Relationship," 163.

54. CLAP was formed in June 1966 in a meeting of thirty associations. It was registered in December 1967 and funded by the Social Action Fund. The Ile de France archives of CLAP are held at the departmental archives in Seine-Saint-Denis.

55. *Apprendre à lire et à écrire: Introduction à la relation parole/écriture: Matériel collectif*, n.d., Dossiers 2–6, Bibliothèque nationale de France—site François Mitterrand.

56. *Apprendre à lire et à écrire: Introduction à la relation parole/écriture*, n.d., Dossier 1, Bibliothèque nationale de France—site François Mitterrand.

57. *Apprendre à lire et à écrire: Introduction à la relation parole/écriture*, n.d., Dossier 3, Bibliothèque nationale de France—site François Mitterrand.

58. "Rapport d'activité du SSFNA, 1970–1971," Nord 2585 W 14.

59. "Rapport d'activité du SSFNA, 1970–1971."

60. "Rapport d'activité du ssfna, 1969–1970," an 19860399 art. 24.

61. Donzelot, *Policing of Families*, 103.

62. The ddass was created by Decree no. 64-783 of 30 July 1964, *Journal officiel de la République française*, 1 August 1964. The ddass subcontracted ssfna social workers to aid with resettlement applications as discussed in chapter 4.

63. Cécile Braquehais, "La réforme du service social des directions départementales de l'action sanitaire et sociale," *La Revue Française de Service Social* 94 (1972): 6.

64. Braquehais, "La réforme du service social des directions départementales de l'action sanitaire et sociale," 7.

65. "Rapport d'activité du ssfna, Bureau de Lille," 1971, Nord 2585 W 2.

66. "Réunion des Assistantes Sociales au Siège," 21–22 February 1972, Nord 2229 W 166.

67. "Rapport sur l'orientation du service, Bureau de Vienne," 27 July 1972, Nord 2229 W 166 (emphasis added).

68. "Réunion des Assistantes Sociales au Siège," 21–22 February 1972, Nord 2229 W 166.

69. Donzelot, *Policing of Families*, 96. While there were over seventy thousand licensed social workers in France in the early 1970s, the majority were employed by public offices and enjoyed greater benefits and higher salaries. These "polyvalent" social workers were not hired by specialized social aid associations for North Africans, which emphasized basic Arabic and internships within these associations during coursework.

70. "Planification familiale et sexualité–Compte-rendu de la réunion pédagogique," appendix IV, 27 May 1974, ssfna, Personal Papers, Nelly Forget.

71. ssfna, "Règlement intérieur," n.d., Nord 2585 W 215.

72. "Les Travailleuses familiales exerçant les fonctions de monitrices familiales à Roubaix," in "Rapport d'activité du ssfna," 1969–70, Nord 2585 W 14.

73. "Les Travailleuses familiales exerçant les fonctions de monitrices familiales à Roubaix."

74. Data from coursework reports compiled in Nord 2229 W 142.

75. Forget, "Réflexions sur les cours au ssfna," 22 February 1972, Nord 2229 W 166.

76. "Table ronde relative à l'ensemble des problèmes que pose actuellement l'Enseignement Ménager Familial," 22 April 1969, an 19770393 art. 2.

77. "Enquête sur les cours de femmes étrangères," *Alphabétisation et Promotion* 13 (April 1971): 3. This survey followed an earlier 1971 clap survey on the same topic with similar findings. For the questionnaire itself and a summary of results, see Génériques, amana 60.

78. "Enquête sur les cours de femmes étrangères," 5. By "self-sufficient," the survey meant that women wished to go shopping alone, to be able to accomplish administrative and bureaucratic tasks, to understand their doctors, and perhaps find work.

79. "Enquête sur les cours de femmes étrangères."
80. "Rapport d'activité du SSFNA," 1971–72, Nord 2585 W 14.
81. "Conflits familiaux liés à l'inadaptation et l'action éducative," in "Rapport d'activité du SSFNA," 1969–70, Nord 2585 W 14.
82. "Les adolescents: Essai statistique commenté dans la région parisienne," in "Rapport d'activité du SSFNA," 1969–70, Nord 2585 W 14.
83. "Les adolescents: Essai statistique commenté dans la région parisienne."
84. H. de Charette, "Note de Synthèse" Ministry of Labor, July 1973, AN 19950493 art. 6.
85. See chapter 4.
86. Board of Directors Meeting, "Programme d'action sanitaire et sociale du Fonds d'Action Sociale pour les travailleurs migrants pour l'année 1971," 22 December 1970, AN 19830245 2. For more on funding logic, see chapter 3.
87. Laurens, *Une politisation feutrée*, 121–22.
88. Dossier A—, no. 1186, Nord 2229 W 9.
89. See chapter 1; on the period after empire, see Vergès, *Wombs of Women*.
90. Detrez to A. Wolff, I.N.E.D., 27 November 1970, Nord 2229 W 165. For historical interpretations of white flight that foreground racism in the context of the United States, see Kruse, *White Flight*; Sugrue, *Origins of the Urban Crisis*.
91. Valabrègue, *L'homme déraciné*, 101. For Valabrègue's work on family planning, see *Contrôle des naissances et planning familial*. For context, see Barrusse, "Denatality Complex.'"

6. A NEW POLITICS OF IMMIGRATION

1. On the office as well as Mosaïque, see Laurens, "De la 'Promotion culturelle des immigrés,'" 29. On offices for cultural rapprochement and the end of empire, see Escafré-Dublet, *Culture et immigration*.
2. This initiative was originally known as the "Semaine des rencontres français-immigrés" under the previous secretary of state for immigrant workers, Paul Dijoud, and was reimagined by Stoléru in 1977.
3. The Institut national audiovisuel conserves the records of Mosaïque. This episode can be found through their online database, http://inatheque.ina.fr/doc/TV-RADIO/DA_VDC13002465/mosaique-emission-du-15-octobre-1978?rang=3 (accessed 26 May 2023). I initially viewed this episode digitally, though access is now restricted to media professionals through INA Médiapro.
4. The 1957 Treaty of Rome creating the European Economic Community granted freedom of movement to families from member countries of the EEC. In 1974 the EEC included the original six member countries (Belgium, France, West Germany, Italy, Luxembourg, and the Netherlands) as well as Denmark, Ireland, and the United Kingdom. Halting all immigration, as France did in 1974, violated this agreement, so members of the EEC were technically still allowed to cross

the border. Spain and Portugal, while not members, were granted exceptions. At the time Algerians significantly outnumbered other North African populations: there were about 270,000 Moroccans and just fewer than 150,000 Tunisians. In fact, annual Algerian immigration had dropped off even before Boumediene's freeze from a high point of 41,000 workers admitted in 1971 to 21,000 in 1973 (though this number only includes documented workers, not their families or people entering on tourist visas). See "Notes du Ministre du travail no. 27," 21–27 October 1974, Dossier 3, Archives nationales de France—Pierrefitte-sur-Seine (hereafter AN) 19990118 art. 12.

5. See Girard, "Attitudes des français," 850; or my analysis in chapter 5.

6. Léon Blum's Popular Front government originally created the office in 1938, and Giscard d'Estaing hoped to appeal to the left by calling back to this moment as he organized his new administration. See Weil, *La France et ses étrangers*, 108–9.

7. State officials for immigration had previously worked in the Ministry of Health or Social Affairs. After Social Affairs was divided in 1970 into Labor and Public Health and Social Security, most migration-related offices moved to Labor. On the end of the Ministry of Social Affairs, see Robcis, *Law of Kinship*, 144.

8. See, for example, Labour's approach to "race relations" in Great Britain in the 1965 and 1968 race relations bills as analyzed by Chin, *Crisis of Multiculturalism in Europe*, 88–93.

9. Postel-Vinay, "Communiqué concernant la politique de l'immigration," 4 July 1974, AN 19990118 art. 12. See also his note, "Politique de l'immigration" for the Conseil des Ministres, 1 July 1974, AN 19950493 art. 6.

10. Postel-Vinay's resignation letter is included in the appendixes to Weil, *La France et ses étrangers*, 527, in which Postel-Vinay makes clear that the social programming and worker/family housing that he was promised when he took the position would not be funded in their entirety, leading to his resignation.

11. On Giscard d'Estaing's logic for the freeze, see Weil, *La France et ses étrangers*, 112–16; Viet, *La France immigrée*, 358–68; both see this period as a "missed opportunity," in Weil's words.

12. Circulars of 5 and 9 July 1974, respectively. See AN 19880084 arts. 1, 2, and 3 on these decisions.

13. Weil, *La France et ses étrangers*, 115.

14. Chin, *Crisis of Multiculturalism in Europe*, 81. On the case of West Germany, see Stokes, *Fear of the Family*.

15. On relations with independent West African countries in the 1970s, see Mann, *From Empires to NGOs*, chap. 4.

16. Muriel Cohen uncovered internal memos and letters suggesting the goals of the suspension; see Cohen, *Des familles invisibles*, 332–33.

17. "Suspension de l'immigration et dérogations à cette mesure, lettre du ministère de l'Intérieur au préfet de l'Aube," 3 February 1975, AN 19990260 art. 1.

18. On the "management of multicultural societies," see Chin, *Crisis of Multiculturalism in Europe*, 91.

19. Dijoud, "Communication sur la condition des travailleurs immigrés et la politique de l'immigration," Conseil des Ministres, 9 October 1974, AN 19990118 art. 12.

20. Chin, *Crisis of Multiculturalism in Europe*, 114.

21. Weil, *La France et ses étrangers*, 131–34.

22. Compte rendu of first meeting of Doublet Commission, 13 January 1975, AN 19990260 art. 19, Dossier 4, available by extract.

23. "Rapport sur l'immigration familiale," Doublet Commission, n.d., 27, AN 19990260 art. 19, Dossier 4.

24. Muriel Cohen similarly interprets the Doublet Commission—"new commission, same ideas"—but does not compare it to the Tillion Commission; see *Des familles invisibles*, 335–39.

25. Compte rendu of Doublet Commission, 31 January 1975, AN 19990260 art. 19, Dossier 4.

26. "Note pour M. Le Directeur [Doublet] a/s group de travail immigration familiale," 10 March 1975, AN 19990260 art. 19, Dossier 4.

27. "Note de synthèse sur les propositions du group immigration familiale," n.d., AN 19990260 art. 19, Dossier 4.

28. Dijoud to Tillion, 10 January 1975, Génériques, AMANA 57.

29. SSFNA, "Rapport Moral, 1974–1975," AN 19870440 art. 52.

30. Tillion, *Republic of Cousins*.

31. On religion, religious difference, and sexual inequality, see Scott, *Sex and Secularism*. On the way French definitions set the basis for exclusion, see Fernando, *Republic Unsettled*.

32. "Les Femmes Immigrées," 1 July 1975, Génériques, AMANA 57. I also found a copy of this report in its entirety at the Centre des Archives du Féminisme 2 AF 176.

33. "Les Femmes Immigrées."

34. Theme III.2, "Les Femmes Immigrées."

35. Theme III, "Les Femmes Immigrées."

36. Theme VI, "Les Femmes Immigrées."

37. Scott, "Vexed Relationship," 164. Scott draws a further link between labor power and sexual power to explain the civilizational discourse that marginalizes Muslim immigrants in Europe.

38. Decree no. 76-383 of 29 April 1976 "relatif aux conditions d'entrée et de séjour en France des membres des familles des étrangers autorisés à résider en France," *Journal officiel de la République française* (hereafter JO), 1 May 1976.

39. Paul Dijoud as cited by Anicet Le Pors in "Conséquences de mesures concernant les travailleurs étrangers," Senate meeting, 8 November 1977, p. 2602, AN 20010399 art. 5. See the transcript of this entire remarkable exchange for the Communist critique of the family reunification policy as well.

40. According to Dijoud, Algerian families and families from Francophone Africa—apart from families from Gabon, Guinea, and Madagascar, now a part of the general immigration regime—were not authorized for family resettlement through the National Immigration Office. "Note d'information no. 1 réseau national d'accueil," 30 June 1975, AN 19990118 art. 1, Dossier 3.

41. Ministry of Labor, "Le nouveau régime de l'immigration des familles étrangères en France," 5 May 1976, AN 19990260 art. 19, Dossier 3.

42. Decree no. 76-383 of 29 April 1976 "relatif aux conditions d'entrée et de séjour en France des membres des familles des étrangers autorisés à résider en France," *JO*, 1 May 1976.

43. LeBon, "'La féminisation' de la main d'œuvre étrangère en France," Génériques, AMANA 57.

44. Under the new circular, in 1976 a total of 29,071 families from outside the EEC entered France, but only 2,584 were Algerians, or 8 percent of the entrances. This number went up only slightly the next year, to 10 percent of the 26,958 families admitted. Though Algerians had historically made up a majority of non-EEC migration, under this new circular their arrivals were limited. See "Immigration familiale: Éléments statistiques, 1976–1982," Ministère des Affaires Sociales et de la Solidarité Nationale, 30 August 1983, AN 19990260 art. 20.

45. LeBon, "'La féminisation' de la main d'œuvre étrangère en France." On the de-skilling of women's labor, see Downs, *Manufacturing Inequality*.

46. See especially Frader, *Breadwinners and Citizens*.

47. Data from INSEE, *Annuaire statistique de la France*, quoted in Riboud, "Analysis of Women's Labor Force Participation," 180. On women's roles in this shift, see also Fishman, *From Vichy to the Sexual Revolution*; Duchen, *Women's Rights and Women's Lives*.

48. Editorial, "Les Femmes immigrées et la formation," *Migrants Formation*, no. 14–15 (March 1976): 3. I consulted this journal at the Centre des Archives du Féminisme (hereafter CAF) 2 AF 176.

49. Claude du Granrut, Secrétaire Générale du Comité du Travail Féminin, "Les femmes immigrées et le travail professionnel," *Migrants Formation*, no. 14–15 (March 1976): 75.

50. Compare the Ministry of the Interior's numbers with statistics cited in Lebon's report, "La féminisation de la main d'œuvre étrangère en France," Génériques, AMANA 57. Lebon compares the percentage of women nationals active in the workforce to the overall active national population: 30 percent of Portuguese

women were active in the labor force in 1975 alongside 28.2 percent of Spanish women, 21.4 percent of women from the EEC, as well as 30.2 percent of Yugoslav women and only 8.1 percent of Tunisian women, 6.3 percent of Moroccan women, and 5.2 percent of Algerian women. The numbers are strikingly different, though the perception they created is the same: Algerian women were much less likely to be engaged in the workforce across these studies.

51. SSFNA Team, "En quinze ans, la migration des femmes maghrébines a changé de visage," *Migrants Formation*, no. 14–15 (March 1976): 10.

52. SSFNA Team, "En quinze ans, la migration des femmes maghrébines a changé de visage," 11.

53. SSFNA Team, "En quinze ans, la migration des femmes maghrébines a changé de visage," 12.

54. "L'activité des cours jumélés en E.S.F. et alphabétisation sur le secteur de Dunkerque en 1977–1978," ASSFAM-SSFNA Rapport d'activité, 1978–79, appendixes, AN 19890108 art. 96.

55. "L'activité des cours jumélés en E.S.F. et alphabétisation sur le secteur de Dunkerque en 1977–1978."

56. Jocelyne Streiff and Sossie Andizian, "Projet d'Étude: Des résistances des femmes immigrées à la formation," IDERIC, n.d., AN 19950493 art. 2.

57. Streiff and Andizian, "Projet d'Étude."

58. Isabelle Leonetti and Florence Lévy, "Modes d'insertion des femmes immigrées," *Migrations/Études* 11 (1978): 9. Conserved in CAF 2 AF 176.

59. For more analysis of Sayad's body of work, see Saada, "Abdelmalek Sayad."

60. Sayad, "Three Ages of Algerian Emigration," 45–48. See also Saada, "Abdelmalek Sayad," 37.

61. Sayad uses this language in "Exemplary Immigration," 78.

62. Nasiali, *Native to the Republic*, 101.

63. The new system was based on 1973 legislation that systematized social aid organizations' efforts to greet and process new migrants at ports of entry through the National Immigration Office. See Ministry of Labor circular no. 10-73, 30 May 1973.

64. "Réseau national pour l'accueil, l'information et l'orientation des travailleurs étrangers et des membres de leurs familles," 12 December 1975, Génériques, AMANA 14.

65. The Social Service for Aid to Emigrants (SSAE) is a different case. Since its creation, the SSAE geared its outreach to all emigrants in France. For more, see Chibrac, *Les pionnières du travail social*.

66. Fournier, Director of the Bureau for Population and Migrations, to the Director of the Social Action Fund, 24 February 1975, AN 1987044 art. 48.

67. Fournier to Director of the Social Action Fund, 24 February 1975.

68. Board of Directors, Social Action Fund Meeting, 3 October 1974, AN 19870258 art. 59.

69. Sabatier to Raymond, President of the FAS, 20 June 1974, AN 19870258 art. 59.

70. Stoléru to Monsieur le Préfet attesting to Convention signed 9 October 1978, letter from 2 January 1979, AN 20010310 art. 5.

71. Board of Directors Declaration, 4 April 1979, Archives départementales du Nord 2585 W 215. Announced in *JO*, 11 April 1979.

72. "Bilan, ESF," 1979–80, Vitry-sur-Seine, Archives départementales de Paris 3587 W 1.

73. According to his secretary of state for immigrant workers, Lionel Stoléru, Giscard d'Estaing lost in 1977 and 1978 because of voter dissatisfaction with his focus on social issues, such as abortion and women's equality. See Stoléru, *La France à deux vitesses*, 42.

74. Prime Minister Raymond Barre introduced *aide au retour* to the Parliament on 26 April 1977. Stoléru, the secretary of state for the condition of manual labor (the new secretary of state for migrant workers), outlined the original principles in a letter to departmental directors on 30 May 1977. See AN 19930417 art. 1.

75. Stoléru to Departmental Directors, Ministry of Labor, 30 May 1977, AN 19930417 art. 1.

76. Stoléru to Departmental Directors, 30 May 1977.

77. Viet, *La France immigrée*, 387.

78. Stoléru to Departmental Directors, Ministry of Labor, 18 July 1977, AN 199930417 art. 1.

79. Those who did not have ONAMO papers were in the country illegally and did not have the right to work in any case, making them targets for deportation (but not *aide au retour*).

80. "L'aide au retour des travailleurs étrangers," June 1979, AN 20010399 art. 8. Further, according to the report of the Bureau of Population and Migrations, Algerians made up 21 percent of foreigners in France compared to 22 percent who were Portuguese and 14.5 percent who were Spanish. The National Immigration Office processed the numbers of *aide au retour* recipients and paid out the stipends from the Social Action Fund.

81. "L'aide au retour des travailleurs étrangers," June 1979, AN 20010399 art. 8.

82. Memo from Ministère du Budget (Papon) to Prime Minister, 15 April 1980, AN 19930417 art. 8. This decision was not unilateral and was made with input from the Bureau of Population and Migrations and Stoléru.

83. Memo from Ministère du Budget to Prime Minister, 11 April 1980, AN 19930417 art. 8.

84. Viet, *La France immigrée*, 387.

85. "Immigration familiale: Réunion du 3 October 1977 chez le Directeur de la Population et des Migrations au Ministère du Travail," AN 19990260 art. 19, Dossier 1.

86. Anicet Le Pors to the Senate, "Consèquences de Mesures Concernant les Travailleurs Étrangers," Sénat, meeting of 8 November 1977, AN 20010399 art. 5.

87. "Conseil d'État Section de Contentieux: Requête et Mémoire Ampliatif," 4 November 1977, AN 19930417 art. 1.
88. GISTI, *Immigration familiale, fascicule 1.*
89. "L'accord franco-algérien du 18 septembre 1981: Historique de la négociation," AN 19930417 art. 9.
90. Viet, *La France immigrée*, 387.
91. Weil, *La France et ses étrangers*, 189.
92. Note for the Secretary General from the Ministry of Foreign Affairs, 9 October 1979, AN 19930417 art. 8.
93. Speech by Lionel Stoléru to the Council of Europe, "La politique française de l'immigration," 6–8 May 1980, AN 19930417 art. 1.

CODA

1. On Gutemberg and *cités de transit*, see Cohen and David, "Les cités de transit."
2. Transcript of interview with "Colette," "Des Cités-Ghetto," Fonds Monique Hervo, Institut d'Histoire du Temps Présent ARC 3019 11.
3. François Mitterrand, *La France au Pluriel*, 9, as cited in Silverstein, *Algeria in France*, 163.
4. Consider this quote: "C'est blesser un peuple au plus profond de lui-même que de l'atteindre dans sa culture et sa langue. Nous proclamons le droit à la différence." François Mitterrand quoted in Viet, *La France immigrée*, 417. Emile Chabal makes this point in *Divided Republic*, 190. For historical interpretations of *droit à la différence*, in addition to Chabal, see especially Escafré-Dublet, *Culture et immigration*, chap. 5.
5. Chabal, *Divided Republic*, 190.
6. Gérard Noiriel famously posited a French analogue in 1989 in *French Melting Pot*, though my findings here challenge his republican reading of French immigration policies.
7. The March for Equality and Against Racism was first known as the "Marche des Beurs." The protest began with thirty or so organizers in southern France and swelled to over one hundred thousand Maghrebi, French, and Maghrebi-French protesters in Paris months later in late 1983. Despite the movement's desire to transform the conversation about North Africans in France, French administrators continued to frame immigration as the root of social problems. One popular association that emerged through these movements, SOS Racisme, quickly became a de facto wing of the Socialist Party. The march's original organizers had demanded a "right to rights," but SOS Racisme narrowed the focus to settling issues with migrants' residency permits. The emergence of the far-right National Front also may have shaped Socialist ambivalence toward these grassroots movements. The National Front gave voice to racist and xenophobic argument that immigration

caused France's supposed social and racial degradation. Its popularity contributed as well to the Socialists' growing ambivalence toward the droit à la différence. On these movements, see Hajjat, *Wretched of France*; Gordon, *Immigrants and Intellectuals*.

8. Bell, *François Mitterrand*, 104–7.
9. For a new, differing interpretation on austerity, see Fulla, "Neoliberal Turn That Never Was."
10. Rosanvallon, *La crise de l'État-providence*.
11. Chappel, "Old Volk," 798.
12. Offner, *Sorting Out the Mixed Economy*, 280.
13. Sayad, "Exemplary Immigration," 74.
14. On the impossibility of integration, see Sayad, "Weight of Words," 222–23.

BIBLIOGRAPHY

ARCHIVES AND MANUSCRIPT MATERIALS

Archives départementales de Paris—Paris, France
  Fonds ASSFAM (special permission): 3587 W
Archives départementales du Nord—Lille, France (Nord)
  Fonds SSFNA du Nord (special permission): 2229 W, 2585 W
Archives du Ministère des Affaires Étrangères—La Courneuve, France (AMAE)
  Afrique du Nord: Algérie 0034SUP
  Sécretariat d'État chargé des affaires algériennes 260QO
  Service de Liaison avec l'Algérie 29QO
Archives nationales de France—Pierrefitte-sur-Seine, France (AN)
  Note that archives of the Fifth Republic are cataloged by year and in order of
    deposit rather than by ministry. This especially affects research on the Social
    Action Fund and Bureau of Population and Migrations, whose deposits are
    scattered across years.
  Abdelmalek Sayad 20150645
  Cecile Braquehais 19770393
  Charles de Gaulle 5AG
  Conseil National des Musulmans Français 20120054
  Direction de la Population et des Migrations
  Georges Mauco 577AP
  Nafissa Sid Cara 103AJ, 19830229
  SAMAS/SLPM FIa
  Social Action Fund (FAS)
Archives nationales d'outre-mer—Aix-en-Provence, France (ANOM)
  Cabinet Civil des Gouverneurs Généraux CAB
    14CAB Delouvrier
  Ministére d'État chargé des affaires algériennes 81F
  Sections administratives specialisées en Algérie SAS

Bibliothèque de Documentation Internationale Contemporaine—Nanterre, France
    Fonds Cimade F delta 2149 (special permission)
Bibliothèque Marguerite Durand—Paris, France
    Conseil National des Femmes Françaises CNFF
Bibliothèque nationale de France—site François Mitterrand—Tolbiac, Paris, France
    Fonds Comité de Liaison pour l'Alphabétisation et Promotion (CLAP)
Bibliothèque nationale de France—site Richelieu—Paris, France (BNF)
    Fonds Germaine Tillion (special permission)
Centre des Archives du Féminisme—Angers, France (CAF)
    Fonds Conseil National des Femmes Françaises
Génériques—Paris, France
    Fonds AMANA
Institut d'Histoire du Temps Présent—Paris, France (IHTP)
    Fonds Hélène Lienhardt ARC 2011
    Fonds Monique Hervo ARC 3019
Private Archives of Nelly Forget—Paris, France

PUBLISHED WORKS

Abi-Mershed, Osama. *Apostles of Modernity: Saint-Simonians and the Civilizing Mission in Algeria*. Stanford: Stanford University Press, 2010.

Adams, Geoffrey. *The Call of Conscience: French Protestant Responses to the Algerian War, 1954–1962*. Waterloo ON: Wilfrid Laurier University Press, 1998.

Ahmed, Leila. *A Quiet Revolution: The Veil's Resurgence, from the Middle East to America*. New Haven: Yale University Press, 2012.

———. *Women and Gender in Islam: Historical Roots of a Modern Debate*. New Haven: Yale University Press, 1993.

Allen, Theodore W. *The Invention of the White Race*. Vol. 1, *Racial Oppression and Social Control*. 2nd ed. New York: Verso, 2012.

Ambler, John S. *The French Welfare State: Surviving Social and Ideological Change*. New York: New York University Press, 1991.

Amrane, Djamila. *Les femmes algériennes dans la guerre*. Paris: Plon, 1991.

Amster, Ellen J. *Medicine and the Saints: Science, Islam, and the Colonial Encounter in Morocco, 1877–1956*. Austin: University of Texas Press, 2013.

Andersen, Margaret Cook. "The Office de la Famille Française: Familialism and the National Revolution in Morocco." *French Politics, Culture & Society* 34, no. 3 (Winter 2016): 44–62.

———. *Regeneration through Empire: French Pronatalists and Colonial Settlement in the Third Republic*. Lincoln: University of Nebraska Press, 2015.

Asad, Talal. *Formations of the Secular: Christianity, Islam, Modernity*. Stanford: Stanford University Press, 2003.

Asseraf, Arthur. "Weapons of Mass Representation: Algerians in the French Parliament, 1968–1962." In *Algeria Revisited: History, Culture and Identity*, edited by Rabah Aissaoui and Claire Eldridge, 79–96. London: Bloomsbury Academic, 2017.

Ath-Messaoud, Malek, and Alain Gillette. *L'immigration algérienne en France*. Paris: Editions Entente, 1976.

Auclert, Hubertine. *Les femmes arabes en Algérie*. Paris: Plon, 1900.

Bailkin, Jordanna. *The Afterlife of Empire*. Berkeley: University of California Press, 2012.

Balibar, Etienne. "Algeria, France: One Nation or Two?" In *Giving Ground: The Politics of Propinquity*, edited by Joan Copjec and Michael Sorkin. London: Verso, 1999.

———. *We, the People of Europe?: Reflections on Transnational Citizenship*. Translated by James Swenson. Princeton: Princeton University Press, 2004.

Ballantyne, Tony. *Entanglements of Empire: Missionaries, Maori, and the Question of the Body*. Durham NC: Duke University Press, 2014.

Bancel, Nicolas, Pascal Blanchard, and Françoise Vergès, eds. *La république coloniale*. Paris: Pluriel, 2006.

Barnett, Michael. *Empire of Humanity: A History of Humanitarianism*. Ithaca NY: Cornell University Press, 2011.

Barrusse, Virginie De Luca. "The 'Denatality Complex': The Demographic Argument in the Birth Control Debate in France, 1956–1967." *Population* 73, no. 1 (2018): 9–34.

Barton, Nimisha. "'French or Foreign, So Long as They Be Mothers': Immigrant Women, Welfare, and the Politics of Pronatalism in Interwar Paris." *Journal of Women's History* 28, no. 4 (2016): 66–88.

———. "Marrying into the Nation: Immigrant Bachelors, French Bureaucrats, and the Conjugal Politics of Naturalization in the Third Republic." *French Politics, Culture & Society* 34, no. 3 (2016): 23–43.

———. *Reproductive Citizens: Gender, Immigration, and the State in Modern France, 1880–1945*. Ithaca NY: Cornell University Press, 2020.

Beaman, Jean. "Are French People White? Towards an Understanding of Whiteness in Republican France." *Identities: Global Studies in Culture and Power* 26, no. 5 (2019): 546–62.

———. *Citizen Outsider: Children of North African Immigrants in France*. Oakland: University of California Press, 2017.

———. "Citizenship as Cultural: Towards a Theory of Cultural Citizenship." *Sociology Compass* 10, no. 10 (2016): 849–57.

Beaujon, Danielle. "Policing Colonial Migrants: The Brigade Nord-Africaine in Paris, 1923–1944." *French Historical Studies* 42, no. 4 (2019): 655–80.

Beauvoir, Simone, de. *The Ethics of Ambiguity*. New York: Citadel Press, 1948.

Bell, David S. *François Mitterrand: A Political Biography*. Cambridge: Polity Press, 2005.

Belmessous, Saliha. *Assimilation and Empire: Uniformity in French and British Colonies, 1541–1954*. Oxford: Oxford University Press, 2013.

Bennett-Coverley, Louise. "Colonisation in Reverse." In *Writing Black Britain, 1948–1998*, edited by James Procter, 16–17. Manchester: Manchester University Press, 2000.

Bennoune, Mahfoud. *The Making of Contemporary Algeria, 1830–1987*. Cambridge: Cambridge University Press, 1988.

Berman, Sheri. "Civil Society and the Collapse of the Weimar Republic." *World Politics* 49, no. 3 (1997): 401–29.

Betts, Raymond. *Assimilation and Association in French Colonial Theory, 1890–1914*. 2nd ed. Lincoln: University of Nebraska Press, 2005.

Blanc-Chaléard, Marie-Claude. *En finir avec les bidonvilles: Immigration et politique du logement dans la France des Trente Glorieuses*. Paris: Publications de la Sorbonne, 2016.

Blanc-Chaléard, Marie-Claude, and Pierre Milza. "Les Italiens à Paris depuis 1945." In *Le Paris des Étrangers depuis 1945*, edited by Antoine Marès and Pierre Milza. Paris: Editions Sorbonne, 1995.

Blanchard, Emmanuel. *Histoire de l'immigration algérienne en France*. Paris: La Découverte, 2018.

———. *La police parisienne et les Algériens (1944–1962)*. Paris: Editions Nouveau Monde, 2011.

Blanchard, Pascal, Nicolas Bancel, and Sandrine Lemaire, eds. *La fracture coloniale: La société française au prisme de l'héritage colonial*. Paris: Cahiers Libre, 2005.

Blum, Françoise. "Regards sur les mutations du travail social au XXe siècle." *Le Mouvement Social*, no. 199 (2002): 84–94.

Boittin, Jennifer Anne. *Colonial Metropolis: The Urban Grounds of Anti-Imperialism and Feminism in Interwar Paris*. Lincoln: University of Nebraska Press, 2010.

Borrmans, Maurice. *Statut personnel et famille au Maghreb de 1940 à nos jours*. Paris: Mouton, 1977.

Bourdieu, Pierre, and Abdelmalek Sayad. *Le déracinement: La crise de l'agriculture traditionnelle en Algérie*. Paris: Editions de Minuit, 1964.

Bowlan, Jeanne M. "Civilizing Gender Relations in Algeria: The Paradoxical Case of Marie Bugéja, 1919–39." In *Domesticating the Empire: Race, Gender, and Family Life in French and Dutch Colonialism*, edited by Julia Clancy-Smith and Frances Gouda, 175–92. Charlottesville: University Press of Virginia, 1998.

Branche, Raphaëlle. *La guerre d'Algérie: Une histoire apaisée?* Paris: Seuil, 2005.

———. *La torture et l'armée pendant la guerre d'Algérie*. Paris: Gallimard, 2011.

Brower, Benjamin. *A Desert Named Peace: The Violence of France's Empire in the Algerian Sahara, 1844–1902*. New York: Columbia University Press, 2009.

Brown, Megan. *The Seventh Member State: Algeria, France, and the European Community*. Cambridge MA: Harvard University Press, 2022.

Burgess, Greg. "The Demographers' Moment: Georges Mauco, Immigration, and Racial Selection in Liberation France, 1945–46." *French History and Civilization* 4 (2011): 167–77.

Burton, Antoinette. *After the Imperial Turn: Thinking with and through the Nation.* Durham NC: Duke University Press, 2005.

———. *Burdens of History: British Feminists, Indian Women, and Imperial Culture, 1865–1915.* Chapel Hill: University of North Carolina Press, 1994.

Byrnes, Melissa. "French Like Us?: Municipal Policies and North African Migrants in the Parisian *Banlieues*, 1945–1975." PhD diss., Georgetown University, 2008.

———. "Liberating the Land or Absorbing Community: Managing North African Migration and the Bidonvilles in Paris's Banlieues." *French Politics, Culture & Society* 31, no. 3 (Winter 2013): 1–20.

———. *Making Space: Neighbors, Officials, and North African Migrants in the Suburbs of Paris and Lyon.* Lincoln: University of Nebraska Press, 2024.

Cabanes, Bruno. *The Great War and the Origins of Humanitarianism, 1918–1924.* Cambridge: Cambridge University Press, 2014.

Cahill, Cathleen. *Federal Fathers and Mothers: A Social History of the United States Indian Service, 1869–1933.* Chapel Hill: University of North Carolina Press, 2011.

Camiscioli, Elisa. *Reproducing the French Race: Immigration, Intimacy, and Embodiment in the Early Twentieth Century.* Durham NC: Duke University Press, 2009.

Carby, Hazel. *Imperial Intimacies: A Tale of Two Islands.* New York: Verso, 2019.

Chabal, Emile. *A Divided Republic: Nation, State, and Citizenship in Contemporary France.* Cambridge: Cambridge University Press, 2015.

———. *France since the 1970s: History, Politics, and Memory in an Age of Uncertainty.* London: Bloomsbury Academic, 2015.

Chafer, Tony. *The End of Empire in French West Africa: France's Successful Decolonization.* London: Bloomsbury Academic, 2002.

Chapman, Herrick. *France's Long Reconstruction: In Search of the Modern Republic.* Cambridge MA: Harvard University Press, 2018.

Chappal, James. "Old Volk: Aging in 1950s Germany, East and West." *Journal of Modern History* 90, no. 4 (December 2018): 792–833.

Charrad, Mounira. *States and Women's Rights: The Making of Postcolonial Tunisia, Algeria, and Morocco.* Berkeley: University of California Press, 2001.

Chibrac, Lucienne. *Les pionnières du travail social auprès des étrangers: Le Service social d'aide aux émigrants, des origines à la Libération.* Rennes: Editions ENSP, 2005.

Childers, Kristin Stromberg. *Fathers, Families, and the State in Modern France, 1914–1945.* Ithaca NY: Cornell University Press, 2003.

———. *Seeking Imperialism's Embrace: National Identity, Decolonization, and Assimilation in the French Caribbean.* Oxford: Oxford University Press, 2016.

Chin, Rita. *The Crisis of Multiculturalism in Europe: A History.* Princeton NJ: Princeton University Press, 2017.

———. *The Guest Worker Question in Postwar Germany.* Cambridge: Cambridge University Press, 2009.

Choi, Sun Eun. *Decolonization and the French of Algeria: Bringing the Settler Colony Home*. London: Palgrave Macmillan, 2016.

Clancy-Smith, Julia. *Mediterraneans: North Africa and Europe in the Age of Migrations, 1800–1900*. Berkeley: University of California Press, 2010.

———. "A Woman without Her Distaff: Gender, Work, and Handicraft Production in Colonial North Africa." In *Social History of Women and Gender in the Modern Middle East*, edited by Margaret L. Meriwether and Judith E. Tucker. Boulder CO: Westview Press, 1999.

Clancy-Smith, Julia, and Frances Gouda, eds. *Domesticating the Empire: Race, Gender, and Family Life in French and Dutch Colonialism*. Charlottesville: University Press of Virginia, 1998.

Clift, Ben. "The Fifth Republic at Fifty: The Changing Face of French Politics and Political Economy." *Modern & Contemporary France* 16, no. 4 (2008): 383–98.

Cohen, Mathilde, and Sarah Mazouz. "Introduction: A White Republic? Whites and Whiteness in France." *French Politics, Culture & Society* 39, no. 2 (Summer 2021): 1–25.

Cohen, Muriel. *Des familles invisibles: Les Algériens de France entre intégrations et discriminations (1945–1985)*. Paris: Editions de la Sorbonne, 2020.

———. "Les circulations entre France et Algérie: Un nouveau regard sur les migrants (post)coloniaux (1945–1985)." *French Politics, Culture & Society* 34, no. 2 (2016): 78–100.

———. "Regroupement familial: L'exception algérienne, 1962–1976." *GISTI/Plein Droit* 95, no. 4 (2012): 19–22.

Cohen, Muriel, and Cédric David. "Les cités de transit: Le traitement urbain de la pauvreté à l'heure de la décolonisation." *Métropolitiques*, 29 February 2012. https://metropolitiques.eu/Les-cites-de-transit-le-traitement.html.

Cole, Joshua. *Lethal Provocation: The Constantine Murders and the Politics of French Algeria*. Ithaca NY: Cornell University Press, 2019.

———. *The Power of Large Numbers: Population, Politics, and Gender in Nineteenth-Century France*. Ithaca NY: Cornell University Press, 2000.

Conklin, Alice. *In the Museum of Man: Race, Anthropology, and Empire in France, 1850–1950*. Ithaca NY: Cornell University Press, 2013.

———. *Mission to Civilize: The Republican Idea of Empire in France and West Africa, 1895–1930*. Stanford: Stanford University Press, 1997.

Connelly, Matthew. *A Diplomatic Revolution: Algeria's Fight for Independence and the Origins of the Post–Cold War Era*. Oxford: Oxford University Press, 2003.

Cooper, Frederick. *Citizenship between Empire and Nation: Remaking France and Africa, 1945–1960*. Princeton: Princeton University Press, 2014.

———. *Colonialism in Question: Theory, Knowledge, History*. Berkeley: University of California Press, 2005.

Cooper, Frederick, and Ann Laura Stoler, eds. *Tensions of Empire: Colonial Cultures in a Bourgeois World*. Berkeley: University of California Press, 1997.

Cooper, Melinda. *Family Values: Between Neoliberalism and the New Social Conservatism.* New York: Zone Books, 2017.

Cornaton, Michel. *Les camps de regroupement de la guerre d'Algérie.* Paris: Harmattan, 1998.

Couette, Pierre. *Marie-Renée Chéné (1911–2000) pionnière de l'action sociale.* Pierre Couette, 2012.

Crapanzano, Vincent. *The Harkis: The Wound That Never Heals.* Chicago: University of Chicago Press, 2011.

Curtis, Sarah. *Civilizing Habits: Women Missionaries and the Revival of French Empire.* Oxford: Oxford University Press, 2010.

Darwin, John. *Unfinished Empire: The Global Expansion of Britain.* London: Bloomsbury, 2014.

Daughton, J. P. *A Divided Empire: Religion, Republicanism, and the Making of French Colonialism, 1880–1914.* Oxford: Oxford University Press, 2008.

———. *In the Forest of No Joy: The Congo-Océan Railroad and the Tragedy of French Colonialism.* New York: W. W. Norton, 2021.

Daughton, J. P., and Owen White, eds. *In God's Empire: French Missionaries in the Modern World.* Oxford: Oxford University Press, 2012.

Davidson, Naomi. *Only Muslim: Embodying Islam in Twentieth-Century France.* Ithaca NY: Cornell University Press, 2012.

Davis, Muriel Haleh. *Markets of Civilization: Islam and Racial Capitalism in Algeria.* Durham NC: Duke University Press, 2022.

de Grazia, Victoria. *How Fascism Ruled Women: Italy, 1922–1945.* Berkeley: University of California Press, 1993.

———. *Irresistible Empire: America's Advance through Twentieth-Century Europe.* Cambridge MA: Harvard University Press, 2005.

Déléry, Antoine. *Joseph Folliet: Parcours d'un militant catholique.* Paris: Cerf, 2003.

DeLey, Margo. "French Immigration Policy since May 1981." *International Migration Review* 17, no. 2 (Summer 1983): 196–211.

Denéchère, Yves. "Les 'enfants de Madame Massu': Œuvre sociale, politique, et citoyenneté pendant et après la guerre d'Algérie (1957–1980)." *Revue d'Histoire Moderne et Contemporaine* 64, no. 3 (July–September 2017): 125–50.

Desan, Suzanne. *The Family on Trial in Revolution France.* Berkeley: University of California Press, 2004.

Diebolt, Evelyne. *Les femmes dans l'action sanitaire, sociale et culturelle, 1901–2001: Les associations face aux institutions.* Paris: Femmes et Associations, 2001.

Donzelot, Jacques. *The Policing of Families.* Translated by Robert Hurley. New York: Pantheon Books, 1977.

Doré-Audibert, Andrée. *Des Françaises d'Algérie dans la guerre de liberation: Des oubliées de l'histoire.* Paris: Karthala, 1995.

Doublet, Jacques. "Réflexions sur dix années de legislation." In *Réflexion sur les presta-tions familiales: Dix années de fonctionnement*, edited by Jacques Doublet, Pierre Laroque, Emmanuel Rain, and Albert Sauvy. Paris: UNCAF, 1958.

Downs, Laura Lee. *Manufacturing Inequality: Gender Division in the French and British Metalworking Industries, 1914–1939*. Ithaca NY: Cornell University Press, 1995.

Dubois, Laurent. *Avengers of the New World: The Story of the Haitian Revolution*. Cambridge MA: Harvard University Press, 2005.

Duchen, Claire. *Feminism in France: From May '68 to Mitterrand*. New York: Routledge, 1986.

———. *Women's Rights and Women's Lives in France, 1944–1968*. New York: Routledge, 1994.

Duclert, Vincent, and Pierre Encrevé, eds. *Rapport sur les camps de regroupement et autres textes sur la guerre d'Algérie*. Paris: Mille et Une Nuits, 2003.

Durham, Brooke. "Une aventure sociale et humaine: The Service des Centres Sociaux in Algeria, 1955–1962." In *Education and Development in Colonial and Postcolonial Africa: Policies, Paradigms, and Entanglements, 1990s–1980s*, edited by Damiano Matasci, Miguel Bandeira Jerónimo, and Hugo Gonçalves Dores, 55–82. London: Palgrave Macmillan, 2020.

Dutton, Paul V. *Origins of the French Welfare State: The Struggle for Social Reform in France, 1914–1947*. Cambridge: Cambridge University Press, 2002.

Edwards, Kathryn M. *Contesting Indochina: French Remembrance between Decolonization and Cold War*. Berkeley: University of California Press, 2016.

Eichner, Carolyn J. *Feminism's Empire*. Ithaca NY: Cornell University Press, 2022.

———. "La Citoyenne in the World: Hubertine Auclert and Feminist Imperialism." *French Historical Studies* 32, no. 1 (Winter 2009): 63–84.

Eldridge, Claire. *From Empire to Exile: History and Memory within the Pied-Noir and Harki Communities, 1962–2012*. Manchester: Manchester University Press, 2016.

Escafré-Dublet, Angélique. "Aid, Activism, and the State in Post-War France: Amana, a Charity Organization for Colonial Migrants, 1945–1962." *Journal of Modern European History* 12, no. 2 (2014): 247–61.

———. *Culture et immigration: Immigration et politiques culturelles*. Paris: La documentation française, 2013.

Ewald, François, *The Birth of Solidarity: The History of the French Welfare State*. Translated by Timothy Scott Johnson. Durham NC: Duke University Press, 2020.

———. *L'État providence*. Paris: Grasset, 1986.

Fanon, Frantz. "Algeria Unveiled." In *A Dying Colonialism*, translated by Haakon Chevalier, 35–68. 1959. New York: Grove Press, 1965.

———. *Black Skin, White Masks*. Translated by Charles Lam Markmann. New York: Grove Press, 1967.

————. *Wretched of the Earth.* Translated by Richard Philcox. 1963. New York: Grove Press, 2004.

Farge, Arlette. *The Allure of the Archives.* Translated by Thomas Scott-Railton. New Haven CT: Yale University Press, 2015.

Farge, Arlette, and Michel Foucault. *Disorderly Families: Infamous Letters from the Bastille Archives.* Edited by Nancy Luxon. Translated by Thomas Scott-Railton. Minneapolis: University of Minnesota Press, 2016.

Fassin, Didier. *Humanitarian Reason: A Moral History of the Present.* Berkeley: University of California Press, 2012.

Fenet, P. A., and François Ewald, eds. *Naissance du Code Civil.* Paris: Flammarion, 1989.

Fernando, Mayanthi. *The Republic Unsettled: Muslim French and the Contradictions of Secularism.* Durham NC: Duke University Press, 2014.

Fishman, Sarah. *From Vichy to the Sexual Revolution: Gender and Family Life in Postwar France.* Oxford: Oxford University Press, 2017.

Folliet, Joseph. *Droit de Colonisation: Étude morale, sociale, et internationale.* Paris: Bloud & Gay, 1933.

Fontaine, Darcie. "After the Exodus: Catholics and the Formation of Postcolonial Identity in Algeria." *French Politics, Culture & Society* 33, no. 2 (Summer 2015): 97–118.

————. *Decolonizing Christianity: Religion and the End of Empire in France and Algeria.* Cambridge: Cambridge University Press, 2016.

Foster, Elizabeth. *Faith in Empire: Religion, Politics, and Colonial Rule in French Senegal, 1880–1940.* Stanford: Stanford University Press, 2013.

Foucault, Michel. *The Birth of Biopolitics; Lectures at the Collège de France, 1978–1979.* Translated by Graham Burchell. New York: Picador, 2010.

————. *Discipline & Punish: The Birth of the Prison.* Translated by Alan Sheridan. New York: Vintage, 1995.

————. *The History of Sexuality.* Vol. 1, *An Introduction.* Translated by Robert Hurley. New York: Vintage, 1990.

————. *Security, Territory, Population: Lectures at the Collège de France, 1977–1978.* Translated by Graham Burchell. New York: Picador, 2009.

————. *"Society Must Be Defended": Lecture at the Collège de France, 1975–1976.* Translated by David Macey. New York: Picador, 2003.

Fourastié, Jean. *Les Trente Glorieuses ou la révolution invisible de 1946 à 1975.* Paris: Fayard, 1979.

Frader, Laura Levine. *Breadwinners and Citizens: Gender in the Making of the French Social Model.* Durham NC: Duke University Press, 2008.

————. "French History: Old Paradigms, Current Tendencies, New Directions." *French Politics, Culture & Society* 32, no. 2 (Summer 2014): 21–33.

Frader, Laura Levine, and Herrick Chapman, eds. *Race in France: Interdisciplinary Perspectives on the Politics of Difference*. New York: Berghahn Books, 2004.

Frader, Laura Levine, and Sonya O. Rose, eds. *Gender and Class in Modern Europe*. Ithaca NY: Cornell University Press, 1996.

Franklin, Elise. "A Bridge across the Mediterranean: Nafissa Sid Cara and the Politics of Emancipation during the Algerian War." *French Politics, Culture & Society* 36, no. 2 (Summer 2018): 28–52.

———. "Defining Family, Delimiting Belonging: Algerian Migration after the End of Empire." *Gender & History* 31, no. 3 (2019): 681–98.

Frey, Marc, and Jost Dulferr, eds. *Elites and Decolonization in the Twentieth Century*. London: Palgrave Macmillan, 2011.

Fuchs, Rachel. *Contested Paternity: Constructing Families in Modern France*. Baltimore: Johns Hopkins University Press, 2008.

Fulla, Mathieu. "The Neoliberal Turn That Never Was: Breaking with the Standard Narrative of Mitterrand's *tournant de la rigueur*." *Contemporary European History* 32, no. 1 (2023): 1–22.

Garavini, Giuliano. *After Empires: European Integration, Decolonization, and the Challenge from the Global South*. Oxford: Oxford University Press, 2012.

Genty, Jean-René. *L'immigration algérienne dans le Nord/Pas-de-Calais, 1909–1962*. Paris: Harmattan, 1999.

Germain, Félix. *Decolonizing the Republic: African and Caribbean Migrants in Postwar Paris, 1946–1974*. East Lansing: Michigan State University Press, 2016.

Girard, Alain. "Attitudes des français à l'égard de l'immigration étrangère." *Population* 26, no. 5 (1971): 827–75.

GISTI. *Immigration familiale, fascicule 1, Evolution de l'immigration familiale et grandes lignes de la réglementation actuelle*. Paris: CIEMM, 1979.

Gordon, Daniel. *Immigrants and Intellectuals: May '68 and the Rise of Anti-Racism in France*. Pontypool, UK: Merlin Press, 2012.

Green, Maia. *The Development State: Aid, Culture, and Civil Society in Tanzania*. Woodbridge, UK: James Currey, 2014.

Green, Nancy L. "French History and the Transnational Turn." *French Historical Studies* 37, no. 4 (2014): 551–64.

Grimaud, Nicole. *La politique extérieure en Algérie,1962–1978*. Paris: Karthala, 1984.

Guerrand, Roger-Henri, and Marie-Antoinette Rupp. *Brève histoire du service social en France: 1896–1976*. Toulouse: Privat, 1978.

Gutman, Amy, ed. *Democracy and the Welfare State*. Princeton: Princeton University Press, 1988.

Hajjat, Abdellali. *La Marche pour l'égalité et contre le racisme*. Paris: Editions Amsterdam, 2013.

———. *The Wretched of France: The 1983 March for Equality and Against Racism.* Translated by Andrew Brown. Bloomington: Indiana University Press, 2022.

Hall, Stuart. "Race—The Sliding Signifier." In Hall, *The Fateful Triangle: Race, Ethnicity, Nation,* edited by Kobena Mercer, 31–79. Cambridge MA: Harvard University Press, 2017.

Handler, Joel. *Social Citizenship and Workfare in the United States and Western Europe: The Paradox of Inclusion.* Cambridge: Cambridge University Press, 2004.

Hargreaves, Alec. *Multi-Ethnic France: Immigration, Politics, Culture, and Society.* 2nd ed. New York: Routledge, 2007.

Harris, Dustin Alan. "A Capital of Hope and Disappointments: North African Families in Marseille Shantytowns and Social Housing." *French Politics, Culture & Society* 40, no. 1 (Spring 2022): 48–82.

———. "The Centre d'Accueil Nord-Africain: Social Welfare and the 'Problem' of Muslim Youth in Marseille, 1950–1975." *French History* 33, no. 3 (2019): 444–70.

———. "Maghrebis in Marseille: North African Immigration and French Social Welfare in the Late Colonial and Postcolonial Eras." PhD diss., University of Toronto, 2018.

Hartman, Saidiya. "Venus in Two Acts." *Small Axe* 12, no. 2 (June 2008): 1–14.

Harvey, David. *A Brief History of Neoliberalism.* Oxford: Oxford University Press, 2007.

Hayward, Jack, ed. *From de Gaulle to Mitterrand: Presidential Power in France.* New York: New York University Press, 1993.

Hegel, G. W. F. *Hegel's Philosophy of Right.* Translated by S. W. Dyde. London: George Bell and Sons, 1896.

Hendrickson, Burleigh. *Decolonizing 1968: Transnational Student Activism in Tunis, Paris, and Dakar.* Ithaca NY: Cornell University Press, 2022.

———. "From the Archives to the Streets: Listening to the Global 1960s in the Former French Empire." *French Historical Studies* 40, no. 2 (2017): 319–42.

Hervo, Monique. *Chroniques du bidonville.* Paris: Seuil, 2001.

Heuer, Jennifer Ngaire. *The Family and the Nation: Gender and Citizenship in Revolutionary France, 1789–1830.* Ithaca NY: Cornell University Press, 2007.

Hmed, Choukri. "Loger les étrangers 'isolés' en France: Socio-histoire d'une institution d'État: La Sonacotra (1956–2006)." PhD diss., Sorbonne, 2006.

Hobsbawm, Eric. *The Age of Extremes: A History of the World, 1914–1991.* London: Vintage, 1996.

Horne, Alistair. *A Savage War of Peace: Algeria, 1954–1962.* New York: New York Review of Books, 2006.

Horne, Janet R. *A Social Laboratory for Modern France: The Musée Social & the Rise of the Welfare State.* Durham NC: Duke University Press, 2002.

House, Jim, and Neil MacMaster. *Paris 1961: Algerians, State Terror, and Memory.* Oxford: Oxford University Press, 2006.

Hurston, Zora. *Their Eyes Were Watching God.* Urbana: University of Illinois Press, 1991.

Jennings, Eric. *Vichy in the Tropics: Pétain's National Revolution in Madagascar, Guadeloupe, and Indochina, 1940–1944.* Stanford: Stanford University Press, 1998.

Jobs, Richard. *Riding the New Wave: Youth and the Rejuvenation after the Second World War.* Stanford: Stanford University Press, 2007.

Johnson, Jennifer. *The Battle for Algeria: Sovereignty, Health Care, and Humanitarianism.* Philadelphia: University of Pennsylvania Press, 2016.

———. "Contradictions of Sovereignty: Development, Family Planning, and the Struggle for Population Control in Postcolonial Morocco." *Humanity: An International Journal of Human Rights, Humanitarianism, and Development* 11, no. 3 (Winter 2020): 259–79.

———. "The Origins of Family Planning in Tunisia: Reform, Public Health, and International Aid." *Bulletin of the History of Medicine* 92, no. 4 (Winter 2018): 664–93.

Johnston-White, Rachel. "The Christian Anti-Torture Movement and the Politics of Conscience in France." *Past & Present* 257, no. 1 (2021): 318–42.

Jordi, Jean-Jacques, and Mohand Hamoumou. *Les harkis: Une mémoire enfouie.* 2nd ed. Paris: Editions Autrement, 2008.

Judt, Tony. *Postwar: A History of Europe since 1945.* New York: Penguin Books, 2006.

Katz, Ethan. *Burdens of Brotherhood: Jews and Muslims from North Africa to France.* Cambridge MA: Harvard University Press, 2015.

Kellou, Dorothée. "A Microhistory of the Forced Resettlement of the Algerian Muslim Population during the Algerian War of Independence (1954–1962): Mansourah, Kabylia." Master's thesis, Georgetown University, 2012.

Kimble, Sara L. "Emancipation through Secularization: French Feminist Views of Muslim Women's Condition in Interwar Algeria." *French Colonial History* 7 (2006): 609–41.

Koonz, Claudia. *Mothers in the Fatherland: Women, the Family, and Nazi Politics.* London: St. Martin's Griffin, 1988.

Koven, Seth, and Sonya Michel. "Womanly Duties: Maternalist Politics and the Origins of Welfare States in France, Germany, Great Britain, and the United States, 1880–1920." *American Historical Review* 95, no. 4 (1990): 1076–108.

Kozakowski, Michael. "From the Mediterranean to Europe: Migrants, the World of Work, and the Transformation of the French Mediterranean, 1945–1974." PhD diss., University of Chicago, 2014.

Kruse, Kevin. *White Flight: Atlanta and the Making of Modern Conservatism.* Princeton: Princeton University Press, 2005.

Kuby, Emma. *Political Survivors: The Resistance, the Cold War, and the Fight against Concentration Camps after 1945.* Ithaca NY: Cornell University Press, 2019.

Kunzel, Regina. *Fallen Women, Problem Girls: Unmarried Mothers and the Professionalization of Social Work, 1890–1945.* New Haven: Yale University Press, 1993.

Lamri, Sophie. "Algériennes' et mères Françaises exemplaires (1945–1962)." *Le Mouvement Social* 199 (2002): 61–81.

Laurens, Sylvain. "De la 'Promotion culturelle des immigrés' à 'l'interculturel' (1974–1980): Discours d'État sur une catégorie d'État." *Cultures et Conflits* 107 (Fall 2017): 15–41.

———. *Une politisation feutrée: Les hauts fonctionnaires et l'immigration en France (1962–1981).* Paris: Belin, 2009.

Lazreg, Marnia. *The Eloquence of Silence: Algerian Women in Question.* New York: Routledge, 1994.

———. *Torture and the Twilight of Empire: From Algiers to Baghdad.* Princeton: Princeton University Press, 2007.

Lebovics, Herman. *True France: The Wars over Cultural Identity, 1940–1945.* Ithaca NY: Cornell University Press, 1994.

Lefebvre, Henri. *The Production of Space.* Translated by Donald Nicholson-Smith. 1974. Oxford: Blackwell, 1991.

Legg, Charlotte Ann. *The New White Race: Settler Colonialism and the Press in French Algeria, 1860–1914.* Lincoln: University of Nebraska Press, 2021.

LeSueur, James. *Uncivil War: Intellectuals and Identity Politics during the Decolonization of Algeria.* 2nd ed. Lincoln: University of Nebraska Press, 2005.

Levy, Jonah D. "From the Dirigiste State to the Social Anaesthesia State: French Economic Policy in the *Longue Durée.*" *Modern & Contemporary France* 16, no. 4 (2008): 417–35.

Lewis, Gail. *"Race," Gender, and Social Welfare: Encounters in a Postcolonial Society.* London: Polity Press, 2000.

Lewis, Mary Dewhurst. *Boundaries of the Republic: Migrant Rights and the Limits of Universalism in France.* Stanford: Stanford University Press, 2007.

———. *Divided Rule: Sovereignty and Empire in French Tunisia, 1881–1938.* Berkeley: University of California Press, 2013.

———. "Legacies of French Slave-Ownership, or the Long Decolonization of Saint-Domingue." *History Workshop Journal* 83, no. 1 (April 2017): 151–75.

Lipsky, Michael. *Street-Level Bureaucracy: The Dilemmas of the Individual in Public Services.* New York: Russell Sage Foundation, 1980.

Lorcin, Patricia. *Imperial Identities: Stereotyping, Prejudice, and Race in Colonial Algeria.* 2nd ed. Lincoln: University of Nebraska Press, 2014.

Lorcin, Patricia, and Todd Shepard, eds. *French Mediterraneans: Transnational and Imperial Histories.* Lincoln: University of Nebraska Press, 2016.

Lyons, Amelia. *The Civilizing Mission in the Metropole: Algerian Families and the French Welfare State during Decolonization.* Stanford: Stanford University Press, 2013.

———. "French or Foreign? The Algerian Migrants' Status at the End of Empire (1962–1968)." *Journal of Modern European History* 12, no. 1 (2014): 126–45.

———. "Invisible Immigrants: Algerian Families and the French Welfare State in the Era of Decolonization." PhD diss., University of California, Irvine, 2004.

———. "Social Welfare, French Muslims, and Decolonization in France: The Case of the Fonds d'action sociale." *Patterns of Prejudice* 43, no. 1 (February 2009): 65–89.

MacMaster, Neil. *Burning the Veil: The Algerian War and the "Emancipation" of Muslim Women, 1954–1962*. Manchester: Manchester University Press, 2012.

———. *Colonial Migrants and Racism: Algerians in France, 1900–1962*. New York: St. Martin's Press, 1997.

———. "The 'Seuil de Tolérance': The Uses of a 'Scientific' Racist Concept." In *Race, Discourse, and Power in France*, edited by Maxim Silverman. Aldershot, UK: Avebury, 1991.

Mahmood, Saba. *Politics of Piety: The Islamic Revival and the Feminist Subject*. Princeton: Princeton University Press, 2011.

Mann, Gregory. *From Empires to NGOs in the West African Sahel: The Road to Nongovernmentality*. Cambridge: Cambridge University Press, 2014.

Marker, Emily. *Black France, White Europe*. Ithaca NY: Cornell University Press, 2022.

———. "Obscuring Race: Franco-African Conversations about Colonial Reform and Racism after World War II and the Making of 'Colorblind' France, 1945–1950." *French Politics, Culture & Society* 33, no. 3 (Winter 2015): 1–23.

Markovitz, I. L., ed. *Studies in Power and Class in Africa*. New York: Oxford University Press, 1987.

Marshall, T. H. *Citizenship and Social Class, and Other Essays*. Cambridge: Cambridge University Press, 1950.

Massenet, Michel. *L'angoisse au pouvoir*. Paris: Plon, 1959.

———. *Sauvage Immigration*. Paris: Editions du Rocher, 1994.

Math, Antoine. "Les allocations familiales et l'Algérie coloniale: À l'origine du FAS et de son financement par les régimes de prestations familiales." *Revue des politiques sociales et familiales* 53 (1998): 35–44.

Mayer, Ann Elizabeth. "Reform of Personal Status Laws in North Africa: A Problem of Islamic or Mediterranean Laws." *Middle East Journal* 49, no. 3 (Summer 1995): 432–46.

Maynard-Moody, Steven, and Michael C. Musheno. *Cops, Teachers, Counselors: Stories from the Front Lines of Public Service*. Ann Arbor: University of Michigan Press, 2003.

Mazower, Mark. *Dark Continent: Europe's Twentieth Century*. London: Vintage, 2000.

———. *Governing the World: The History of an Idea, 1815 to the Present*. New York: Penguin Books, 2012.

———. *No Enchanted Palace: The End of Empire and the Ideological Origins of the United Nations*. Princeton NJ: Princeton University Press, 2009.

McDougall, James. *A History of Algeria*. Cambridge: Cambridge University Press, 2017.

Merle, Robert. *Ahmed Ben Bella*. Paris: Gallimard, 1965.

Miller, Jeannette E. "A Camp for Foreigners and 'Aliens': The Harkis' Exile at the Rivesaltes Camp (1962–1964)." *French Politics, Culture & Society* 31, no. 3 (2013): 21–44.

Mittelstadt, Jennifer. *From Welfare to Workfare: The Unintended Consequences of Liberal Reform, 1945–1965*. Chapel Hill: University of North Carolina Press, 2005.

Mortimer, Robert A. "Algerian Foreign Policy: From Revolution to National Interest." *Journal of North African Studies* 20, no. 3 (2015): 466–82.

Muehlebach, Andrea. *The Moral Neoliberal: Welfare and Citizenship in Italy*. Chicago: University of Chicago Press, 2012.

Murray-Miller, Gavin. "Imagining the Trans-Mediterranean Republic: Algeria, Republicanism, and the Ideological Origins of the French Imperial Nation-State, 1848–1870." *French Historical Studies* 37, no. 2 (2014): 303–30.

Nasiali, Minayo. *Native to the Republic: Empire, Social Citizenship, and Everyday Life in Marseille since 1945*. Ithaca NY: Cornell University Press, 2016.

———. "Native to the Republic: Negotiating Citizenship and Social Welfare in Marseille 'Immigrant' Neighborhoods since 1945." PhD diss., University of Michigan, 2010.

———. "Ordering the Disorderly Slum: 'Standardizing' Quality of Life in Marseille Tenements and Bidonvilles, 1953–1962." *Journal of Urban History* 38, no. 6 (November 2012): 1021–35.

Naylor, Ed. *France's Modernising Mission: Citizenship, Welfare, and the Ends of Empire*. London: Palgrave Macmillan, 2019.

———. "'Une âne dans l'ascenseur': Late Colonial Welfare Services and Social Housing in Marseille after Decolonization." *French History* 27, no. 3 (2013): 422–47.

Naylor, Philip C. *France and Algeria: A History of Decolonization and Transformation*. Gainesville: University Press of Florida, 2000.

Noiriel, Gérard. *État, nation, et immigration: Vers une histoire du pouvoir*. Paris: Gallimard, 2001.

———. *The French Melting Pot: Immigration, Citizenship, and National Identity*. 2nd ed. Translated by Geoffroy de Laforcade. Minneapolis: University of Minnesota Press, 1996.

Nord, Philip G. *France's New Deal: From the Thirties to the Postwar Era*. Princeton: Princeton University Press, 2012.

———. "The Welfare State in France, 1870–1914." *French Historical Studies* 18, no. 3 (1994): 821–38.

Offner, Amy. *Sorting Out the Mixed Economy: The Rise and Fall of Welfare and Developmental States in the Americas*. Princeton: Princeton University Press, 2019.

Orloff, Ann Shola. "Gender and the Social Rights of Citizenship: The Comparative Analysis of Gender Relations and Welfare States." *American Sociological Review* 58, no. 3 (1993): 303–28.

Ottaway, David, and Marina Ottaway. *Algeria: The Politics of a Socialist Revolution.* Berkeley: University of California Press, 1970.

Palier, Bruno. "Les transformations du modèle social français hérité de l'après-guerre." *Modern & Contemporary France* 16, no. 4 (2008): 437–50.

Pandey, Gyanendra. *Routine Violence: Nations, Fragments, Histories.* Stanford: Stanford University Press, 2005.

Pattieu, Sylvain. "BUMIDOM 1963–82: Organizing Overseas Migrations to the Metropole, Actions and Contradictions." Translated by Tyler Stovall. In *The Black Populations of France: Histories from Metropole to Colony,* edited by Sylvain Pattieu, Emmanuelle Sibeud, and Tyler Stovall, 123–38. Lincoln: University of Nebraska Press, 2021.

Peabody, Sue, and Tyler Stovall, eds. *The Color of Liberty: Histories of Race in France.* Durham NC: Duke University Press, 2003.

Pedersen, Susan. *Family, Dependence, and the Origins of the Welfare State: Britain and France, 1914–1945.* Cambridge: Cambridge University Press, 1993.

Peterson, Terrence. "Counterinsurgent Bodies: Social Welfare and Psychological Warfare in French Algeria, 1956–1961." PhD diss., University of Wisconsin–Madison, 2015.

———. "Think Global, Fight Local: Recontextualizing the French Army in Algeria, 1954–1962." *French Politics, Culture & Society* 38, no. 2 (Summer 2020): 56–79.

Planche, Jean-Louis. *Sétif 1945: Chronique d'un massacre annoncé.* Paris: Perrin, 2006.

Pollard, Miranda. *Reign of Virtue: Mobilizing Gender in Vichy France.* Chicago: University of Chicago Press, 1998.

Ponty, Janine. "Une intégration difficile: Les polonaises en France dans le premier vingtième siècle." *Vingtième Siècle. Revue d'histoire,* no. 7 (July–September 1985): 51–58.

Prakash, Amit. *Empire on the Seine: The Policing of North Africans in Paris, 1925–1975.* Oxford: Oxford University Press, 2022.

Prochaska, David. *Making Algeria French: Colonialism in Bône, 1870–1920.* Cambridge: Cambridge University Press, 1990.

Prost, Antoine. "L'évolution de la politique familiale en France de 1938 à 1981." *Mouvement Social* 129 (1984): 101–9.

Pulju, Rebecca J. *Women and Mass Consumer Society in Postwar France.* Cambridge: Cambridge University Press, 2011.

Rabinow, Paul. *French Modern: Norms and Forms of the Social Environment.* Chicago: University of Chicago Press, 1989.

Rahal, Malika. *Algérie 1962: Une histoire populaire.* Paris: La Découverte, 2022.

Rater-Garcette, Christine. *La professionalisation du travail social: Action sociale, syndicalism, formation (1880–1920).* Paris: Harmattan, 1998.

Reid, Donald. "The Worlds of Frantz Fanon's 'l'Algérie se dévoile.'" *French Studies* 61, no. 4 (2007): 460–75.

Riboud, Michelle. "An Analysis of Women's Labor Force Participation in France: Cross-Section Estimates and Time-Series Evidence." *Journal of Labor Economics* 3, no. 1 (1985): S177–S200.

Robcis, Camille. *Disalienation: Politics, Philosophy, and Radical Psychiatry in Postwar France.* Chicago: University of Chicago Press, 2021.

———. *The Law of Kinship: Anthropology, Psychoanalysis and the Family in France.* Ithaca NY: Cornell University Press, 2013.

Roberts, Mary Louise. *Civilization without Sexes: Reconstructing Gender in Postwar France, 1917–1927.* Chicago: University of Chicago Press, 1994.

Roediger, David R. *The Wages of Whiteness: Race and the Making of the American Working Class.* 1991. 3rd ed., New York: Verso Books, 2007.

Rogers, Rebecca. *A Frenchwoman's Imperial Story: Madame Luce in Nineteenth-Century Algeria.* Stanford: Stanford University Press, 2013.

Rosanvallon, Pierre. *The Demands of Liberty: Civil Society in France since the Revolution.* Translated by Arthur Goldhammer. Cambridge MA: Harvard University Press, 2007.

———. *La crise de l'État-providence.* Paris: Seuil, 1981.

———. *La démocratie inachevée: Histoire de la souveraineté du peuple en France.* Paris: Gallimard, 2003.

———. *Le peuple introuvable: Histoire de la représentation démocratique en France.* Paris: Gallimard, 2002.

———. *Le sacre du citoyen: Histoire du suffrage universel en France.* Paris: Gallimard, 2001.

———. *The New Social Question: Rethinking the Welfare State.* Translated by Barbara Harshaw. Princeton: Princeton University Press, 2000.

Rosenberg, Clifford. *Policing Paris: The Origins of Modern Immigration Control between the Wars.* Ithaca NY: Cornell University Press, 2006.

Rosental, Paul-André. *L'intelligence démographique: Sciences et politiques des populations en France (1930–1960).* Paris: Odile Jacob, 2003.

Ross, Kristin. *Fast Cars, Clean Bodies: Decolonization and the Reordering of French Culture.* Cambridge MA: MIT Press, 1996.

Rowe, Mike. "Going Back to the Street: Revisiting Lipsky's *Street-Level Bureaucracy.*" *Teaching Public Administration* 30, no. 1 (March 2012): 10–18.

Rudolph, Nicole. *At Home in Postwar France: Modern Mass Housing and the Right to Comfort.* New York: Berghahn Books, 2015.

Ruedy, John. *Modern Algeria: The Origins and Development of a Nation.* Bloomington: Indiana University Press, 1992.

Saada, Emmanuelle. "Abdelmalek Sayad and the Double Absence: Toward a Total Sociology of Immigration." *French Politics, Culture & Society* 18, no. 1 (Spring 2000): 28–47.

———. *Empire's Children: Race, Filiation and Citizenship in the French Colonies.* Translated by Arthur Goldhammer. Chicago: University of Chicago Press, 2012.

Sacriste, Fabien. *Germaine Tillion, Jacques Berque, Jean Servier et Pierre Bourdieu: Des ethnologues dans la guerre d'indépendance algérienne.* Paris: Harmattan, 2011.

Saïdi, Hédi. *Mémoire de l'immigration et histoire coloniale.* Paris: Harmattan, 2007.

Salah, Ali. *La communauté algérienne dans le Département du Nord.* Lille: Université de Lille, 1973.

Sambron, Diane. *Femmes musulmanes: Guerre d'Algérie, 1954–1962.* Collection Mémoires Histoire. Paris: Editions Autrement, 2007.

Sayad, Abdelmalek. "An Exemplary Immigration." In Sayad, *Suffering of the Immigrant,* 63–87.

———. *Immigration ou les paradoxes de l'altérité: La fabrication des identités culturelles.* Paris: Raisons d'Agir, 2014.

———. *The Suffering of the Immigrant.* Translated by David Macey. Cambridge: Polity Press, 2004.

———. "The Three Ages of Algerian Emigration." In Sayad, *Suffering of the Immigrant,* 28–62.

———. "The Weight of Words." In Sayad, *Suffering of the Immigrant,* 216–24.

Schields, Chelsea. *Offshore Attachments: Oil and Intimacy in the Caribbean.* Berkeley: University of California Press, 2023.

———. "A Science of Reform and Retrenchment: Black Kinship Studies, Decolonisation, and the Dutch Welfare State." *Contemporary European History* 32, no. 2 (2023): 1–19.

Scott, Joan Wallach. *Gender and the Politics of History.* New York: Columbia University Press, 1999.

———. *Only Paradoxes to Offer: French Feminists and the Rights of Man.* Cambridge MA: Harvard University Press, 1996.

———. *The Politics of the Veil.* Princeton: Princeton University Press, 2007.

———. *Sex and Secularism.* Princeton: Princeton University Press, 2019.

———. "The Vexed Relationship of Emancipation and Equality." *History of the Present* 2, no. 2 (Fall 2012): 148–68.

Seferdjeli, Ryme. "'Fight with Us Women, and We Will Emancipate You': France, the FLN, and the Struggle over Women during the Algerian War of National Liberation 1954–1962." PhD diss., London School of Economics and Political Science, 2004.

———. "French 'Reforms' and Muslim Women's Emancipation during the Algerian War." *Journal of North African Studies* 9, no. 4 (2009): 19–61.

Semley, Lorelle. *To Be Free and French: Citizenship in France's Atlantic Empire.* Cambridge: Cambridge University Press, 2017.

Sessions, Jennifer. *By Sword and Plow: France and the Conquest of Algeria.* Ithaca NY: Cornell University Press, 2011.

Sewell, William. *Logics of History: Social Theory and Social Transformation.* Chicago: University of Chicago Press, 2005.

———. *Work and Revolution in France: The Language of Labor from the Old Regime to 1848*. Cambridge: Cambridge University Press, 1980.

Shepard, Todd. "Algeria, France, Mexico, UNESCO: A Transnational History of Anti-Racism and Decolonization, 1932–1962." *Journal of Global History* 6, no. 2 (July 2011): 273–97.

———. "Algerian Nationalism, Zionism, and French Laïcité: A History of Ethnore-ligious Nationalisms and Decolonization." *International Journal of Middle East Studies* 45, no. 3 (August 2013): 445–67.

———. *The Invention of Decolonization: The Algerian War and the Remaking of France*. Ithaca NY: Cornell University Press, 2006.

———. "Making Sovereignty and Affirming Modernity in the Archives of Decolonization: The Algeria-France 'Dispute' between the Post-Decolonization French and Algerian Republics, 1962–2015." In *Displaced Archives*, edited by James Lowry, 21–40. Oxford: Routledge, 2015.

———. *Sex, France, and Arab Men*. Chicago: University of Chicago Press, 2017.

———. "'Something Notably Erotic': Politics, 'Arab Men,' and the Sexual Revolution in Post-Decolonization France, 1962–1974." *Journal of Modern History* 84, no. 1 (March 2012): 80–115.

Sidi-Moussa, Nedjib. "Devenirs Messalistes (1925–2013): Sociologie Historique d'une Aristocratie Révolutionnaire." PhD thesis, Université Paris 1–La Sorbonne, 2013.

Silverstein, Paul. *Algeria in France: Transpolitics, Race, and Nation*. Bloomington: Indiana University Press, 2004.

Simon, Catherine. *Algérie, les années pieds-rouges: Des rêves de l'indépendance au désenchantement (1962–1969)*. Paris: La Découverte, 2009.

Sinha, Mrinalini. *Specters of Mother India: The Global Restructuring of an Empire*. Durham NC: Duke University Press, 2006.

Sloan, Elizabeth. "Welfare and Warfare: Social Action for Algerian Migrants in Metropolitan France during the Algerian War." PhD diss., Stony Brook University, 2012.

Slobodian, Quinn. *Globalists: The End of Empire and the Birth of Neoliberalism*. Cambridge MA: Harvard University Press, 2018.

Smith, Bonnie. *Ladies of the Leisure Class: The Bourgeoises of Northern France in the Nineteenth Century*. Princeton: Princeton University Press, 1982.

Spire, Alexis. *Étrangers à la carte: L'administration de l'immigration en France, 1945–1975*. Paris: Grasset, 2005.

———. "Semblables et Pourtant Différents: La citoyenneté paradoxale des 'Français musulmans d'Algérie,' en metropole." *Genèses* 4, no. 53 (2003): 48–68.

Stamler, Hannah. "Decorating Mothers, Defining Maternity: The Invention of the French Family Medal and the Rise of Profamily Ideology in 1920s France." *French Politics, Culture & Society* 40, no. 1 (Spring 2022): 83–106.

Stein, Sarah Abrevaya. *Saharan Jews and the Fate of French Algeria*. Chicago: University of Chicago Press, 2014.

Stokes, Lauren. *Fear of the Family: Guest Workers and Family Migration in the Federal Republic of Germany*. Oxford: Oxford University Press, 2022.

———. "An Invasion of Guest Worker Children: Welfare Reform and the Stigmatisation of Family Migration in West Germany." *Contemporary European History* 28 (2019): 372–89.

———. "The 'Market-Conforming' Family: Foreign Families, the 'Grandmother Solution' and the West German Welfare State." *Contemporary European History* 32, no. 2 (May 2023): 221–34.

Stoler, Ann Laura. *Carnal Knowledge and Imperial Power: Race and the Intimate in Colonial Rule*. 2nd ed. Berkeley: University of California Press, 2010.

———. *Imperial Debris: On Ruins and Ruination*. Durham NC: Duke University Press, 2013.

———. *Race and the Education of Desire: Foucault's History of Sexuality and the Colonial Order of Things*. Durham NC: Duke University Press, 1995.

Stoléru, Lionel. *La France à deux vitesses*. Paris: Flammarion, 1992.

Stora, Benjamin. *Algeria, 1830–2000: A Short History*. Translated by Jane Marie Todd. Ithaca NY: Cornell University Press, 2001.

———. *Ils venaient de l'Algérie: L'immigration algérienne en France (1912–1992)*. Paris: Fyard, 1991.

———. *La gangrène et l'oubli: La mémoire de la guerre d'Algérie*. Paris: La Découverte, 1991.

Stora, Benjamin, and Mohammed Harbi. *La guerre d'Algérie: 1954–2004*. Paris: R. Laffont, 2004.

Sugrue, Thomas. *The Origins of the Urban Crisis: Race and Inequality in Postwar Detroit*. Rev. ed. Princeton: Princeton University Press, 2014.

Surkis, Judith. "Custody Battles and the Politics of Franco-Algerian Divorce, 1962–1992." *Journal of Modern History* 94, no. 4 (2022): 857–97.

———. "Ethics and Violence: Simone de Beauvoir, Djamila Boupacha, and the Algerian War." *French Politics, Culture & Society* 28, no. 2 (Summer 2010): 38–55.

———. *Sex, Law, and Sovereignty in French Algeria, 1830–1930*. Ithaca NY: Cornell University Press, 2019.

———. *Sexing the Citizen: Morality and Masculinity in France, 1870–1920*. Ithaca NY: Cornell University Press, 2006.

———. "When Was the Linguistic Turn? A Genealogy." *American Historical Review* 117, no. 3 (2012): 700–722.

Sutton, Keith. "Population Resettlement—Traumatic Upheavals and the Algerian Experience." *Journal of Modern African Studies* 15, no. 2 (June 1977): 279–300.

Thénault, Sylvie. *Histoire de la guerre d'indépendance algérienne*. Paris: Flammarion, 2005.

———. *Violence ordinaire dans l'Algérie coloniale: Camps, internements, assignations à résidence*. Paris: Odile Jacob, 2012.

Thomas, Martin. "Intelligence and the Transition to the Algerian Police State: Reassessing French Colonial Security after the Sétif Uprising, 1945." *Intelligence and National Security* 28, no. 3 (2013): 377–96.

Tillion, Germaine. *Algeria: The Realities*. Translated by Ronald Matthews. New York: Knopf, 1958.

———. *The Republic of Cousins: Women's Oppression in Mediterranean Society*. Translated by Quintin Hoare. London: Al Saqi Books, 1983.

Tocqueville, Alexis de. *Democracy in America*. Translated by George Lawrence. Edited by J. P. Mayer. 1840. New York: Harper Perennial, 2006.

Tumblin, Jesse. *The Quest for Security: Sovereignty, Race, and the Defense of the British Empire, 1989–1931*. Cambridge: Cambridge University Press, 2020.

Tyre, Stephen. "From *Algérie Française* to *France Musulmane*: Jacques Soustelle and the Myths and Realities of 'Integration,' 1955–1962." *French History* 20, no. 3 (August 2006): 276–96.

Valabrègue, Catherine. *Contrôle des naissances et planning familial*. Paris: La Table Ronde, 1960.

———. *L'homme déraciné: Le livre noir des travailleurs étrangers*. Paris: Mercure de France, 1974.

Varon, Jeremy. *Bringing the War Home: The Weather Underground, the Red Army Faction, and Revolutionary Violence in the Sixties and Seventies*. Berkeley: University of California Press, 2004.

Vergès, Françoise. *The Wombs of Women: Race, Capital, Feminism*. Translated by Kaiama L. Glover. Durham NC: Duke University Press, 2020.

Vétillard, Roger. *Sétif, Mai 1945, Massacres en Algérie*. Paris: Editions de Paris, 2008.

Viet, Vincent. *La France immigrée: Construction d'une politique, 1914–1997*. Paris: Fayard, 1998.

Vince, Natalya. *The Algerian War, the Algerian Revolution*. Cham, Switzerland: Palgrave Macmillan, 2020.

———. *Our Fighting Sisters: Nation, Memory, and Gender in Algeria, 1954–2012*. Manchester: Manchester University Press, 2015.

———. "Transgressing Boundaries: Gender, Race, Religion, and 'Françaises Musulmanes' during the Algerian War for Independence." *French Historical Studies* 33, no. 3 (2010): 445–74.

Wadowiec, Jaime. "The Afterlives of Empire: Gender, Race, and Citizenship in Decolonized France." PhD diss., Binghamton University, 2014.

———. "Muslim Algerian Women and the Rights of Man: Islam and Gendered Citizenship in French Algeria at the End of Empire." *French Historical Studies* 36, no. 4 (2013): 649–76.

Weber, Eugen. *Peasants into Frenchmen: The Modernization of Rural France, 1870–1914*. Stanford: Stanford University Press, 1976.

Weil, Patrick. *How to Be French: Nationality in the Making since 1789*. Durham NC: Duke University Press, 2008.

———. *La France et ses étrangers: L'aventure d'une politique de l'immigration de 1938 à nos jours*. Paris: Gallimard, 1991.

———. "Racisme et discrimination dans la politique Française de l'immigration, 1938–1945/1974–1995." *Vingtième Siècle. Revue d'histoire*, no. 47 (July–September 1995): 77–102.

Wildenthal, Lora. *German Women for Empire, 1884–1945*. Durham NC: Duke University Press, 2001.

Wilder, Gary. *Freedom Time: Negritude, Decolonization, and the Future of the World*. Durham NC: Duke University Press, 2014.

———. *The French Imperial Nation-State: Negritude and Colonial Humanism between the Two World Wars*. Chicago: University of Chicago Press, 2005.

———. "From Optic to Topic: The Foreclosure Effect of Historiographic Turns." *American Historical Review* 117, no. 3 (2012): 723–45.

Zehraoui, Ahsène. *Les travailleurs algériens en France: Étude sociologique de quelques aspects de la vie familiale*. Paris: Maspéro, 1971.

INDEX

A., Ourdia, 125, 127–29
A., Saïd, 110–11
A., Tassadit, 150–51
acculturation, 38, 40–41, 82, 171. *See also* assimilation
adaptation, 29, 38, 39–40, 42, 86, 105, 147–48
Algeria, 5–6, 23–25, 45–46, 99
Algerian difference, 22–23, 35, 43, 135–36, 138–39
Algerian family: as burden on the welfare state, 82, 103–6, 165, 183–84; and concerns over birthrate, 32, 74, 118, 150–51; gendered understandings of, 35–36, 42, 91, 135–36, 138, 160; maladaptation of, 81, 115, 119, 137, 151–52, 158
Algerian government, 6, 99, 106–7
Algerian independence: consequences of, 70, 76, 97–99, 107; continuities across, 82; as rupture, 6, 127. *See also* decolonization as process
Algerian migrants: and access to social benefits, 3, 38, 78–80, 90, 125; living conditions of, 86–87; restrictions placed on, 6, 25–26, 29, 106, 114; as threats, 16, 29, 85, 93, 103, 148–49

Algerians: cultural difference of, 158–60, 163–64, 170; and exclusion from rights, 6, 12, 22, 24–26, 32, 37, 43, 179
Algerian War, 69–70, 75; and Battle of Algiers, 57, 64; memory of, 13, 17, 185, 187n8; social aid during, 9, 47, 51–57, 59–63, 70. *See also* military social aid programs
Algerian women: emancipation of, 40–41, 60, 62–65, 136, 158, 160–61; femininity of, 30, 114, 146–48, 159–60, 167–68; as primary targets of social work, 52–55, 58–59, 63, 81–82, 130–32, 198n8; and work, 117–18, 154, 161, 166–68, 201n53
ANAS (National Association of Social Workers), 47–48, 53, 59
army. *See* military social aid programs
assimilation, 13, 119, 168–69. *See also* acculturation
ATOM (Association for Aid to Overseas Workers), 80

belonging, 37, 163, 169, 185. *See also* citizenship
bidonvilles, 49–50, 64, 85, 87–88, 108, 109–10. *See also* housing

www.ingramcontent.com/pod-product-compliance
Lightning Source LLC
Chambersburg PA
CBHW030425290125
21028CB00008BB/184